A Family's Joys and Sorrows
in the Beautiful, Remote
Yampa River Canyon

T·H·E
Mantle
Ranch

Queeda Mantle Walker

WESTWINDS
PRESS®

THE PRUETT SERIES

First Edition

Library of Congress Cataloging-in-Publication Data

Walker, Queeda Mantle, 1933-
  The Mantle Ranch : a family's joys and sorrows in the beautiful, remote Yampa River Canyon / Queeda Mantle Walker. -- 2nd ed.
     p. cm.
  ISBN 978-0-87108-350-0 (pbk.)
  ISBN 978-0-87108-980-9 (e-book)
  1. Mantle, Evelyn Fuller, 1907-1978. 2. Walker, Queeda Mantle, 1933- 3. Women ranchers--Colorado--Yampa River Valley--Biography. 4. Ranchers--Colorado--Yampa River Valley--Biography. 5. Ranch life--Colorado--Yampa River Valley. 6. Yampa River Valley (Colo.)--Biography. I. Title.
  CT275.M4573W36 2011
  978.8'12033092--dc23
  [B]
                                                    2011019433

WestWinds Press®
An imprint of

GRAPHIC ARTS
BOOKS®

P.O. Box 56118
Portland, OR 97238-6118
(503) 254-5591
www.graphicartsbooks.com

COVER PHOTO: *From Burro Park overlook of Castle Park. Upper and lower Red Rock Benches beyond, with Blue Mountain above all.*
BOOK & COVER DESIGN: *Bob Schram/Bookends*

Dedication

To My Mother,

Evelyn Fuller Mantle

Acknowledgments

OR ME, THIS JOURNEY THROUGH THE LIVES of my parents, my siblings, and myself, has been one of discovery of family love and the importance of devoted friends. I particularly want to say that my mother, Evelyn Mantle is my hero and example of strength of character and of accomplishment. She was steadfast through the greatest of trials. This book is about her most of all.

My present family has listened for nine long years to me talk of this book. I appreciate their patience and interest. My brother Lonnie wrote some episodes for me, told me stories, sorted and indexed our collection of old pictures and sent me beautiful color photos of his.

I particularly want to thank Dr. Richard Geesaman for his friendship and help. He read, proofed, encouraged me, pushed and shoved me into finishing. Without him I would never have got the job done. He even brought my publisher, Fred Pruett, to my house and introduced us.

My dear friend Doris Karren Burton has printed some of my stories in her publication "The Outlaw Trail Journal" which she edits for the Uintah County Library History Center in Vernal, Utah. She has given me permission to tell these stories again in this book. She also encouraged me endlessly. Thanks, also, to Katherine Shank Rinker for the photos she contributed.

Sam Haslem and Eula Chew Wise and Doris Karren Burton generously shared their family pictures with me and I am grateful. We shared so much fun as kids! God blessed us with our wonderful parents.

QUEEDA MANTLE WALKER
Boulder, Colorado,
November 2004

Preface

I LIVED ON THE MANTLE RANCH from the time of my birth in 1933, until 1954 when I graduated from the University of Colorado. This is a family story; a story of my parents, my siblings, and me, living the kind of life that most people today can scarcely imagine. At times our life was filled with incredible hardships, but it was not without its own brand of special joy and fulfillment. It was a wonderful place to grow up and remains my favorite place on earth with a special trove of memories.

But in a larger sense this is the story of my mother, Evelyn Fuller Mantle, a loving, caring hard working woman, who never complained, though she would often have been justified in doing so. Mother recognized early on that she was going to have to take care of most of the things around the ranch that needed doing and if she lacked the skills and knowledge at the outset, she trained herself and in the process became one of the most accomplished people I have ever known.

Although a very private person, Mother revealed much of her life to me over the years. She and her first cousin, Eva, who lived in New York, corresponded regularly. They had been like sisters before Evelyn's family moved west. After mother's death in 1978, Eva made a special trip to visit me in Colorado. She presented me with several boxes of letters written to her from Mother, which she had lovingly saved all those years. She gave them to me with the understanding that I was to write a story of mother's life. These tender letters, together with stories Mother shared with me, form the foundation of this book.

My father, Charley Mantle was a true character and of course plays an indispensable part in this story, too. Often as hard and ruthless as the land that shaped him, he could also be loving in his own special way. A born mimic and story-teller, he spoke in a carefree, colorful way, pulling no punches. Accordingly, to present him as he really was, I have taken the liberty of imagining what he might have said in particular situations.

Contents

The Mantle Ranch Country

KEY TO MAP

1. Castle Park
2. Castle Rock
3. Mantle Homestead cabin
4. New House, the heart of Mantle Ranch
5. Crows Nest Cliff
6. Laddie Park where Evelyn and children climbed out to first Bench School
7. Mantle Cave
8. Joe's Grave–foot trail to get to the ladder when Hells Canyon flooded
9. Hells Canyon–lower section
10. Red Rock Canyon
11. Red Rock Ranch, Tom Blevins cabin
12. Second airport
13. Second Bench School–at Red Rock
14. Chew Ranch at Pool Creek
15. Wind Cave in Pool Creek Canyon
16. Steamboat Rock
17. Yampa River flows into the Green River at Steamboat Rock

18. Sand Canyon–horse trail and road out west side of canyons
19. Winter horse trail starts over treacherous Blue Mountain
20. Pearl Park
21. Roundtop
22. Martha's Peak
23. Upper Hells Canyon Gorge–where crickets entered
24. Mantle Summer Cow Camp
25. Horse trail between Martha's Peak and Hells Canyon Gorge
26. Rat Spring
27. Serviceberry Gap
28. Water tank at Serviceberry Gap where the pipeline ended
29. Quaker Spring where the pipeline began
30. Hardings Hole
31. Mouth of Johnson Canyon where it empties into the Yampa at Bull Canyon

32. Johnson Draw where Mantle Ranch Road ended until 1938 when it reached the rim of Hells Canyon
33. Mantle Ranch Road finished into Hells Canyon in 1941, now cars could drive out without the help of Henry Horse
34. Red Rock Bench Road from the west was finished into Hells Canyon in 1944
35. Schoonover Pasture and dehorning corrals
36. Youghall
37. East Mantle Ranch Road switch backs at Thanksgiving where the road climbs to the top of Blue Mountain, then east on to Elk Springs
38. Cattle drives traveled on east through East Cactus to Deer Lodge
39. Outlaw Park
40. Warm Springs
41. Location of trailer for the first Bench School

Introduction

I T WAS AUGUST 12, 1926, IN VERNAL, UTAH. "I do!" she said. "I've done it – it is over," she thought. The couple embraced but did not kiss in front of the two witnesses and the justice of the peace. They turned and walked out into the hot summer day. The horses that had brought them here were waiting patiently outside at the hitching rack. Mounting, the couple rode off toward the east and their new life together.

This is the story of the life of these two young people. The place where they lived is in the very northwest corner of Colorado where Colorado, Utah, and Wyoming join. The Green River coming out of Wyoming from the north, and the Yampa River coming from the east out of the mountains of Colorado, join here in a maze of magnificent, deeply eroded, canyons. Their home was to be situated along the Yampa (or Bear) River, in one of the nation's most isolated places, ten miles east of the confluence of the Green and Yampa Rivers. It remains today, rugged, intimidating country, little touched by any human influence.

The present day towns of Craig, Colorado, and Vernal, Utah, joined by Highway U.S. 40 form the southern boundary of the area. The northern boundary of their home is the north side of the Yampa River, where Douglas Mountain raises its red stone cliffs high above the river, forming an almost impassable barrier to the rich grasslands of Browns Park to the north. The Mantle Ranch lies within the boundaries of Dinosaur National Monument, established by presidential proclamation on October 4, 1915, only a few years before Charley Mantle's arrival.

Between Highway 40 and the Yampa River looms Blue Mountain, a dominant landmark of the area, rising two thousand feet above the surrounding country. Blue Mountain begins on the west at the Utah state line and runs east to within a few miles of the town of Elk Springs. A large land mass, the mountain stretches some twenty miles east to west and ten miles north to south. In appearance, the mountaintop looks like great rolling hills of grassland and sagebrush. There is little water and what there is is very precious. During the summer, the mountain is caressed by a cool breeze. No evergreen trees crown its summit, but a few pinon and junipers may be found around the edges.

The north side of Blue Mountain abruptly sweeps down two thousand feet to a long fairly flat bench that runs up to the very rim of the cliff that is the south shore of the Yampa River. This bench is anywhere from two miles to five miles wide from the base of the mountain to the canyon rim. It is beautiful wild pastureland, supplied with water from some very nice springs along the side and base of Blue Mountain. The north slope of Blue Mountain as well as the bench were excellent grazing lands for herds of cattle as well as large herds of deer and wild horses. All of this area, despite its rather rolling vista, is cut with deep crevasses and bare rock jutting from the earth. The vegetation is tough and unyielding, and the general weather condition is dry and windy. The people who live there must become tough and unyielding as well.

Within the sandstone canyon walls the Yampa River is eroded to as deep as eleven hundred feet. It curves sharply and wanders its way to the Green River. Along its shores are lush, green, small parks and side canyons full of feed. Keeping the cattle on those areas to graze but to not be marooned and endangered by floods and ice is a job for only a real cowman.

When Evelyn went with Charley to spend her life with him in this rugged area there was no road, no electricity, no running water, no telephone. There was no doctor or grocery store, nor any living soul to depend on but yourself. Their only communication with the outside world was attained by a horseback ride of more than forty miles up the steep rough north side of Blue Mountain, then over the top of the mountain and down the south side. Any time they "went to town" they stayed with rancher friends who would put them and their horses up for the night. It was a hard life, particularly for Evelyn, who had none of the modern conveniences of the day and yet it was a life that supplied its own special compensations.

1

Charley and Evelyn

VELYN FULLER WAS A BEAUTIFUL chestnut haired, hazel eyed girl of nineteen on her wedding day. Her parents, along with Evelyn and her younger brother, Frank, had come to Blue Mountain, Colorado to homestead when Evelyn was only fourteen. They lived in a one-room dugout and tried to whip a living from the arid land.

One day the handsomest man Evelyn had ever seen came riding up to their house. He wore a white shirt with a black silk scarf tied loosely at his neck, and a wide brimmed white hat placed at a jaunty tilt on his head. He was riding a shimmering sorrel horse who strutted and danced with uneasiness at having a man mounted on his back for the first time. The man dismounted from the horse in a cloud of dust as the horse bolted in terror to the end of his lead rope and stood trembling and wild-eyed. The man maneuvered his horse to a hitch rack and tied him up. Then he turned, removed his hat, faced Evelyn with a broad smile, and said "Howdy, I'm Charley Mantle. I heard you folks had moved in here and I come over to say hello."

Charley Mantle wasn't much interested in the girl of fourteen. However, she was very interested in him. She was "horsecrazy" and never got enough of being near them. Throw in a romantic looking cowboy and she could see that this homesteading was going to be fun. He broke horses for a living. Charley was twenty-eight years old and he lived just across Turner Creek from the Fullers, where he had set up his horse training camp.

Evelyn's family came from a comfortable life and a large, loving extended family in Syracuse, New York. Evelyn was born in Cicero, New York on February 18, 1907. Trouble at home had caused her parents to move west. They left home with a team of horses, a little farm equipment, and only the barest essentials. Evelyn was eight and her brother Frank, six. En route, they stopped and farmed in Nebraska for a few years. Mrs. Fuller became sick with tuberculosis and the family was advised to move to the drier, healthier climate of Phoenix, Arizona. As soon as Mrs. Fuller was sufficiently improved, they travelled to high, dry western Colorado, where Mr. Fuller worked in the coal mines and held different jobs in the northwestern part of the state. Homesteading offered an opportunity and the Fuller family moved to the even higher and drier top of Blue Mountain in the very northwest corner of

Colorado. Here, at this little homestead, the now fourteen-year-old Evelyn met Charley Mantle in 1921.

Each winter the Fullers would leave the snowbound mountain and move to a lower elevation. Mr. Fuller would get some kind of work, and the kids would go to school. Evelyn's favorite school was the high school in Hayden, Colorado. She made many friends there and it was the longest she had ever been in school in one place. When there was no work to be had nearby, Mr. Fuller had to seek employment in other places. Evelyn boarded with a friend in town, while her mother, father, and brother lived wherever there was work.

Evelyn was a talented athlete. She ran track events and played basketball in high school. Being an accomplished "tomboy," and very outgoing, she was invited to every event in the community. She and her friend "spied" from a cliff high above the rowdy little coal mining town of Mount Harris. They marveled and shivered with excitement, and feared being caught as they watched the wild night life far below them. Even as a teenager, Evelyn required the most that was possible from herself. Her grades were high, her reputation impeccable, and her enjoyment of life day by day was complete.

But, what Evelyn liked best of all was Blue Mountain!

Charley

CHARLEY MANTLE WAS BORN IN VERNAL, UTAH, IN AUGUST, 1893. He lost both his parents the same summer, when he was thirteen. His father had been killed in a wagon wreck during the summer, and his mother died the same year in childbirth, when the last of their six children, a baby girl, was born. Left on their own were four boys and two girls.

The two youngest children, Lena and Brian, were adopted into homes. Joe, the next in age, found a home with some folks named Jenkins. He wasn't officially adopted, but took their name anyway. Nancy was taken in by a family who treated her as a servant, but at least she had food and a place to stay. Lewellen and Charley, the oldest boys, were taken in by their father's five brothers, who were bachelors. The uncles put them in school and tried to do right by them, but it was a pretty meager existence. Charley went through fourth grade, then struck out on his own. Jobs for a kid paid very little, even though Charley was a top cowhand at this young age. He worked for one cow outfit for four years just to buy his first saddle. In every outfit he worked for he soon became recognized as an expert with horses.

Charley was drafted into the U.S. Cavalry during World War I. For training, he was sent to Fort Hood, Texas along the Rio Grand river on the Mexican border. There he was subjected to the strict regimentation, and the insults and the senseless orders of overbearing sergeants. Having been a man since he was thirteen years old Charley found all this unbearable. Besides, he had never been so hot in his life. There was no escape from the heat or the Army. His only pleasure was in working with the cavalry horses. His talent for handling horses was soon recognized, and he was put in charge of the horses and was soon teaching horsemanship to recruits.

Charley was transferred to Fort D.A. Russell, Cheyenne, Wyoming (today's Warren Air Force Base), where he continued to work with the cavalry horses. Soon after his transfer the war ended and he was discharged from the Army. He was sick of constantly being around so many people, and had had his fill of people telling him what to do. Accordingly, upon being discharged, he hurried back to his beloved northwest Colorado. He had saved up a little money and started looking for a small ranch that would be so remote he'd never have to be crowded with people again.

Soon after returning to Colorado, Charley found just the kind of place he was after, though several years would pass before he was able to acquire the property. Looking off the north side of Blue Mountain he saw spread before him the land he dreamed of. Two thousand feet below him, the steep side of Blue Mountain levelled out into flat sage covered benches of good pasture land. Beyond the benches began the no-man's land that Charley dreamed of. One thousand-foot cliffs dropped straight and sheer into the gorge carved out by the Bear River. Along the river were fertile green parks, alluring little side canyons, and a land well protected from the elements. Here flourished vegetation he had seen nowhere else in the surrounding country. There was plenty of perfect winter shelter for cattle, too. There were no roads, however, and the only way to get into the country of his dreams was to ride a horse over Blue Mountain and down the dangerous rocky trails off the mountain into the uncharted canyons.

Charley Mantle in a U.S. Cavalry uniform about 1918.

Here in this beautiful land, deep in one of its many canyons, Charley found an old man living in a cabin. Billy Hall had applied for a homestead, but had not been able to complete the requirements to claim it. Yes, he would sell out his interest for just a little money and even throw in the few cows he had. Accordingly, in 1924, Charley paid him cash and moved in. He soon found that ranching was fun and solitude was wonderful, but he needed money for improvements and more cattle. He set up a camp on top of Blue Mountain where there were a lot of homesteaders and ranchers running cattle on their summer range. Best of all, there were a lot of wild horses running free and the ranchers were glad to have them caught and taken off their range.

Since Charley Mantle soon developed the reputation of being the best horse trainer in the country, people brought their horses to him to be broke. They also bought horses from him that he had caught and broke from the herds of wild horses in the area. He would not accept the spoiled and mean horses to break. He wanted to turn out gentle working horses with healthy mouths. He knew he would have a market for saddle horses, so he set to work and built a round corral. A round corral with no corners to get hurt in was necessary when training wild young horses. He visited the neighbors and gathered up some of their range horses to break for them. He built wild horse traps in the trails the wild horses used.

A trap was an inconspicuous corral constructed of natural trees, brush, rocks. It would have two very long wings built parallel out from it which would become wider and wider as they were extended. The trick was for the wings and corral to be so camouflaged that the wild horses would not see their mistake until they were too far inside the wings to turn back. They were being hotly pursued by shouting, wild-riding cowboys, so the horses were not likely to notice the trap. That of course was true only once, and after that the horses who had been captured in a trap were forever wary of potential traps. It was a huge game between cowboys and horses. The wild stallions enjoyed their victories in escaping just as much as the cowboys enjoyed their more infrequent victories. An escaped stallion would many times stand atop a distant hill and snort and squeal his victory at the frustrated cowboys.

2

Life on Blue Mountain

VELYN DIDN'T LIVE VERY FAR from the round corral where Charley camped and broke horses on Blue Mountain. She would drop by and hang her foot over the corral poles and watch him work by the hour. He usually wouldn't pay any attention to her except to occasionally tease her. She saw him constantly chewing and enjoying something, so she asked him if he had any more. He said yes and pulled out his plug of chewing tobacco and cut her off a chunk with his pocket knife. She stuck it in her mouth, chewed hard, made a face and swallowed it. She felt sick and ran home as fast as she could with Charley's taunting laugh in her ears. Still she worshiped and daydreamed that someday he would fall in love with her. To him she was just a little neighbor girl, but fun to have around while he worked. She constantly begged him to ride a horse, so one day he gave in and let her ride a gentle horse. He didn't have a saddle for her, so she had to ride bareback. She begged to ride along with him when he took the broncs out on training rides. He thought she would soon tire, but she rode every day just as long as her parents would let her. They rode all over Blue Mountain, the handsome man on a bronc, and the young girl riding bareback.

Evelyn watched in fascinated horror Charley's process of changing a wild-eyed bronc to a gentle saddle horse. Ranch horses were not broke to ride until they got their full growth at about three or four years of age. Until that time they ran free on the range; 1,000 pounds of muscle and terror when one day they were gathered and herded into a corral by a bunch of racing, shouting cowboys. There they were fore-footed, which meant they were roped by their front feet, then jerked down and cowboys piled on them. While the horse kicked and squealed he was fitted with a hackamore. Evelyn thought her tears of anguish for the poor horse were a secret from Charley. They weren't, and he was sorry his little friend was so upset, but he couldn't let on. When the horse was finally let up his hackamore rope was tied to a big log. The log would move a little when the horse pulled on it with all his strength. He soon became too tired to pull the log any more, so faced it straddle-legged, waiting to run away if it should attack him. At last he would approach and sniff the log and find it not terrifying at all, and most importantly, it wouldn't follow him if the hackamore rope hung slack. Evelyn would beg Charley at this point to free the horse for awhile and let him rest. He would laugh and call her a sissy, then go on with his work. At this point the work of the horse trainer, or bronc stomper, or horse breaker as he was called would begin. Most horses responded to gentle treatment and liked the learning process, but some were born stubborn and tested his patience and skill as a trainer.

Evelyn had become Charley's faithful shadow and she was a constant worry to him. She was a horse lover, and wanted to pet and caress the poor horse. Still a wild animal who could instantly become crazed with fear was a horse too dangerous for her to be near. At times he had to be curt and hard in his orders for her to stay away from the horse.

Charley relentlessly worked with the horse, becoming familiar and even a refuge from harm to him. The horse finally accepted a saddle blanket being thrown under, over, and onto his back. When the horse finally relaxed and was not afraid of the blanket it was put in place on his back and the whole process started over with the saddle. The flapping and creaking of the parts of the saddle were mostly ignored by the tired horse, and he would throw one last fit as the cinch was tightened under his belly.

Then, under much protest from Evelyn, the horse was tied to the old familiar log again. It was usually about dinner time by now, so Charley would go eat while the horse snorted and sulked and became accustomed to this new thing attached to his body. Usually Evelyn would get Charley to come outside and eat with her, since she wasn't allowed to go inside. She brought bread and meat, and he usually ate jerky and cold pancakes, with a hot cup of coffee.

When the horse calmed down, Charley would return and fit it with a hackamore. This was a rawhide braided nose band hung from a twisted horsehair or strong leather head stall. It was fitted with two reins as well as a rope for leading and tying the horse up. These also were made of twisted horsehair or braided rawhide. The lead rope would be knotted around the chin end of the nose band, making it snug, with the front just above the nostrils. A bit was never put into the horses mouth until he learned to stop and turn with the hackamore.

Charley taught the horse to turn by pulling on a rein and by tying the rein to the saddle horn tight enough to bend the horse's stiff, unyielding neck in the direction he would then have to turn when he moved. The position was very tiring on the neck muscles and the horse soon found that yielding to the pull of the rein was the comfortable thing to do. All this was very time consuming and left Charley with little leisure time. Neighbors usually dropped by and Charley loved to sit in the shade and entertain them with his comic, masterfully spun yarns. He could imitate anyone he knew in their looks, mannerisms, and speech, and gleefully did so. People would sit spellbound for as long as he would perform. Everybody knew they would be next on his list.

By this point in the training process, the horse knew the basics of stopping and turning, and his nose and chin were so sore from the rubbing and chafing of the hackamore during the learning process that he would respond quickly to pressure exerted. It was time for Charley to mount the horse. Evelyn's heart stopped as he pulled his hat down tight, mounted the horse quickly and grace-fully and clamped himself into the saddle as if glued there. The first reaction of the horse would be to plant all four feet solid on the ground and stand stiff-legged like a coiled spring. To make him take the first step was the trainer's biggest challenge. The horse was big and powerful and full of fear and as such its behavior was completely unpredictable. He might walk peacefully forward, although not likely. He might explode straight forward in a long leap, jerk his head down between his front legs, and ram both front feet into the ground with all the force of his 1,000 pounds, or he might explode straight up onto his hind feet and fall over backward. Of a certainty, whichever method he chose, at some point he would decide to run away with this man on his back. In his blind fear he wouldn't look where he was going and might fall into a hole, run into a tree, or fall off a cliff. Since the two horsehair reins were all Charley had to control the great horse, he would usually take this first ride in a round corral with high pole sides and no corners to injure horse or rider. Through this hair-raising part, Evelyn's emotions ran from paralyzing fear for Charley to worshipful wonder and pride in his beautiful performance. In the corral Charley would teach the horse to move forward easily after being mounted, not explode into frantic, dangerous acts. He would teach him to turn to the right and the left, and to stop and back up within a few hours.

Evelyn lived for the next step. It was to ride the horse outside the corral, and she often got to ride along on a gentle horse. The tricky part of this was for Charley to get on the horse and set down tight before the horse realized he was no longer confined to the corral. The horse's first instinct was to lunge and buck and run. Charley had to get him into a spin to stop the charge and help the horse remember his recent lessons. The biggest disservice the trainer could do the horse at this point was to get bucked off. The horse would never be dependable from that day on if he bucked his rider off. A horse trainer who ruined horses in this way was soon shunned by all the ranchers and could find no work with them.

Evelyn was growing older and becoming a beautiful girl. She was secretly in love with Charley. He began to notice, too, how she had changed from the young girl he had once teased and with whom he had ridden endlessly over the country-side. All the girls shamelessly chased this handsome, graceful raven haired cowboy with the soft brown eyes and he enjoyed it. However, he was determined to never fall in love and certainly never get married. Other young men began to notice Evelyn and she was asked out quite often. Charley began to notice this popularity, and he felt strangely uneasy about it.

There was an old abandoned school house made of red stone on top of Blue Mountain. It was called the Red Onion because it was built of red sand-stone quarried nearby. Once every couple of months there was a dance at the Red Onion. A fiddler, usually Marcus Jensen, was hired and all the residents of Blue Mountain and from a radius of some fifty miles around would attend. People would bring their babies and lots of food and spend a couple of days camping out. Mostly the young people would come with their families or in

Evelyn Fuller and a group of young people on Blue Mountain.

groups and not much actual dating went on. If the girls arrived on horses they would jump off their horse with their sack of dancing clothes and run into the bushes to change. Everybody would dress up and the dancing and yarn-spinning and merriment would go on late into the night. Charley was a prankster and teased everyone and was very popular and totally unavailable for any lasting commitment to any woman. He began to notice that most of Evelyn's dances were taken and the older folks began to snicker about how he wasn't getting around to dancing with all the girls so much any more because he spent most of his time trying to cut in on Evelyn.

One day before a dance at the Red Onion Charley rode over to Evelyn's place. He finally got around to asking her if she would like to ride over to the dance with him tomorrow. Since it was only a couple of miles away her parents gave permission. He showed up the next day dressed at his very finest, even with his boots shined. He was leading a saddled horse that Evelyn recognized as his finest pacing mare. This mare was coveted by all of the horse loving people on Blue Mountain, and Charley would not let anyone else ride her. Evelyn's breath caught in her throat. Could it possibly be that he would let her ride that horse she loved? He tipped his hat to her, and said, "I brought along Pacer. 'Thought you might like to ride her to the dance.'" She was so excited at getting to ride this wonderful horse that Charley found he had cheated himself out of her undivided attention for the evening. Before the next dance he asked if he might again pick her up and take her to the dance. She accepted and this time he showed up with a big horse they could both ride together on.

Evelyn turned seventeen in February and when she finished school in the little town of Hayden, Colorado she and her family returned to Blue Mountain. It was none too soon for her, because she couldn't wait to see Charley. She had bragged to her friends about knowing the most handsome cowboy in the world. There was a fairly large group of young people on Blue

Mountain that summer and it would prove to be a dream summer for all of them. They all worked very hard, but took time out to play. They traveled in a drove from the dance at the Red Onion to the dance fifty miles away in Browns Park, as well as to all the local rodeos each town put on. One of their favorite trips was to ride their horses to a point just under the north rim of Blue Mountain. There the snow banks lasted late into the summer and they would have snowball fights, stuff each other's necks with snow, and make ice cream from the thick creamy syrup they brought.

That summer Charley suddenly developed a huge interest in the group and spent every minute he could with them. Many times he left his brother Wellen at the horse camp training the horses so he could be away. He even slyly invited the whole group to accompany him down into his canyon land paradise. He knew Evelyn's parents would never consent to him taking her there alone with him. He also was afraid if he showed her too much personal interest they might not let her see him at all any more.

3

First Canyon Trip

HARLEY INVITED ALL HIS FRIENDS TO THE RANCH. Those that were able to come, put some jerky and biscuits in their pocket, tied a bedroll behind their saddle, and in the early dawn rode to the head of Hells Canyon where they all met for the ride down off Blue Mountain. They expected to spend two days, because it was too far and too hard on the horses to make the roundtrip in a day. They followed a dim and steep, rocky trail along the rim of the yawning gorge that spring runoff water in Hells Canyon had been cutting in its steep plunge off the mountain for many centuries. At the foot of the mountain they dropped into the bottom of Hells Canyon. As they followed it down, sheer sandstone cliffs grew ever higher on each side. At last the canyon ended and they were face to face with the even taller sun-bathed wall that was the north side of the Yampa (Bear) River, into which Hells Canyon emptied its waters.

The Bear River ran right by Charley's homestead. Here, the young people splashed and swam and sunned themselves. In the same water they were playing in they had their fishing lines set. They used big hooks and big bait because they had heard some spectacular fish could be caught here. Evelyn threw her baited hook into the water. She was holding her willow fishing pole and daydreaming as she watched the fluffy white clouds sailing over the towering canyon walls. Suddenly, a powerful yank on her line brought her to her feet yelping for help. Three men leaped to her side and helped her hold the line from being jerked away. For a long time they struggled with the unseen monster on the end of the line. Finally the struggling lessened, and between the four of them they were able to start pulling whatever it was in toward the shore. A great head with a wide gaping mouth and eyes incredibly far apart progressed slowly toward the bank, then great flaring gills came into view and finally a glistening white body reflecting many colors. It was the biggest fish they had ever seen. They estimated it must weigh eighty pounds. They had heard stories of whitefish in the Bear river so huge that it took a horse to pull it out of the water, but had just supposed these were nothing more than exaggerated fish stories.

All the swimmers were out of the water watching the beaching of the fish, and no one much wanted to get back in the water. Talk turned to just how do you cook an eighty-pound fish for supper. Then Charley came to the rescue. He put his lariat rope around the big fish just behind the front fins and dragged it behind his horse to a nearby grove of cottonwood trees. He threw his rope over a limb, dallied the lariat rope around his saddle horn and backed his horse up until the fish's tail cleared the ground. He gave instructions to the men to clean and skin the fish just as they would a buckskin. He told the girls to make a ring of rocks and make a big fire in it, using dried tree limbs.

Charley's friend Rial went with him and they turned their horses toward Charley's cabin just up the creek. Soon they returned with their arms full and the two bronky horses they rode snorting and skittish beneath them. No wonder, because they carried a coffee pot, two dutch ovens, a big iron skillet and a big flour sack full of other supplies. Now was Charley's chance to show off his unusual skill. He could cook! He filled the coffeepot with water and dumped in a couple handfuls of coffee grounds and put the pot on hot coals. He made a big dutch oven full of biscuits and covered its lid with smoldering coals. He cut up beef tallow in the other dutch oven and the skillet and put them on low coals. He asked the men to cut steaks crosswise of the grain from the giant fish. These he salted and peppered and dipped lightly in flour. He added hotter coals under the skillets and when the fat was clear and hot he gently filled the pans with fish steaks.

While the feast was cooking each person whittled the bark off of and flattened a green willow stick to use as a fork. Charley carefully watched the coffee pot and at the first rolling boil he added a cup of cold water and pushed the hottest coals out from under the pot. He turned over the fish steaks, revealing a golden brown crust. He then brushed the coals off the top of the biscuit Dutch oven, lifted the lid and let his friends smell the wonderful aroma of fresh baked bread. The sight of the fat, golden biscuits made everybody's mouth water. By then the fish steaks were done perfectly on both sides. "Dig in," Charley said. So each person helped themselves to a biscuit, opened it up, and lifted out a fish steak to place on the biscuit. While everybody sampled the first marvelous bite Charley put on more steaks to fry.

The dinner was delicious and the company comfortable in the soft shade of the cottonwood trees. They finished off the coffee from the deformed enamel and tin cups Charley and Rial had gathered up. Someone suggested in a loud voice to Evelyn that she should propose to Charley since he was such a good cook. One of the girls added, "Yes, Evelyn, especially since you don't know how to cook." They told stories and bragged of their accomplishments and shared their dreams. Charley got to spinning yarns as he was well known for and they could have stayed right there all the rest of the day. However, their precious day was slipping by much too fast and they had many things they wanted to do in this awesome paradise.

Rial Chew was the son of the rancher who had homesteaded ten miles away, where the Bear River flowed into the Green River. He was fascinated by the Indian artifacts and the caves they had lived in, which abounded in this canyon country. There were flint chips of broken and half finished arrowheads over the entire country in these canyons and on the benches at the foot of Blue Mountain. Often, but not often enough to dampen the thrill of it, one would find a complete arrowhead lying on top of the ground where rain and wind had bared it from the earth and left it lying, clean and shining.

Rial talked Evelyn and two others into going with him to scale a cliff and explore a cave whose dark mouth shone thirty feet up the face of the cliff. After a thorough investigation of all possible ways of reaching the cave they decided on one route. A wide ledge of rock led gradually up the side of the cliff. As the ledge came closer to the cave it became narrower and narrower until it ended five feet from the cave. Rial led them up the ledge. As the trail grew narrower they all took off their boots so they could grip the sandstone with their bare toes. Rial put Evelyn in the front. When they came to the end of the ledge Rial said, "Ok, here's the plan. Since Evelyn is the smallest and a good climber she is going first. There are some little cracks and pockets in the rock that she can get her toes into. Just in case she falls I am going to put my lariat around her and we will all keep ourselves braced to hold her. Eager to get into the cave at any cost, Evelyn let Rial tie the lariat around her and off she went. Toe-hold by painful finger-grip, she inched around the cliff toward the cave. The sun was hot, shining directly onto the sheer buff-colored cliff. She began to sweat, and her toes and fingers became slippery. Before each step she methodically rubbed her toe on the sandstone cliff to dry it. The muscles in her legs began to ache and knot. Her arms became numb with the strain. She kept up a constant chatter telling her friends to get ready to catch her because she wasn't going to make it. Then miraculously an eight-inch-wide bench appeared in the shadow of a crack in the cliff. Gasping with pain and trembling, she rested on this tiny bench until the pain went away. Her heart leaped as she realized that this was a path that led directly over the next three feet and into the mouth of the cave. Could this have been a complete path centuries ago over which Indians could have travelled freely to and from the cave?

Giving an unladylike whoop, Evelyn lunged down the path and into the cave. She ducked just in time to avoid a frightened bat as it abandoned the cave. Before her was a wonder such as she had never before seen, but she knew it was important because it had been built by human hands. Finally the urgent, angry shouting of her friends got through to her. She leaned out of the cave and looked around the cliff at them. "You oughta see what's in here!" Rial begged for her attention, and finally got it. He said, "Are there any brush or trees growing in the mouth of the cave?" "No, she said." " Well, is there a big loose rock you can get the rope around that would hold me?" he asked patiently. She said, "Yes, but it is so big it would take most of your rope to go around it." He said, "That's all right because we have two ropes. I'll knot them together, and leave the loop in one for you to put around the rock."

Evelyn did as she was instructed, resenting every minute she had to wait before looking over the inside of the cave. She ripped her pants and skinned her elbow but was finally able to get the lariat loop around the huge rock that had long ago fallen from the roof of the cave. Rial was the first to test the rope and was able to pull himself easily around the narrow path. After him came the others. When everybody was safely in the cave, they were finally free to explore it. The cave mouth was about thirty feet wide by fifteen feet high in the middle. In the front of the cave, from the side they were on to a little past the middle was a mound of fine sand mixed with small rocks. This mound protected the depth of the cave from view. Beginning where the mound ended were short stone structures built by long ago inhabitants. As the quiet group approached they saw that they were storage bins, expertly built with flat, narrow sandstone slabs. They were round, about two feet deep and sealed on the outside by a reddish dirt which had been made into a thick plaster and patted into place with human hands, leaving prints of fingers and whole hands. The bottom of the storage bins was the solid rock of the cliff and the lids were expertly chipped, round, thin chunks of sandstone. Barely breathing, hushed with awe, the visitors lifted a lid. Inside was a stubby corncob with a few kernels of corn still in it. Beside it lay some pieces of dry squash rind. Lining one of the bins was a woven basket. Within another they found a piece of soft leather which they guessed was tanned buckskin. Carefully replacing everything as they found it they proceeded to explore the rest of the cave.

The cave was deep enough that after climbing across the mound in front the visitors had to advance a bit at a time, pausing to let their eyes adjust to the shadows. Delicious fear of ghosts of the past washed over them. Would they find mummies and was a witch doctor's magic protecting this ancient home? The sides of the cave were lined with sandstone which had fallen from the roof over the years. In one place where the original floor was visible they found a human bed made of cedar bark. A thick mat of the reddish bark of the native cedar trees had been laid down in an area the size of a cot for one short person. The bark had been stripped from the trees, then rubbed between the Indian's hands until it separated into long, soft strips. The bottom layer was thick and coarse. The next layer was rubbed finer, and so on until the top layer had obviously been worked until it was fluffy and soft. Pack rats had taken advantage of the already prepared bark at one end of the bed and carried it off to their own nest.

On the floor of the cave they found a camp fire site. The original sand in the bottom of the cave had been very shallow, so the sand rock underneath where the fire had been was blackened. The fire area was covered with ashes and blackened sand. Most surprising of all to the visitors were the large pieces of charcoal, as if the fire were only last week, not centuries ago. The extreme dryness of the cave had preserved everything within it. The young people's imaginations ran wild, their apprehension disappeared, and they chattered and dug in the sand until all at once it was night.

Now they had a problem. They could climb straight down the cliff on the ropes, but how could they get the ropes back? A lariat rope was a very expensive tool every cowboy had to have, and none of these young people could afford to lose a rope. It was finally decided that Rial would wait in the cave while the other three climbed down and rode to camp for another rope. Well after dark, when the three excited explorers arrived at camp Charley had begun to worry about them. Evelyn animatedly told him Rial was trapped in an Indian cave and couldn't get down without help. Disdainful of people who wasted their time with their noses glued to the ground looking for arrowheads, or risking their lives climbing around into caves, Charley said, "Serves him right. Just leave him there overnight and maybe he will learn not to get into places he can't get out of." He had made a mistake! Evelyn launched into a berating such as he had not experienced since his army days. Her face was red and her hazel eyes were a searing yellow in her wrath at Charley wanting to leave their friend high in a cave overnight. "I didn't mean it. I was only foolin'. We'll go right now," he said. Never had he saddled his horse any faster, grabbed two lariat ropes and headed up the canyon with Evelyn to get Rial. They tied the ropes together and Rial looped it around the big rock in the cave. Then holding both ends of the rope together he climbed down the cliff, pulling the rope down after him. Evelyn and Rial rode side by side back to camp, chattering about the cave. Charley felt left out and lonely.

Everyone was exhausted from the day of playing, and threw down their bed rolls and crawled in, asleep as their heads hit the ground. They awoke to a strange and beautiful sight. As the sun rose its light crept slowly down the sheer, towering sandstone cliffs of the canyon. Charley had been up and prepared a breakfast of flap-jacks, fish steaks and coffee. They wolfed it down, surprised at how hungry they were. They wrapped the leftover fish in pancakes and stuffed them in their pockets and saddle bags for lunch. Rial had already wrangled the horses, so they were waiting ready to be saddled.

They broke camp as quickly as possible because they didn't want to waste any of their precious time. Before they saddled their horses, they jumped them into the river in the deep water where they themselves had swum the day before. The riders hung onto the horses' manes and tails and let themselves be pulled along. Some horses refused to do it, and none of them seemed to enjoy it much, so this activity didn't last long. They all got out, refreshed, saddled up and started the return journey.

It would be hard on the horses today, because they had to climb the steep north face of Blue Mountain. Charley was anxious to get back on Evelyn's good side. He could tell that she was totally fascinated by the ancient Indian cave they had found the night before, so he took them on a roundabout route up the mountain. First he took them out onto the bench above the canyons, where they tied up their horses and searched for arrowheads. All of them had their pockets full of flint chips and a few found almost perfect arrowheads. Rial, as usual with the sharpest eyes, was the only one that found a perfect arrowhead. It was small and dainty with intricately worked shoulders, and made of a pink-tinted flint. Evelyn was very impressed and showed it.

Next Charley led them afoot up a hot little draw full of potholes which caught the runoff rain water. Along the sides of the canyon were numerous small caves and nooks in the sandstone walls. There were burn marks in several places on the roofs and especially where there was a small hole worn through the roof of the cave affording ventilation for a fire. In the caves they found big chunks of flint worked to a sharp edge on one side and blunt on the other. They were just the size for an Indian to hold in his hand and cut meat or scrape hides. There were stone storage bins containing bits and pieces, indicating that the ancient Indians had probably smoked and dried their corn and squash and meat then stored it in the bins.

Charley had a hard time getting the group moving out of the little draw. Evelyn was by his side again, her eyes shining, and chattering about Indians. He finally got them mounted by promising that if they would leave right now he would show them more. Only after they were mounted did he point out to them numerous round circles built of rocks on the ground. He told them that the circles were where teepees had been erected by the Indians on their yearly return here.

Charley led them past the trail they had come off Blue Mountain the day before, and they rode along the foothills. Finally he turned his horse toward the mountain. The cedar trees and pinyons were thick and there was only the faint remnant of a trail, but Charley followed it easily. The trees broke away into a rocky, grass covered clearing as the trail started up the steep mountain. Charley turned his horse sharply to the right and rode along the line of the trees to a giant pinyon tree. There he stopped and sat grinning, saying nothing. Finally Rial gave a shout as he saw long slender poles, and shorter, sturdier poles leaned up into the tree all around it. Teepee Poles! Travois Poles! Evelyn asked Charley to explain why the poles were leaned in the tree. He said, "It looks to me like when the Indian hunters went up the mountain to hunt they left their teepee poles behind. I would guess when the women came to carry the meat off the mountain they brought horses and travois poles to pack it. You know they tied a pole on either side of a horse's shoulders, with the poles stuck out behind and a load tied between them. The back of the sticks dragged along the ground and the horse could carry and pull a lot of meat that way."

The group reluctantly got back on their horses and started the long climb home. The mystery of the ancient Indians churned in their heads. They would remember this trip for the rest of their lives and would always think of Charley's homestead as Paradise.

4

Busby, 1924-25

CHARLEY WAS HAVING A TERRIBLE TIME GETTING HELP. He missed Wellen (Lewellen), too. They had been buddies since their parents died. They worked perfectly together and besides Charley was very worried about him. Wellen hadn't written in a long time. His hitch in the army must be about over and Charley reasoned that he should be coming home.

One day in early February, Charley decided to ride out to the post office and see if there was any news. He rode into Youghall in Bear Valley on the east end of Blue Mountain* just at dark, put his horse in the little corral and threw him enough hay for the night. He knocked on the door but nobody answered. He went on in and found nobody at home. The stove was cold, and it didn't look like anybody would be coming back soon. He started a fire in the stove, fixed himself a little supper and a pot of coffee, then began to look around. The post office part of the room was padlocked so he couldn't look for any mail.

He was tired and decided to go to bed. He went out and got his bedroll off the saddle and spread it out on a cot by the stove. Something caught his eye on the floor under the table. He picked it up, and found it to be a letter addressed to him. It was from his brother Lewellen, who wrote that he had become very ill and was in the Fitzsimmons Veterans Hospital in Denver. He said he was not doing good and would have to stay awhile, and would not be able to come back and help Charley the following spring as he had planned. Wellen said he knew Charley had to have some help and he had met a young feller who he figured just might work out with a little training. He went on to explain that the guy's name was E.L. Busby, but went by the name of Busby or Buzz from Missouri. He had come out to see the West and wanted to be a cowboy more than anything in the world. He was working there at the hospital where he and Wellen had become friends. Wellen allowed he sure didn't think Charley had anything to lose because Busby seemed like he would do anything he set his mind to.

---

*Pronounced "You-all." Nothing remains of Youghall today, save for the foundation of one building. It was about twenty miles from the ranch

Desperate for help, Charley wrote to Wellen telling him to send Busby on out. He would meet him at Youghall store on May first. All he had to do was get himself and his bedroll there, and Charley would meet him with a saddled horse. He told Wellen to assure the kid that Charley would sure teach him to be a cowboy. He gave Wellen the names of people who would come and get Charley if he, Wellen, needed help. Charley offered to come to the hospital when Wellen was ready to come home.

Busby took the bus to Craig, then the stage to Sunbeam. He tried every way he could think of to get on up to Youghall, but without a horse it seemed impossible. An old man finally felt sorry for Busby and lent him a horse. Busby rode on to Blue Mountain and finally found Youghall on May first. The post-master was not happy to see Busby or the horse. He could see he would be the one that would have to feed them both no matter how this turned out. The postmaster said there was no way Charley would just happen to come out and get him. However, Busby seemed like a nice kid, so he fed him and let him hang around. Busby did what chores he could to sort of pay his way, and waited.

Just at dark a cowboy rode up over the rim from the west leading a saddled horse. Busby was so happy he nearly cried. He walked quickly to meet Charley with outstretched hand and said, "Howdy, I'm your new hand." Charley had trouble suppressing his smile at the sight of the eager young man, dressed in slacks, a light shirt, loafers, and a floppy old hat. He liked the kid immediately. His honesty and eagerness were immediately obvious, and he was there ready to work.

Next morning before daylight they were up and saddled. After breakfast, Charley paid the postmaster for the keep on the old man's horse until some-body coming through could take him back to Sunbeam. Then they mounted up and rode toward the rim. Busby wasn't sure what the rim was, but in any case, it was great because he was now a cowboy in the old West. When they reached the rim he found it to be the rocky edge of Blue Mountain. Far below him stretched a wild looking country of sagebrush and canyons like no other country he had ever seen. His cowboy idol sat easily on his horse alongside him and said, "Busby, you are gonna' be a cowboy. This is where you begin."

They slipped off the rim on a steep little trail toward a small ravine where Charley was holding some cattle. The cattle needed to be driven down off the mountain into West Cactus, then on to the ranch, some thirty miles distant that same day. The oak brush on the side of the mountain tore up Busby's loaf-ers, socks, thin cloth pants, and shirt. Parts of his clothes were ripped off his body, the remainder just hung in tatters. His ankles were bleeding, his arms and legs scratched and sore, and the insides of his legs were rubbed raw. He had so many saddle sores he could scarcely sit. But through it all he whooped and hol-lered at the cattle to keep them from shading up in the brush, and worked hard keeping the herd together. Charley marvelled at the toughness of the kid.

At dark they arrived at the ranch, shoved the cattle down the river and turned out their tired horses. Busby went to the creek to wash his wounds and

Charley fixed them a huge supper of biscuits and jerky gravy. The dugout looked as good as the Denver Cosmopolitan Hotel to Busby. He washed the dishes, then hit his bed and slept motionless until daylight.

The next morning Busby woke to find Charley cooking breakfast. Embarrassed at being still in bed, he leaped up, then sat back down, tenderly. Every part of him hurt. Not wanting to lose his chance to be a cowboy, he put on his best smile, got up and went and sat in the cold creek water awhile until the burning stopped. When he came in, Charley had made him a big breakfast of pancakes and jerky gravy. The coffee was a life saver and he was eternally thankful when Charley stayed seated through two whole cups.

After breakfast Charley said, "Some young feller forgot and left his boots under the bed. He was about your size. Try em' on and if they fit, they're yours." The fine leather cowboy boots fit as if they had been made for him, and Busby wore them proudly. He didn't have to fake his new bow legged walk. His knees and other sore parts just couldn't bear to touch.

Charley caught him a fresh horse and Busby saddled it for the day's work. He was tremendously relieved that the horse was perfectly gentle, and even seemed to like him a little. Charley tied a coiled lariat rope on Busby' saddle and they rode off, moving the cows down the river and out Red Rock Canyon. On Red Rock bench they waited until the cattle had scattered out and began to graze. Then they dragged dead trees and brush with their lariat ropes by the saddle horns until they had a good supply and built a makeshift but tight brush fence across a narrow part of Red Rock Canyon so the cattle couldn't go back.

On the way home Charley stopped to pick up a rather forlorn looking horse tied to a log. Busby was baffled as to why a man would treat a horse like that. As Charley walked toward the horse it reared and tried to strike him. So Charley left the rope on him, untied it from the log and mounted his own horse. He got fairly close to the new horse, dallied the lead rope around his saddle horn and rode off. The new horse bellered, reared to his full height and threw himself on the ground. Charley let him up and rode off again. After throwing himself a couple of more times, the horse planted all four feet and refused to do anything, but Charley just rode off and the horse's neck stretched until it wouldn't stretch any more. Finally, he gave a great leap and began following Charley's saddle horse. Charley said "Good Boy!" and led him to the river where he drank long and deep. He led him around awhile longer, then moved the log to a new grassy location and tied the horse back to it. As they rode toward the house, Charley said, "That is your saddle horse as soon as you heal up and get so's you can ride him."

Next day as Busby was pulling on his new boots Charley said, "You know that same young feller left his chaps hangin' on the wall. Try 'em on. If they fit they're yours." Just like the boots, the fine leather chaps fit Busby perfectly. How proud he was of how he looked. His first chore every day was to milk the cow. He earned every drop he got from the wild old range cow, but somehow the process seemed more dignified in his cowboy duds.

Over the summer Charley and Busby branded calves, repaired trails, watered the hay field, and spent every spare minute building a cabin. Charley would get Busby started, then ride off to Blue Mountain to his horse training camp. He would sometimes leave the canyon in the morning on a half-broke bronc, and return that night on an even snakier one, leading a completely unbroken animal. Busby got to go up on the mountain quite often and loved doing so, but he always had to ride some bronc when he did. He gradually developed into an excellent rider and put hours of training into the horses that Charley got started. The horse Charley had told him would be his saddle horse eventually turned out to be much too gentle and obedient for Busby, so Charley told him he would sell him, and Busby could have his choice of the wild horses they would break that winter.

The building of the cabin had to be put on hold until fall, because Charley had gotten an unusually large number of horses to break that summer. He wanted to get them finished before the big wild horse chase in the fall when there would be more new horses to work with.

At last the horses were all processed and returned to their owners as nice ranch horses. They would all be used for the fall work by their owners and would become whatever it was their destiny to be. Some would become roping horses for rodeo cowboys, some would be little girl's pets. Most would be cow ponies. They would move herds, carry baby calves, rope cattle for branding and doctoring, catch wild cattle on the range and turn them toward home. They would be a vital part of some rancher's family.

Excitement was running high about the fall wild horse gather. Charley told Busby he was a good enough cowboy and could help. First, though, they had to get some chores done on the home place. They closed up the horse camp, and headed down the mountain with a string of long-legged, stout horses that were built for speed and endurance. Charley had bought some oats in Vernal, and they fed the horses grain every day to harden them up.

Charley sharpened up the old scythe and applied linseed oil to the aging handle. He told Busby it was a mowing machine and showed him how and where to use it. Busby would make big slashing half circles from right to left through the tall grass with the twenty-four-inch blade. He soon found that he must go all the way in one sweep or the hay wouldn't lay down evenly and made a big mess. At first the stubs and holes in the dirt he left made his work look like that of a toothless donkey, but finally he mastered the system and came to take great pride in how short and smooth his blade cut, and how the hay lay out smooth and shining in the sun. When he went in for supper that night Charley bragged on him and said, "I never seen a young feller who could use a scythe so good." Next day after the sun had dried the hay Busby went out and stacked it in long rows with a pitch fork. Then Charley came dragging a skid of light boards by his saddle horn. He told Busby to pile as much hay on the skid as he could. Then Charley dragged the skid off and dumped the hay under an overhanging cliff with a tumble-down brush fence thrown up in front of it. After they got it all hauled in, then Charley said, "Busby you need to stack that neatly and tromp each layer so it will stay fresh. I'd help you but I got to shove some cattle out east." Busby was not happy with his assignment.

Charley could see that Busby was still mad at him the next day. It looked like time for a little fun, so late in the afternoon he said, "Get your horse. We gotta go get some meat." They rode to Rat Spring on the north face of Blue Mountain and waited for the big bucks to come off the mountain to water. Carefully, Charley chose one, then handed Busby the 30-30 rifle. Shaking with excitement, Busby raised the rifle, carefully sighted in, and pulled the trigger. The big buck dropped, shot in the heart. The two men cleaned the deer, then threw it over Busby's saddle and he walked home leading his horse. He was so proud and happy that the long walk seemed short. They skinned and cooled the deer overnight. Next morning Charley fried up a big skillet of the fresh meat for breakfast. Then he said, "Now we have to cut it in thin strips and cut off all the fat." It took nearly all day. They laid the strips out on a long board salvaged from a heap of driftwood along the river. Then they salted it heavily on both sides to keep the flies from blowing it. Charley had a partial roll of rusty barbed wire. They stretched it between corral poles and fence posts and draped the salted meat over it. With four days in the hot sun the meat dried and shrank, becoming jerky. Busby couldn't get enough of it. They put it in clean flour sacks and stored it hanging by nails from the ridge pole of the dugout.

Charley and Busby searched the driftwood piles along the edges of the river that had been left by high spring run-off. They dragged home anything that could be used in building the cabin. What they gathered, along with what logs they had salvaged out of Billy Hall's cabin, looked to them like enough to build the new cabin with.

Busby asked Charley what had happened to Hall's cabin. An explosion of some kind appeared to have blown out one wall and completely collapsed the cabin. Charley told him that for a while after Billy Hall left, Pat Lynch, a hermit who lived in the canyon, stayed there. One of them must have had some dynamite stored in the cabin, because one day Pat was in the cabin and all at once there was a big boom that blew him clear outside. Pat always thought he was being pursued by somebody that wanted to kill him. When the blast tossed him out of the house he yelled, "They have killed me again." Thereafter, the whole area Green River to Charley's place was called "Pat's Hole."

Charley and Busby's prize find was a fine, smooth, straight log from Billy's old house large enough to make a fine center post. They also had a ridge pole and two side logs which would make the foundation for a fine roof.

One day they rode to Vernal for supplies. Charley said they were prosper-ous and to prove it bought them each a new white hat. They had high crowns and broad brims and could be shaped any damn way you wanted them. Busby decided to style his with just a single crease in the top front of the crown. The store manager steamed the crease in for him. It sure did make him look tall. Charley bought them new Levis and a new shirt and scarf apiece, too. Busby bought himself spurs with a little bigger rowel than he needed. He also had jingles on them. Jingles were small metal dangles attached to the shank of the spurs that jingled when he walked. He loved the sound of the jingles and of the big rowels spinning. He was hoping there was a dance coming up soon so he could show off his new stuff. As they rode home in their new duds, leading two pack horses laden with supplies, Busby was the happiest he could ever remember being.

The wild horse roundup was in early November. It was the damndest horse race Busby had ever seen. They jumped a herd of about thirty wild horses just under the north rim of Roundtop. There were five men placed strategically along the rim to give direction to the racing herd. They rode their horses at breakneck speed over rocks and brush and ledges moving the horses ever westward along the north side of Blue Mountain. Some escaped along the way, but they ended up with a good many captured in a camouflaged corral they had built earlier. They roped and tied down the young horses they wanted and turned out the rest. Charley chose five fine looking horses. They haltered them and after much hard work got them down off Blue Mountain to the Tom Blevins place at Red Rock.

They worked hard breaking the horses. Busby fell in love with one and true to his word Charley let him have it. He rode the horse for many years, even when he became the foreman of the famous Square S ranch. Charley and Busby moved back to the ranch to finish training the horses and get on with their ranch work.

Busby was anxious to finish the cabin and worked relentlessly on it. He wasn't happy with the slightly crooked driftwood lumber that framed the door and windows, but it had to do because there was none other. They carefully searched out smooth, slender poles to fit tightly together over the ridge poles. Then they made excursions with a pack horse and gathered thick, whole strips of cedar bark, which they laid tightly across the poles. Then, at last, it was time to cover the roof with a thick blanket of dirt. Busby carefully watered and packed the dirt on the roof so it wouldn't blow off.

Busby was dying to go out and get glass for the windows. Charley finally agreed, only if they rode out the two skittish horses that needed work the most. It was a wild trip, with the horses performing runaway bucking fits through the ledges and trees, along with a few pouting spells where they lay flat on the ground and wouldn't get up. They got to Vernal, had the glass they needed cut to size, spent the night, and in the morning saddled up for the ride home. It just wasn't looking good for the glass or the man carrying it. Finally they wrapped the glass securely in gunny sacks , and Charley set the glass on the roof of a shed. He snubbed Busby's horse's head up close to his own saddle horn, and told Busby to get on. He did, and the two horses treated them to a dusty merry-go-round for about fifteen minutes. Finally Busby's horse recovered some semblance of calm and lined out in a walk. Charley said, "Now Busby, I'll keep his head snubbed up until he settles down. You grab that glass as we go by. Busby carried that glass in his arms all day. When they finally got home he set the glass tenderly on a high rock, and spent

A winter view of Charley Mantle's homestead looking down Hells Canyon.

hours getting the feeling back in his arms. The next morning he told Charley he had to milk the cow himself today because those windows were goin' in. He had them all in and firmly secured with putty by ten o'clock.

How proud the two men were of their new cabin. Last of all they put on the oldest boots they had, then poured lots of water on the cabin floor. They added sand to the mud and tromped it into the mud. Then they added more sand to the mud and stomped some more until they finally got the dirtfloor smooth and practically dust free.

They weaned the calves in December and fed them a little cottonseed cake to get them used to it. When the winters were hard the calves had to know what the cake was and to have developed a taste for it, because it was about all that could keep them alive. In January they brought the thin cows in off the rough pastures and put them on Hospital Hill. It was a little pasture on a hill on the opposite side of the river that you could only get cattle on by sanding the ice on the river and crossing the cows over the ice. The pasture was full of good grass, and they supplemented the cattle's diet with cottonseed cake and doctored them every day until they got their strength back. They had to rope and snub each of them to a tree and give them a creosote bath to rid them of the lice that sapped their strength.

Charley butchered a dry cow in December. The meat aged awhile hanging in a tree, then froze solid. They cut steaks off with an ax as they needed them. Busby got tired of his diet of biscuits, meat and canned tomatoes. One day in early January he rode out the twenty miles to Youghall "to get the mail." He got a ride to Elk Springs and bought some dried fruit, potatoes, carrots and onions. He also got some hard candy for Charley. After that, he went out to check the mail every two weeks. Charley suspected he went because it was his only chance to wear his "real" cowboy hat, boots, spurs and chaps. Busby had ordered a camera, and was nearly ready to die from anticipation. When it finally arrived, he brought it triumphantly home only to discovered that it had no film, so he rode back the forty miles and ordered film, which finally arrived in March. Many of the photos in this book were taken by Busby.

One day during the winter, Charley said, "Busby we gotta build a round corral here to work these horses in. Help me pack up and we'll go cut some posts and poles. They camped out in a really terrible little cramped cave out east of Hells Canyon. For a whole week they cut sturdy tall cedar posts for foundation posts for the corral. They searched out slender, tall trees for the rails. They trimmed them and stacked them so they would dry straight. They left the bark on the cedar poles and posts because Charley said they would last forever that way. Then they moved camp and cut long slender cottonwood poles for the gate poles. They peeled these because Charley said they cured and lasted better that way. They even rode up on the side of Blue Mountain for a few Aspen tree poles for the gate. They would be strong and light and would last a long time.

Just as soon as the ground thawed they built the corral. It was magnificent. Busby and Charley were really proud of their creation. Busby noticed during this time of hard work the complete lack of visiting by Charley's old buddies. Through all the rest of the time they had been around spinning yarns and hanging around helping a little with the horse and cattle work.

When spring came Busby cleaned up and aired out the cabins for the arrival of Charley's sister, Nancy, who was coming for a visit. And Wellen also came home that spring. He was still sick, but recovering and the doctors thought it would do him good to get back to the country he loved.

Evelyn, too, had entered the picture and it was obvious to Busby that his cowboy hero was in love. Busby was a good and dedicated photographer. He took hundreds of excellent pictures, which he would share with Evelyn later on. When he left he made her a gift of the camera. She took pictures with it for many years.

Busby cleaned out the old ditch, repaired the dirt dam in the creek, and irrigated the field so there would be hay that winter, and started thinking about maybe he should be moving on. A government cattle buyer came through the country. He bought any cattle you wanted to sell at a set price. The purpose was just to help keep ranchers and homesteaders from starving out. The cattle buyer hired Busby. Only after checking with Charley that he could do without his help did Busby accept the job. He and his horse left, but he assured Charley that he would be back often, and that they were friends forever. He always said that becoming a cowboy at the hand of Charley Mantle and riding at his side was the most fun he ever had in his life and the experience he treasured the most.

5

The Fullers Visit Charley

AS THE SUMMER WORE ON TOWARD LABOR DAY, Evelyn began to dread the time when she would be leaving Blue Mountain again. The dryfarm homestead was doing very poorly and not producing a living for the Fuller family. She feared they would never return and could not bear the thought of never seeing Charley Mantle again.

Finally the day came when the Fullers had their possessions packed up and were ready to leave for the winter. Evelyn said a tearful goodbye to Charley and promised to see him when school was out next June. For all his efforts to remain aloof his eyes were wet with tears as he hugged her hard and said goodbye.

Mr. Fuller found work in the coal mines at Oak Creek, but Evelyn begged to be able to finish her last year of high school in Hayden. Ruth Folton, a friend of her parents came to see the Fullers and asked if Evelyn might stay with them for the school year. They readily agreed, and Evelyn entered school resolved to extract every bit of knowledge available from every class. She was obsessed with gaining knowledge and was an outstanding student. By year's end, she would be valedictorian. Her teachers said that she seemed destined to be a teacher. Her retention of the materials she studied and her ability to express herself were exceptional.

Evelyn was also very athletic and full of energy. She participated in the girls track events and played baseball after school with the boys team. Evelyn and her friend were starters on the girls basketball team and got to travel to other towns with the team. When the team had a game at Oak Creek, Evelyn was able to visit her parents and spent Christmas vacation with the family. She was shocked to see her mother pale and sickly looking. Her mother was so weak she was hardly able to do the household chores. She coughed a lot and Evelyn often saw blood on her lips.

Evelyn had only been back at school for a week when one day a messenger came to the door of her friend's home. The man said he was a neighbor of the Fuller family in Oak Creek and had sent him to get Evelyn because the family was moving to California. He said that her mother had become very ill with a recurrence of tuberculosis and the doctor had ordered her immediate removal to a lower elevation. With a heavy heart Evelyn said goodbye to her friends, hoping that some miracle would allow her to return to school in Hayden.

One bitter cold, snowy February day, Charley rode out of his canyon home, bound for the post office in Youghall. He couldn't explain why he had felt compelled to make the trip. Usually he did not attempt this treacherous journey during the winter months. He was well stocked with supplies for the winter and besides he had some broncs he was breaking which needed daily riding.

He rode one horse to break a trail in the snow for a second horse and changed mounts frequently as one would get too tired to fight the drifts without relief. Along the way, he suddenly remembered something. This was Evelyn's birthday! February 18. Could it be that he was going to the post office just because it was a silly girl's silly birthday? A new eagerness filled him, and he urged the horses on as fast as they could manage.

When he arrived at the post office in Youghall there was nobody around; it was empty, just as it had been when he found the letter from Wellen. The post office was just a cabin on the east end of Blue Mountain, in Bear Valley, where the postmaster ran a few cattle in the summer and sold a few groceries out of his living room. His home served as a post office for the people on Blue Mountain, as well as for Charley and Rial Chew who lived in the canyon country.

Inside, Charley found the stove still warm, so he added a stick of wood and set the coffee pot to the front of the stove. The post office was behind a window with bars on it. Under the bar was a note scrawled on a scrap of paper. It said "Help yourself. Coffee pot's on. The mail is in a box in back." Charley opened the door with shaking hands and found the box behind the window. He pawed through the little bit of mail. There was a letter addressed to him, but it was from California. He desperately searched through the rest of the mail, but found nothing more for him. Despondent, he poured himself a cup of coffee and sat down on the bench by the stove.

He slowly tore open the envelope and began to read, "My dearest Charley—" Dread filling him, he fumbled to the last page and saw, "Love, Evelyn." She told him how her mother had become ill, and they had to take her to California or she would die. She told him of her heartbreak at leaving school. Most of all she told him she missed him, and nothing in heaven or earth would keep her from returning to Blue Mountain the following spring.

Then Charley prepared to do something he only did in rare circumstances: write a letter. He had the handwriting of a fourth grader long out of practice at writing. He wrote that he was fine, but that he missed her and so did Pacer. He said she had to come back or he would be the saddest cowboy on earth! Charley was embarrassed at the tender things he had said, but he searched out an envelope, put the letter inside and licked it so thoroughly that there was no chance of it flying open. He sent it to the address Evelyn had given him and left three pennies lying on top of it for postage. When Evelyn received the letter she thought it was the most beautiful piece of literature she had ever read.

Charley rested his horses and fed them for the long ride home tomorrow. He felt real good about having made this trip. He also felt a real urgency to get home and fix up the homestead cabin, because he intended to invite Evelyn down for a visit just as soon as she returned to Blue Mountain. In his mind he kept hatching up schemes to keep her from ever leaving him again. There was nothing certain that she would be back this time, but she had told him she would and he knew how determined she could be. He must think of a way to keep her near him forever. Another important thing he must do was to get his ranch work in shape and his cattle settled so he could spend all summer at his horse training camp. Fortunately, Buzz was there to help him with the spring work.

Although the end of May was much too early to be on Blue Mountain, but Charley was there at his horse camp, nonetheless, keeping an anxious eye on the Fuller place for any sign of their return. Finally about noon one day an old pickup turned in to their homestead. These days, Charley had made a habit of riding the high ridges with a good view. He was so excited when he saw the truck turn in that he gave a yelp and spurred the bronc he was riding into a run. Instead of a run the frightened bronc went into a wild running, bucking frenzy that nearly took them off a cliff. Finally regaining control, Charley rode as quickly as he could to the Fuller cabin. Evelyn saw him coming and walked out to meet him. They only shook hands, but the joy at seeing each other shone in their eyes.

Gradually the young people returned to Blue Mountain. Once their spring work was caught up, they began to have time to see each other. They had taffy pulls and square dances at each other's homes. The dances and rodeos came and went. Evelyn was more popular than ever because she had become the most beautiful girl in the country. Charley worried as he saw the competition circling "his" girl. In desperation, one day he asked her parents if they would like to visit his ranch and do some fishing one day soon. The Fullers agreed and on the appointed day they rode down off Blue Mountain into the Canyons. As the day wore on, Evelyn's parents became increasingly worried. This was turning out to be no ordinary little horseback ride. This trip was long and rough and seemed to be leading endlessly into more of the same. To their world-weary eyes it was not at all the beautiful, majestic vacation paradise their daughter had described. Finally, when they thought their bodies could not bear another rock in the trail or another gully to jump, their horses pulled up to a hitching rack made of a crooked green cottonwood pole notched into the top of two sturdy unpeeled cedar posts. In front of them stood a cabin out of their worst nightmares. It was constructed of misshapen logs of every size. It was surrounded by overgrown sagebrush and rabbit brush. Charley's cheery, "Get off and come on in" only confirmed their fears that this really was where they were headed. When the cabin first came into view they had seen a clean shaven young man disappear into the cabin, and smoke had soon started pouring out of the chimney.

As Evelyn's parents pushed open the door they smelled the heavenly scent of fresh coffee and hot biscuits. The dirt floor had been freshly swept and sprinkled down. The unpainted board table was decorated with a lonely Sego Lily in a crushed enamel cup. Holding up the center beam of the cabin was a large, smooth upright log planted firmly into the floor. It seemed the only straight log in the entire structure of the cabin. The varying size logs that made up the walls had varying size cracks between them. These cracks were filled with a compound called "dobbin" made from a mixture of yellow soil. The roof was made of five parallel beams, covered with smaller poles and branches laid in the opposite direction and covered with a layer of cedar bark, on top of which was a thick layer of dirt. The two windows, one on each side, were cut out of the logs, then framed with boards, which obviously had been salvaged as driftwood from the river. The framed four-pane windows were then made to fit inside. They opened upward on leather strap hinges, and were secured in the open position with a leather latch fastened to a beam in the ceiling. The door frame, made of thicker driftwood, with hardly any straight edges, was something to behold. The door hole had come out a little less true than a rectangle, so the door which was made out of straighter boards had just been altered to fit. The door was secured with leather hinges and latch.

Charley introduced the nice looking young man as Buzz. He graciously invited them to sit down on the stools at the table and served them all a cup of coffee. While they gratefully sipped the scalding hot coffee Buzz fried up some buckskin he had cut off a hind leg of deer he had produced from a dingy grey sack, that had at one time been white. When the skillet full of meat was cooked he set it in the middle of the table, and produced a pan full of sourdough biscuits from the oven. Everyone dug in gratefully. They dipped their biscuits into the good brown drippings on the inside of the skillet and ate their fill of buckskin and biscuits. For the moment, Evelyn's parents forgot the apprehension they felt for their daughter. The conversation was easy and entertaining, the cabin was comfortable and cozy, and the food was delicious.

Evelyn eagerly showed her parents the swimming hole and the Indian caves and the enchanting shadows that crept up the towering cliffs with the setting of the sun. They noted the sweet cold water from the generously flowing spring that ran under a cliff in front of the cabin. Charley and Buzz used the spring as their refrigerator. In a small cave deep in the shelter of the cliff, cooled by the spring water below, they had stored their fresh and cured meat, lard, honey, syrup and milk.

Mr. Fuller noticed with relief that there were good corrals built a little way from the house. They were built with straight, strong poles and posts, well constructed and well situated. He also noted that there was an irrigation system originating at a hand shovelled dam under the overhang where the spring water ran. This must be to water the vegetable garden and the hay field, he thought, and set out to look over the crops. He found five or six old fruit trees that had been planted years ago and had not received much care since. They were full of dead wood and missing all the leaves as far up as a deer could stand on its hind legs to reach. However, there was a little fruit on them. It was obvious that no water had been run down the ditch in recent history. Under an overhang he found where a fenced haystack had been. The fence was of dead, untrimmed trees thrown up as a barrier in front of a cavity in the cliff that had obviously been used as a bed ground for cattle. The part where the haystack had been was separated from the rest of the bed ground by a brush fence. Stuck up in a crack he found a hand-held scythe and realized with a jolt that it was this bronc stomper's only mowing machine and he had only one tiny irrigated hay field, so probably only put up enough hay each summer for winter feed for a saddle horse and a milk cow.

The next day Charley took them on a ride around his ranch and showed them his fine pastureland. Deep in the canyons along the Bear River the small parks on each side of the river were lush and green. The hills and flats along the bench at the foot of Blue Mountain grew thick with harder, more substantial feed, which would have more food value than the soft feed along the river. There was a lot of vegetation growing that provided natural salt for the cattle. There were north slopes where the snow would lay giving the cattle a water supply very near to all the plentiful winter feed. There were south slopes to warm the cattle's cold bodies in winter, and produce early spring feed and there was plenty of warm, dry bed ground under the cliffs. He told them of the natural springs which were placed by God himself at just the right intervals. Baby calves and mothers giving milk could travel between them easily in their search for good grass. He explained to them that he had pasture land on top of Blue Mountain for his cattle during the summer. They did so much better in the cool mountain air. The canyons were too hot in summer and the calves couldn't gain and grow as well.

The day passed quickly. The Fullers began to realize that they were dealing with an expert cowman here, but certainly not a farmer. By comparison, Evan Fuller was a farmer who loved the earth and producing crops from it. He was desperately disappointed to realize that Charley Mantle frankly hated farming and was disdainful of farmers. He vowed that as soon as they got home he would try to get Evelyn interested in one of the other young men. This one would never provide her with a home or comfort. Good lord, there wasn't even a potato in the house. How, he wondered, did Buzz and Charley keep from getting scurvy and dying as the sailors of old had when they had no vegetables or fruit to eat.

With considerable relief the Fullers rode out of Charley's canyon paradise the next day.

6

Rial's Ranch

CHARLEY FOUND HIMSELF WANTING TO SPEND all his time with Evelyn, but she wasn't hanging around his corral as much any more. She was popular with men and women alike. She had a kindly, caring way and yet was always ready to join in any adventure offered. Charley noted, too, that Rial had begun showing up on Blue Mountain more often these days and invited everybody to spend the Fourth of July at his ranch. It was agreed that if Charley could lead them on the trail, Rial would be at his ranch waiting when they arrived. Eight people were able to go. They rode a rough, rocky trail, starting just under the rim of Round Top and on west down the steep north face of Blue Mountain. This area was one of the main hideouts of the wild horses Charley caught and broke to ride, so he knew the trail well and led the way.

When they reached the foothills at the base of Blue Mountain the soil changed in color. It was blood red. They watered their horses at Red Rock, where the cool abundant spring pulsed like a heartbeat from its birthplace at the foot of a short red cliff. A short way farther down, the riders ate wild currents off the bushes that grew by a spring that dripped, as if weeping, large quantities of water from a moss-padded hole in the cliff. A cabin was near the dripping spring, but nobody was home. Charley led them up and over a round, flat topped red butte. Lying exposed was a forest of petrified wood. They examined the petrified wood and searched for arrowheads until the shadows started getting long, indicating it would soon be dark.

Charley headed his bronc off through the sagebrush flat toward the canyon walls they could see in the distance. They rode to a point where the land dropped off below them into a shallow canyon. Beyond a creek of lovely rushing water, sheer white cliffs reared into the sky. A long, rambling ranch house of logs, with a dirt roof cuddled along the creek among the trees. Smoke poured from the chimney, and a cool vine covered front porch seemed to invite them in. As they dismounted at the hitch rack and were tying up their horses, Rial came out of the house. With blue eyes sparkling and a big grin on his face, he welcomed them. "Come on in and wash up. Mother has supper on the table."

Next morning they rode off down Pool Creek Canyon. Along the way Rial showed them ancient Indian petroglyphs chipped into the canyon walls. It was a hot July day, and the air in the canyon was still and close. Rial stopped his horse in front of a strange little cave and stood smiling and silent before them. The cave's small mouth seemed cut with a sharp knife from an extra smooth, sheer section of the high canyon wall. It was in the direct sunlight, and so hot the grass was dried and curled beneath their feet. They tied their horses to big sagebrush, their curiosity thoroughly aroused. Suspiciously they approached the cave mouth. Within, they could see that the cave was very shallow, and the back was a flat, sheer wall, just like the wall from which the front had been cut. Approaching to within about six feet of the entrance, they were struck by a rush of cold, moving air. It smelled fresh and clean and carried the feel of moisture. The tall men had to stoop to enter. Standing inside the opening, they could look straight up the long slab of rock in the back until it disappeared into darkness. On either end of the cave the passages became smaller as they disappeared into the darkness. The delicious cool air came on a gentle breeze from both sides. Rial told them folklore of how this cave had spiritual meaning to the Indians.

Feeling cool and refreshed, the group mounted their horses and continued on down the canyon. Soon the narrow canyon ended as its water emptied into the Green River. In awe they gazed across the river to where where a cliff over 1,000 feet high formed the perfect prow of a great steamship, rearing mightily into the blue sky above. its sides were so steep and smooth that their eyes were drawn upward until their necks could no longer stand the strain. The steamship appeared to be sailing into the Green River. Rial told them that this was Steamboat Rock.

They turned their horses up the Green River, riding close to the steep, eroded bank to where the river made a great loop to pass around Steamboat Rock. Rial stopped his horse, faced the Green River, and uttered a long, loud series of yipping cries. To the last yip, the towering, slightly dished-in side of Steamboat Rock returned his call. Echo after echo of the call sounded, becoming fainter until all sound ended. Everyone took their turn calling to the cliff. Some threw their best cattle-moving calls. Some screamed. Some sang. Echo rock returned whatever was given to it. Appropriately, the place was called Echo Park.

They rode on up the river a short way. Emerging from a grove of box elder trees they came upon a sight that would remain in their memories for the rest of their lives. In this semi-desert land of western Colorado water was the king that controlled people's lives. Before them was the merger of two bountiful rivers and the birth of a new, bigger river. From the north, flowing between two steep canyon walls came the great, somewhat greenish colored Green River, while from the east, flowing beneath towering golden cliffs, came the Bear River, sparkling clear and golden. The triangle between the two rivers was a steep drop from the red cliffs of Douglas Mountain to great rounded, white and gold sandstone bluffs. Finally, at the confluence of the rivers it became a beautiful sandy bank with a box elder grove behind it. The two colors of water ran side by side along the foot of Steamboat Rock, finally joining into one soft muted combination of both. They had truly seen the birth of a river!

They waded across the Bear River to the sand bank and sunned and played and splashed. They swam down to Echo Rock and practiced their yells. They hungrily ate their pancake sandwiches and waited a while for them to digest as they lay in the shade of the bank on the moist cool sand. They could not tear themselves away from this beautiful place until well past the hour when they should have departed.

Reluctantly next morning the group of young people said goodbye to Rial and his mother. Charley led them home by a different trail, which took them onto the west end of Blue Mountain, where they emerged onto the almost flat, treeless top of Blue Mountain. They travelled east, passing through range land stocked with big rangy cattle. At the cows' sides were fat, lazy calves who ran and kicked up their heels behind the horses in a playful ritual. As they went along members of the group dropped off to their own cabins. When they came to the Red Onion, Charley and Evelyn said goodbye to the riders who remained, and went off down the draw to Evelyn's cabin. There Charley said a formal goodbye to her, tipped his hat to her parents, and rode on to his own place.

7

Courting and Proposal

THE FOURTH OF JULY TRIP TO RIAL'S RANCH had been a highlight of the summer. The young people all had to work hard and had very little time to get together again until the early August dance at the Red Onion. As July wore on, the Fullers kept Evelyn very busy so she had not been able to visit Charley's camp to see him. And when he came by he was not given a warm welcome nor invited in. It seemed that they were always just leaving or just going out to do something that didn't include him. He became suspicious that they did not want Evelyn to be with him. One day he came by and was able to see Evelyn just a second before her father took her away for something urgent that she needed to do in the cabin. Charley had quickly asked her to meet him tomorrow down by the twin rocks at 11:00 o'clock. They must talk. She agreed.

The next morning, Charley tied his horse to a bushy tree in the shallow dry creek bed and walked a short distance to the twin rocks. A little after 11:00 Evelyn arrived from the other direction, running and out of breath. Charley asked why he was not being permitted to see her any more. Her dark, golden eyes flashing with anger she said, "My father thinks I am falling in love with you. He said, 'No daughter of mine is going to marry a man who lives in a shack with a dirt floor and doesn't even grow a garden for food'. He wants me to start dating other guys and forget you. He said you are too old for me anyway." Charley said, "Are you falling in love with me? I am already in love with you, you know." Evelyn threw herself into his arms and sobbed, "Of course I am in love with you. I have always been in love with you. I can't love anyone else, and don't want to date any other man."

They made plans to meet at next week's dance at the Red Onion. There they would discuss further what they could do to convince her parents to let them see each other. During the next few days Charley made it a point to ride his broncs by the Fuller homestead every day. He would search out Mr. Fuller and visit with him at length about himself, his plans, which included introducing some conveniences at his ranch. He could never force himself to say he would till any soil and plant any seeds, however; cowboys just didn't do that sort of thing. He told him he had a milk cow that provided milk every day. He didn't tell him, however, that it was a wild Hereford range cow that he milked only by pure force after he could get her roped and tied up. He told him of the cedar fence posts he had cut and the fences he was going to build. He told him of his sisters and his brothers and how they had been separated when their parents died, but had remained close and loving. Despite his apprehensions about him as a husband for his daughter, Mr. Fuller began to like Charley and recognized in him a gentleness and caring for others. He even saw a willingness to change and learn new ways of doing things. It became apparent to him why Charley was one of the most liked men in the area. His ability to have fun at whatever he was doing and his outrageous sense of humor were captivating.

Mr. Fuller could do anything with his hands. He was an excellent carpenter, and a good mechanic. He could handle a team of horses as well as anybody in the country. He knew how to prepare the earth for planting, and he knew how and when to plant the seeds of any crop. He knew how to make dams to put irrigation water out on fields. He even knew how to build retainer walls of stone, and how to install rip-rap for flood control. Charley came to respect and admire him in these few days. He found himself eager to go by for the visits now, and their friendship grew rapidly. He began to hope he might get invited up to the house again, but it never happened. He only saw Evelyn from a distance.

The weekend for the big dance at the Red Onion finally arrived. Charley got dressed up in his new Levis, turned up a wide cuff to the outside just the proper width, and put on a white shirt with a black silk scarf tied loosely around his neck. Then he set his good hat at just the right jaunty angle. He patted a little "smell-um-good" on his neck and off a little as he trotted his horse by the neighbor's on his way to the dance. For her part, Evelyn got a fresh haircut, shampooed and carefully rinsed her hair in rain water. Then she sneaked a little of her mother's rouge and a couple of squirts of her perfume, brushed her already shining hair a hundred strokes and put on the new rose dress she had ordered from the Montgomery Ward catalog. Johnny Milheim came by to pick her up in his car and her parents were happy to see her interested in somebody besides Charley. They also went to the dance in their old pickup.

Everybody got right into the party. Each person had brought something to eat to add to the overloaded table. No one wasted a minute to start eating, and continued to do so all through the afternoon and evening. Marcus Jensen fiddled his heart out. The cowboy boots shuffled and clattered and stamped, and happy voices filled the Red Onion. Charley and Evelyn danced together only once, so as not to make themselves the center of Mr. Fuller's attention. Nobody noticed they both disappeared at the same time. Standing a little away from the building, still within plain sight although it was dark, they met to discuss their problem.

Charley told Evelyn how much he had come to like her father. She told him that her father had mentioned that maybe he had misjudged Charley; that he seemed like a real nice man, but just a shame he was too old for Evelyn to date. With a desperate look on his face, and mumbling like a school boy in front of the class, Charley Said, "Evelyn, will you marry me?" "Yes, oh yes," she said.

The next day, Charley rode over to the Fuller cabin. He tied his horse to the hitch rack and went in search of Mr. Fuller. He found him hard at work repairing a wagon bed. Charley said, "Evan, I need to talk to you, can we sit down?" Mr. Fuller had seen his daughter's glowing face, so knew full well what was coming and hoped the handsome cowboy would never manage to get his voice to work. He wasn't about to put him at ease if he could help it.

Finally, Charley croaked, "I'm gonna marry Evelyn! I mean, sir, if it is all right with you, I would like to marry her. I love her and I will be good to her." Evan took a moment to get his thoughts together, and finally said, "Charley, I like you. You are a fine man, and I want to stay friends with you. But, you are fourteen years older than Evelyn. You are almost my age. If you had a child in a year, you would be fifty-one when that child was eighteen years old. That might be fair to the first one, but what if you had four children, say, with two or three years between each one. You would be over sixty when your obligation to the last child was finished. It seems to me Evelyn would have most of the burden of raising the kids. I have seen where you live. You have chosen an impossibly hard life in the hardest place to live I have ever seen. Women can't live like that. They need friends and nice clothes and comfortable houses. Evelyn is used to having fresh vegetables to eat, too. It looked to me like you just eat meat and biscuits. You don't have a car, and there is no road to your ranch. Evelyn couldn't come out to visit her family and friends, and they couldn't drive in to see her. No, Charley, I just can't give you permission to marry my daughter.

Charley stood up, bristling with anger. "She don't want nobody but me, and we're gonna get married whether you give your permission or not." Evan knew this would be Charley's reaction, so had already considered what terms he could negotiate for a conditional yes to the proposal. "All right. You don't have my blessing, but I will accept your proposal, on one condition. I will spend some time down in the canyon at your ranch and help you with a lot of improvements to make Evelyn's life easier. I will have to do it off and on as I can get the time, but I'm sure you won't mind being alone some. Is it a deal?" Relief flooding his face, Charley stuck out his hand, "Good! Let's shake on it."

Charley told Evelyn what her father had said. She felt honored that two such wonderful men were worried about her welfare. Secretly she believed that she could live in a cave and carry water from the river in a gourd and be happy just so long as she was with Charley. They made plans to ride to Vernal, Utah and be married the next week.

When Charley and Evelyn rode into the McCarl ranch just east of Vernal they were greeted heartily by Thede and Pearl. Charley had been a favorite of theirs for a long time. They had known him since he was a kid and he often stayed with them when he came to Vernal on business. They were astounded when Charley introduced them to Evelyn and told them of their wedding plans. He had always vowed he would never get married and they had never seen him really fond of any woman. This was one of the most beautiful girls they had ever seen. Proud and poised, she obviously loved this cowboy and intended to be by

Charley and Evelyn's wedding picture, August 12, 1926.

his side for the rest of her life. Charley said, "I was hopin'" you two would go with us as witnesses when we get married tomorrow."

Motherly Pearl put her arm around Evelyn and led her into the house. "You two are going to stay right here with us, have supper and spend the night. I want to have a long talk with you, Missy. No girl ought to get married without an older woman to talk to first. I want you to ask me about anything you want to know about, and there ain't nothin' too private to ask me. Besides, I'm gonna tell you about a lot of things you need to know that you wouldn't even know to ask me about. Then, in one year I want you to come back here for another talk. We'll keep in touch. You can always count on me and Thede to be your friends." And it was true.

The next morning the four of them drove into Vernal in Thede's car. The first stop was to get a marriage license at the court house. The county clerk told them where to find a justice of the peace. Determined, but nervous, the young man and young girl stood beside each other facing the justice of the peace. Thede and Pearl, stood beside them. They repeated their vows of love, honor, obedience, and faithfulness through sickness and health, for richer or poorer. It was done. Their life together had begun. Hardship, pain, sorrow—yes, but boredom and mediocrity would never rob these two of the destiny that was theirs.

8

Getting Home

ITH A PROMISE TO RETURN SOON TO SEE THEM, Charley and Evelyn waved goodbye to Thede and Pearl and rode off toward Blue Mountain. Just west of Jensen, Utah, they rode through the gate and up to the cabin owned by Charley's bachelor uncles just as darkness was falling. They had been his and his brother Lewellyn's guardians after the death of their parents. The old men were overwhelmed to learn that Charley had gotten married. How the hell was he going to support this pretty little thing? Over supper they questioned him. Was he going to take her up on that mountainside where he broke horses and lived under a cedar tree? Was he going to take her down in those canyons and keep her barefoot and pregnant so she wouldn't run away? They allowed that was the only way an 'upper-crust' woman like her would ever stay down there. Evelyn did the supper dishes while they talked. She found herself hoping that Charley was a better housekeeper than these uncles were. Otherwise, it would take a scrubbing from top to bottom before she would ever live in that cabin with him.

Charley unrolled his 'soogan' from the back of his saddle, spread it on the ground and here they spent their wedding night under the stars on the dry yellow clay bank of a dry creek. Prickly grease-wood and pungent rabbit brush grew all around them, but Evelyn thought it was the most beautiful place in the world because she was the wife of Charley Mantle. He was a gentle, tender lover.

The next morning they saddled up early, ate a big breakfast of salt pork and sourdough pancakes washed down with black coffee, and rode on toward Blue Mountain. They arrived at the Fuller cabin in the late afternoon. Evelyn's parents were resigned to the marriage. They were not happy with it, but gradually found themselves approving. Their daughter's happiness was evident, and Charley was obviously helplessly in love with her, and attentive to her needs. He could see that she was completely exhausted by the strain of the last two days and by the long hard ride today. He had planned to just stop by and show the Fullers that all was well, but when invited, decided to stay the night. It would be just too hard on Evelyn to ride on to his horse camp tonight. He made a mental note that he must remember that Evelyn was an amateur horsewoman and he must give her time to get hardened up and experienced before they rode such long distances. Also, he realized that the rugged country they would be riding into would be very difficult and even frightening to her.

Evelyn went to her room to get ready for bed, but fell sound asleep still in her clothes. Charley took off her boots and covered her up. Meantime, Charley visited into the night with his new in-laws. He told them that he planned to gather up everything at his horse camp and move down to the ranch. He would leave his brother Lewellen there to finish up the few horses that needed some more days of riding before their training was complete. His own string of horses he would pack with his and Evelyn's belongings and take them to the ranch, too. Evan and Julia offered to help Evelyn pack up her things so they would be ready to stick into the panniers on the pack horse.

When Evelyn woke the next morning Charley told her that if she wished to stay with her parents an extra day he would go break camp and come back by and pick her up the following day. She would not hear of it, however, and said that she would have everything packed and he should just return and pick her up early that afternoon. He agreed and trotted off to his camp. Charley was anxious to see how Wellen had done with the horses while he was gone, but when he rode into camp he just sat on his horse looking at the mess. Wellen had obviously been gone. The horses were turned loose in the big pasture and he would have one hell of a time catching them. A porcupine had been in camp, too. Everything was chewed open, shredded and scattered. Even his tent ropes had been chewed in two. Only what was hanging on a slender limb of a small cedar tree was untouched. He knew that was his jerky. All the leather had been chewed on his pack saddles, along with what leather was on the halters and bridles. His rawhide ropes had also been chewed, though not all the way through. Cursing Wellen with a string of explicatives so long he had to draw a breath to continue, he threw a private fit of stomping, punching and cussing there on the mountainside all by himself. Finally, he wondered how Evelyn would have reacted to this fit and thanked his lucky stars she hadn't seen it, and certainly not heard it.

He dug in to clean up the mess and salvage the things he would need for the trip to the canyon. He was not nearly done, and hadn't had time to even try and catch a pack horse when it was time to pick up Evelyn. He didn't know how she would react to this mess, but he just couldn't stand being away from her any longer and he had promised to come back for her in early afternoon. Returning to the Fullers he told them what had happened. His father-in-law just nodded his head as if to say, "Just as I thought—there will be no comforts for my daughter with this man." They stacked Evelyn's possessions inside the cabin and arranged to return with a pack horse for them the next day.

When Evelyn saw the state things were in at the camp, she said, "I'll work on this until dark, and you go catch the horses. Go on and get going or we won't get a thing done before dark. I want to go home! Charley's heart caught painfully in his chest at the joy of hearing her call his ranch in the canyons home. Tearing themselves apart from a kiss, they both went to work. Not nearly done by dark, but unable to continue, Charley cooked up some jerky gravy and hot biscuits for supper, and they fell gratefully into bed.

They were awakened at daylight by a racing horse, and a rider screaming like a wild man. The man yanked his horse to a sliding stop at their bedroll, showering them with dirt. "Charley, what the hell you doin' still in bed?" Charley, barely in control of his fury said, "Wellen, you SOB, where have you been?" The grinning Wellen said, "I had to go to town for some flour." Charley said, "How could getting a sack of flour take so long?" Wellen explained, "I had to get some sugar, too." Charley made Wellen ride off down behind the ridge while he and Evelyn got dressed. Then he built a fire and put on the coffee pot. After a breakfast of jerky gravy and flap jacks the two men saddled up and set out to catch the horses. They had to overtake and rope each animal, so it took a couple of hours. When that was done they returned and helped Evelyn salvage what was left of the camp. After an early lunch of jerky gravy and hot biscuits, washed down with hot coffee, Evelyn was thinking how nice it would be to get down to the ranch and get some variety in their diet.

Wellen stayed in camp as planned with just enough provisions to last until he could polish off the broncs, which were going to need a lot more time to "polish off" after running wild for a week. Charley and Evelyn rode down to the Fuller cabin and finished packing the third pack horse with her belongings. Evelyn hugged her parents and begged them not to worry about her. Charley invited them to come down just any time they could and they would be welcome. They waved goodbye as they rode off. They each rode a horse, and they led three pack horses. This was all their earthly possessions. Evan and Julia cried bitter tears as their daughter rode away. Charley and Evelyn took the trail that led off Blue Mountain, along the edge of the impassable gorge of upper Hells Canyon.

9

A New Home

VELYN'S SPIRITS SOARED. She had everything she wanted. Charley set a brisk pace, as they only had about five hours of daylight left. They passed through the spreading bottoms of the valleys on top of Blue Mountain. The dust kicked up by the horses from the black soil plus the heavy aroma of sagebrush filled the air. They passed a few cows with their calves following on their way to a nearby spring for their evening drink. Gradually the big open valleys changed into limestone formations and craggy terrain covered with juniper and pinyon trees. They surprised five mule deer sleeping in the brush, who jumped up with a great popping of limbs and hurrying hooves. Startled, Evelyn's horse jumped sideways and she had to grab the saddle horn to keep from falling off. They began to see more and more deer moving along the sides of the mountains. The deep gorge of Hells Canyon was on their left, beautiful rose and barefaced lavender stone walls, which sank into deep purple shadows. From the far side of Hells Canyon rose the majestic Round Top mountain. It was the highest peak, from where they could almost see Charley's horse camp on the horizon, where the foot of Roundtop met the top of Blue Mountain.

On their right they could look into a round basin of sagebrush flanked by juniper and pinyon. The basin was cupped into the side of Martha's Peak, which rose almost to the height of Roundtop Mountain. The steep sides of Martha's Peak plunged into the depths of the Hells Canyon Gorge.

Charley led the way into the jumble of jagged limestone outcroppings and thick evergreen trees, the horse's iron-shod hooves made a sharp, brisk clatter on the rocky trail. Experts at carrying a heavy load in their panniers, the horses leaned and maneuvered so as not to bump their load on trees and rocks. Charley was no longer leading them, but had tied their lead ropes to the pack saddles. There was no place for them to go off the narrow trail and it gave them more freedom to maneuver their loads. Evelyn was hard pressed to dodge the trees with her body and the rocks with her legs, while at the same time keeping her hat from being scraped off by a tree. She was so engrossed that she looked up in surprise when all the horses stopped. Charley was sitting on his horse grinning in expectation at her. She turned her head away from the mountain and a world of such beauty she had never beheld spread out far, far below her.

41

She felt almost dizzy from the height.

The afternoon sun left the north side of Blue Mountain in shadows where it stretched off to the west. In the distance were the white cliffs of Rial's Pool Creek Ranch. As the focus of her eyes moved closer the earth changed to blood red and long narrow fingers of red ridges sprang from the flanks of Blue Mountain at Red Rock Ranch. The ridges emerged large and tall from the side of the mountain. They extended far into the sagebrush bench below, gradually decreasing in height until they became short, narrow red aprons of earth at the edge of the gray sagebrush flats. As her eyes traveled to the north she could see a jumble of gigantic yellow sandstone cliffs that sank deep into the earth where they were cut through by the deep gorge of Bear River. Rearing high beyond the river were the rose and lavender cliffs of Douglas Mountain, which blotted out her view to the north.

Her eyes returned to the red hills, and she let her gaze drift slowly toward where she stood. The red ridges became shorter and soon were a part of the narrow strip that was the foothills of Blue Mountain. Stretching out from the foothills was a wide sage flat that dropped off sharply into what she knew were the canyons formed by the Bear River and its tributaries. The golden sandstone was cut deep and sheer. Far below the cliffs she caught a brief glimpse of the Bear River where It appeared from time to time as a shining ribbon in the depths. As her eyes traveled up the river, she could see in many places where the river had cut the gorge in such long, narrow loops that only a tall, thin neck of the towering sandstone separated it from itself. As far as she could see to the east the Bear River had cut its tortuous way through the sandstone cliffs.

Directly below her observation point could be seen the bottom of upper Hells Canyon. She could look back along their trail and see down into the gorge. As they had ridden the trail along the rim of the gorge, thick cedars and pinyons had blocked their view of the depths. The gorge was deep and shrouded in shadows, but she could see where the floods had thrown water high onto the walls. As the gorge narrowed just before each cliff edge she could see where the water had spouted from the narrow passage and flew far into thin air to fall hundreds of feet onto the next outcropping. Finally, at a gate only the Lord could have made, Hells Canyon burst from fury to tranquility. The gate itself was made up of two towering pillars jutting from the mountains on either side of the canyon, which seemed to almost join in forming the narrow gate. The pillars were of rose, lavender, red and coffee colored, glistening stone. Outside the gate from the gorge, the canyon became a shallow stream bed with gently sloping sides. Although dry now, deer trails led into the creek bed from the surrounding hills, indicating good feed and a plentiful water supply nearby.

Charley pointed out to Evelyn the trail down Hells Canyon toward the river and told her they would be riding down it. The openness of the canyon ended abruptly, becoming enclosed in sandstone cliffs. The cliffs were short at the top of the canyon becoming progressively taller and the canyon grew narrower as it descended to the river. Evelyn was breathless at the beauty and wonder of it all. A love for this place that was now her home was born in her that day, and would last until the day she died.

Charley caught up the ropes of the pack horses and began leading them again. He knew that the horses, at being almost home would pass him at a high run and scatter their possessions all the way home if not controlled. The riders, too, looked forward to being home. When they arrived, Charley saw his "milk" cow standing nearby with her calf, so while he still had his horse saddled he ran them into the corral. He rode his horse into the corral and asked Evelyn to shut the gate behind them, but to be ready to open it for him in a minute. He rode to within twenty feet of the calf and then with a quick flick of his wrist a loop not more than four inches larger than the calf's head passed over the head and tightened around its neck. Unceremoniously Charley turned his horse around, dallied the rope around his saddle horn, called to Evelyn to open the gate, and dragged the bawling calf outside the gate. The wild-eyed cow followed close behind looking for somebody to kill over the injustice to her baby. Evelyn held her breath and slammed the gate shut just in time.

There was just enough daylight left to unpack and carry everything inside the cabin. In the clean little cabin the "kitchen" corner was furnished with a tin dish pan, a tub, a washboard, a big pot for heating water and a new water bucket with an enamel dipper. There was also a set of four new enamel coffee cups. Charley explained that, Buzz and some of Charley's friends had gotten together and bought them the new stuff as a wedding gift. Buzz also had told him that the best wedding gift of all was a new double-bed mattress, which they promised somehow to deliver.

The wood box was full and Charley soon had the stove hot and served his new bride a hot cup of coffee. Supper followed. It was jerky gravy, hot biscuits, and canned tomatoes. Evelyn was so tired she didn't even note the addition of the vegetable to their diet. The bed was in the corner. It was a shallow box made of strong, slender poles. Sturdy pole legs held it off the dirt floor. Inside the box, strung tight from the poles was an intricate weaving of rawhide. It made a base, on which a lumpy straw-filled mattress laid. On top of the mattress were a top blanket and a bottom blanket, two dirty crushed feather pillows with no pillow cases, and a beeswax treated tarp was spread over it all. Too tired to care and with the man she loved, Evelyn crawled in and had one of the best night's sleep of her life.

Next morning Charley was up at daybreak. He started the fire in the stove and put on the coffee pot. After awaking Evelyn he disappeared from the cabin while she got dressed. Returning with a bucket of cold, sweet spring water, he put it on the crooked board that served as a washstand outside the door. Evelyn brought in the washbasin and put hot water from the kettle on the stove in it, then took it back outside and mixed cold water with the hot, and washed up. Charley did the same, also carefully shaving with his straight razor that was hanging on the wall above the wash basin.

Charley said, "Come on with me while I milk the cow and then I'll fix our breakfast." He took a battered bucket which was turned upside down on a corner shelf, and they went to the corral. The cow looked up and let out a long, low bawl as if announcing she was ready for the challenger. Charley took his lariat rope and went inside. He roped her around her long horns, then dallied around a corral post and reeled her in, all the time dodging her lunges at him. He snubbed her tight to the post, one horn on each side, then maneuvered another rope around the hocks of her hind legs and tied her hind legs together so tight they touched. Then he told Evelyn to let the calf in. He was hungry and raced right in and started sucking and bunting as if he would eat his mother alive. When he started swallowing long gulps, Charley knew the cow had let down her milk, so he dropped a loop around the calf's head and dragged him over to the fence and tied him up. Then he got his bucket and started milking. He stood on both feet, bending over, squeezing with one hand and holding the bucket with the other, leaping back each time both of the cow's hind feet came flying at the bucket. She finally calmed down, and he squatted beside her, put the bucket on the ground and milked with both hands. The steaming milk made a mountain of soft white foam in the bucket. When he extracted all the milk he could get, he turned the calf loose, loosened the cow's back legs then went outside the fence. He reached through the corral rails and took the rope off her horns. The last Evelyn saw of her she was running as if possessed by the devil with her calf close behind. She wondered just how often they needed milk, and made a mental note to remember to tell Charley about the gentle Guernsey cow she was used to milking.

After a hearty breakfast of coffee, jerky gravy and flap jacks Charley wanted to show her around his place. Fifty yards in front of the cabin was a cliff which rose in benches, one stacked on the back of the other, to about 800 feet. The first cliff was dished out and under it in the cool shade ran a fine stream of spring water. Behind the cabin about 100 yards rose a sheer cliff of about 500 feet. These two cliffs ran parallel to each other, forming Hells Canyon down which they had ridden yesterday, and which could now be seen winding narrow and deep within its walls to the East. Within a half mile of the cabin, Hells Canyon ended at a 1,000 foot sheer, smooth sandstone cliff, colored rose red, yellow, and shades of copper and black. Charley pointed to the buzzards circling above it and told her the cliff was named "The Crow's Nest" because of their ever present nest in the top of a very long vertical chip out of the cliff face. At the foot of this towering cliff Hells Canyon creek joined the Bear River.

Charley strode out in front of the cabin, turned around, and said, "Now this new cabin Buzz and me just built. We never had built anything before, but Buzz is pretty handy. Hall's old cabin was up the hill there where the hole in the ground is. Some dynamite that was stored in it blew it all to hell but we saved some of the logs out of it. I moved into the dugout over here on the right." He pointed to two windows on either side of a door emerging from a mound of dirt. "Now that we have a cabin, we will use the dugout for our bunkhouse. I didn't figure you would like to live in a dugout. Back up there to the right, against the cliff, is a cellar. I guess Hall kept fruit in it and stuff he didn't want to freeze in the winter." They walked up there, and Evelyn could see steps descending to a door. She opened the door and passed into a nice earthen room dug to well below any possible freeze line. It was covered with a thick mound of dirt over the rafters, and a wooden chimney emerged from the back to furnish fresh air for the room. Rough wooden shelves lined the sides.

Charley took Evelyn back to the cabin. Facing the cliff in front of the cabin, he said, "You see that ladder? When there is a flood in the creek the water is too nasty to drink. I climb up that ladder and bring fresh drinking water from the potholes in the slab rocks up on the bench." A very long pole ladder with short poles nailed to it for rungs stretched far across the cut bank of the creek and leaned against the top of the cliff far above. Time and the long span it covered, unsupported, had made it sway in the middle. Charley studied it a minute and said, "I better reinforce that before next spring."

Next, Charley pointed down the creek a short way, and said, "Pat Lynch, the old man who lived in these parts, made his home down there across the creek. He dammed up the creek and made a ditch to water his orchard down there. The trees still bear fruit. Then Old Man Hall made a better dam, and dynamited a ditch out of the rock wall there to carry water to his orchard and grain and hay fields down there where we ate the fish supper that night."

About fifty yards down the canyon, Evelyn saw a jumble of dead trees with a few posts buried along the way that made a fence which closed off Hells Canyon. She knew that at least the saddle horses and the "milk" cow were pastured below that fence.

Then Charley proudly pointed to the corral up the canyon from the cabin. "I cut those twenty-foot cedar posts way up-country, stacked them until winter and skidded them on the snow all the way down here. I found those long, straight aspen poles up on the side of Blue Mountain and cut them and snaked

The rickety ladder in front of the homestead cabin, reaching to the bench above Hells Canyon. The ladder was the only escape when the Yampa River flooded.

45

them out with horses. I peeled them and let them cure lying flat. Mixed with thin cedar poles I think they made the finest round corral in the country. Look at those long straight gate poles. They slide like they were greased. There isn't a knot or splinter on the inside of that corral that could hurt a horse. There isn't a place they could break a leg getting their foot caught in the sides. See the weaning corral? Hall built it, and used the cliff for the back side. The east side of it is dug into the hillside, then lined with timber, which is filled in behind with big rocks and dirt. I wean the calves from their mothers by locking them up in there in December. The bank breaks the wind and the cliff reflects heat so it is warm for them even in real cold weather. I keep the milk cow in there in the winter, too. The rest of the corrals are just old cottonwood poles I used. They keep in a night horse is about all I use them for. They won't hold wild horses or wild cows." He put his arm around Evelyn, and proudly said, "Well, how do you like our home?" "I love it," she whispered.

10

Newlyweds

UGUST PASSED SWIFTLY. Charley and Evelyn swam in the river, made love and rode their horses all over the canyon paradise. They visited the Chew ranch and Evelyn sealed her friendship with Mrs. Chew. The entire Chew family adored her and couldn't believe Charley Mantle could be so lucky, but they worried about whether he would be good to her, since she was so young, and obviously so in love. Mrs. Chew begged Charley to let Evelyn stay with her for a couple of days while Charley and the boys went to check out the wild horse herd and Charley agreed. No sooner had they left the yard than Mrs. Chew told Evelyn to "Grab that apron. I am going to teach you to cook."

For two long, hot days Evelyn was hardly allowed to leave the kitchen. She was taught to kill, clean, cut up properly, and cook a chicken, a fish and a pig. She learned how to can or salt and dry meat to preserve what wasn't eaten before it spoiled. She learned how to clean seemingly spoiled side pork with vinegar then cook it into beans that had been soaked overnight. She learned how to season meats and vegetables and gravy. She even learned how to make a variety of dishes from jerky. Mrs. Chew told her she wouldn't bother with teaching her to make jerky, because she was sure Charley could teach her that.

Mrs. Chew was an expert baker, and she taught Evelyn the basics she would never forget for making baking powder breads, yeast and sour dough breads. They made cakes, cookies and pies. Mrs. Chew stressed and tested Evelyn on the first rule of baking: "The more you maul yeast breads, the better they are, however, the less you maul baking powder breads and pie crust the better they are." She taught Evelyn how to make a starter of yeast for home made bread and to adapt it for sour dough for biscuits and pancakes. She gave her a yeasty starter from her own kitchen, and warned her to always keep it alive by tending it daily.

Last of all, this wise woman told Evelyn that Charley didn't eat vegetables nor ever intended to, but Evelyn must insist that they have vegetables and fruits to eat. She advised her to start on this project immediately while their marriage was so new that Charley would do anything on earth to please her. She told Evelyn which vegetables would keep through the winter, and how to store them. She told her what seeds to buy this fall to plant in the spring for the earliest possible garden. She

Wellen Mantle & Mrs. Chew in front of the Chew ranch house.

told her what would grow on Blue Mountain, in case that is where they would spend their summer. Never had a friend done more for a friend and it would be returned a hundred fold over the years.

As Charley and Evelyn were leaving the Chew ranch, Rial asked them to wait that his mother had something for them to take home. From the shade he lifted four brown gunny sacks. Each contained two grown hens, except one sack, which held one hen and a rooster. Choking with laughter at the look of horror on Charley's face, Rial tied two sacks behind each saddle and sent them off toward home.

By September, Charley could wait no longer. They must ride up onto Blue Mountain to see if Wellen was finished with the horses. Charley needed to get paid for breaking those horses so he would have money to buy winter supplies. Wellen did have the horses finished and had collected the money. He said he was going to go to northern New Mexico and spend the winter on a ranch near Cuba and said he would return in the spring.

When they arrived at the ranch, Evelyn set about making a home out of the cabin. She had collected magazines and newspapers from everybody who had any. She had also found several folds of cheesecloth at her parents house and brought along a collection of nails from her father, because all she had seen around the homestead was horseshoe nails and a few big spikes for building pole corrals. She wished they had been able to afford a new broom, because the old one was worn down to only four inches on one side and was badly misshapen as it angled out to its scraggly tip. Resourceful, though, she went down by the creek and found some slender, leafy willow branches. Tying a bunch of them together, she made a very efficient broom, which she swept the ceiling and the walls of the cabin with. Cobwebs and dust and a few old mouse nests fell to the floor. She went back over it again and again until nothing was left to fall. Then she cut off the small pieces of cedar bark hanging through the layer of branches on the roof. She washed the cheesecloth, using her new washboard and wash tub for the first time. Then she spread the cloth out over sagebrush to dry and bleach in the sun. When it was snowy white, she asked a reluctant Charley to help her. They stretched strips of the cheesecloth tight between the ridge logs of the ceiling and tacked it firmly in place. Evelyn stood in the door and admired the effect. The snowy white cheesecloth brightened up the dark cabin, and would catch any dirt falling out of the roof. It was practically maintenance-free; all she would have to do was take it down occasionally, shake and wash it and put it back up. Charley smiled approvingly over his clever wife's accomplishment.

Next, Evelyn asked Charley to split some short cottonwood wedges for her. These she fit into the cracks between the logs in the walls and around the windows and door, tapping them firmly into place with the hammer. Nails were needed in only a few places. At this point she had to ask for Charley's help again. He and a couple of cowboys who had spent the night were getting ready to go catch wild horses and were reluctant to help. However, remembering Mrs. Chew's warning to train on Charley while the marriage was new, Evelyn insisted that he help her. The three of them made short work of gathering some yellow clay from the bench above the house and smashing up some gray limestone they packed in from the head of Hells Canyon. They brought some sand from the river bed, and mixed this all together in a recipe only they seemed to know, and added water. When the "dobbin" was of the perfect consistency to spread, yet hold its shape, they stuffed it into the cracks between the cabin logs. They tamped and smoothed it with some sticks Charley whittled into smooth paddles. At last, everybody agreed it looked good. The dobbin was stuck firmly into the cracks, then smoothed out onto the logs so that when it dried and shrunk it would block out the cold winter winds. While it was still wet, Evelyn scraped off any that had squeezed through onto the inside, then washed the dobbin traces off the inside walls.

Freed from their domestic chores, the happy cowboys rode off to do their favorite thing, which was to chase wild horses. Charley said he would be gone a couple of days. Evelyn assured him she was not afraid to stay alone, and that she had a project to do that would keep her busy, as indeed she did.

She started tearing up the magazines, beginning in the center with the folded center page, carefully removing the double pages and laying them all the same direction. She separated off the pages that had interesting pictures or cartoons, or something especially interesting on them. When she had a big stack, she decided to test her plan before destroying all the precious magazines. She mixed up some flour and water paste, feeling guilty about using the precious flour, but determined to do what she planned anyway.

Starting at the bottom of the back wall, she pasted magazine pages across the length of the wall, overlapping them well. Then she did a second row, lapping them over the top of the first row. When she came to the height which would be eye level for people sitting at the table, she began using an occasional page from her "special" pile. She continued on to the ceiling, cutting off the top of the last page and tucking the end up above the cheesecloth and gluing it to the wall. Surveying her work, she was thrilled and worked until it got too dark to see, lining the entire cabin. The next morning she was up at daylight, and finished the job. She decided it was just too dangerous to have the paper on the wall around the stove until she got a smooth piece of tin. Then she had an idea of something that might work. She went out to Charley's trash dump, and dug out all the tomato cans. It was slow and tedious work cutting the lids out of the cans. All she had to work with was a dull can opener, but she was persistent and worked until her fingers ached, cutting out the lids from each can. Finished at last, she washed the lids, turned the gold colored side up and nailed them to both walls where the stove sat in the corner. She started at the height of the stove legs from the floor, and nailed the lids as you would shingles, with each lid hiding the nail in the lid before it. There were only enough to cover to just a little above the top of the stove, but she was pleased. She had worried about the hot little stove burning the cabin down, and knew the tin shield would help to prevent that from happening.

Evelyn finished her job by pasting a paper lining around the door and windows that had colored pictures. She wished she had cloth to make curtains, and she wished she had a pretty quilt to replace the tarp on the bed. She wished, too, that she had just a little paint to cover the table and bench. She knew the Indians made paint from native materials, and regretted not knowing how that was done.

Charley had assured Evelyn that there were no rattle snakes in the canyon. He told her the story of the demise of the rattlesnakes. Apparently, there had once been rattlesnakes in the bottom of the canyon along the Bear River downriver from the cabin. An old cowboy named Marigold had told Charley that they used to drive cattle herds through the canyons each fall. They would gather cattle from ranchers who wanted to join the drive along the way, finally coming down Red Rock Canyon to the river. They would hold the cattle for the night in the foothills at the mouth of Red Rock Canyon. There were so many rattlesnakes that the cowboys would circle their sleeping bags with horsehair ropes at night, because rattlers will not cross a hair rope. Marigold said they all hated this stop because of the rattlesnakes. One fall they found that the spring floods in the river had washed off a whole point of sand hills that had extended out into the river, forming a bend. The bend was gone and the river ran straight now, and there were no rattlesnakes. Evidently, that point had been their winter hibernation grounds and the flood had destroyed them all. Never had their been rattlesnakes in the canyon since.

Evelyn didn't really believe this story, and was terrified of snakes, so she set out to clear the brush from around the cabin. Locating an old, dull grub hoe she set to work. The grub hoe had an axe-type blade on one face and a hoe-shaped blade on the opposite face. It was attached to a homemade handle made from a rough cottonwood limb. She worked until her hands were bleeding, and her back was breaking. She had a small area cleared all around the house, and even a little beyond the hitch rack in front. How she wished she had asked Charley to do this back breaking work. Deep in the back of her mind, though, she knew he probably wouldn't have done it and would probably be a little angry with her for taking out the tall brush. They made a good place for tying extra horses, and drying Levis.

Exhausted, but eager to finish the job before Charley returned, Evelyn labored on. She started up the stove and heated a pan of water. With only some lye soap to work with, she scrubbed the windows. They had never been washed before and had to be scraped of dobbin, tree sap, and other matter that stuck to them. After being very sure they were clean, Evelyn thoroughly rinsed them with clear water and then polished them with the few precious remaining newspaper pages. The cabin seemed to come alive with brilliant light. The afternoon sun shone through the sparkling clean west window and touched the wall beyond. The white wallpaper reflected back the light to all parts of the little cabin, making it alive, light, and cheery. Evelyn felt the swelling pride that only a new bride can feel when she makes her new house into a home. She dusted the stove, wiped down the ever-present coffee pot on the back of the stove, hung the frying pan back on the wall, set the "grub box" that was sitting on the floor in order, then sprinkled down the dirt floor.

Outside, Evelyn swept the entire area she had cleared with her new willow broom. She took special care with the very front of the cabin, arranging, hanging, folding, and organizing the jumble of stuff Charley had thrown against the cabin wall. Some of it, she took to the bunk house. Saddles and pack outfits she took around to the side of the cabin and carefully arranged them. She kept telling herself that Mrs. Chew would have wanted her to put her foot down while she still could about all this ugly trash in front of the house. Finally she was through. She stood by the hitch rack and surveyed the work she had done. The cabin's new dobbin and shining windows made it look bigger. Removing the things piled against the front, and clearing the brush from around it had made a tremendous improvement. The cabin looked cozy and inviting. A shiver of delight shot through Evelyn. She must get cleaned up and fixed up, because Charley would be coming home soon, and she couldn't wait to show him what she had done.

Charley rode in just before dark. Excited and anxious to see his new bride, he had ridden as fast as his bronc could manage, all the way from Red Rock. He had left the two cowboys at Red Rock with the wild horses they had caught. Charley was tired and hungry, and wished his new bride was a better cook, but it didn't matter because she was learning, and besides, he grinned to himself as he thought about how much he loved her.

Charley gave his best cow-moving yell, directed straight at the Crow's Nest. Echoing back, and rolling off the walls of Hells Canyon, Hallu-u-u-u-u—hallu-u-u-u—hall-uu reached Evelyn's ears a half mile away at the cabin. She rushed out to the hitch rack and eagerly waited for Charley. Showing off like a kid, he spurred his horse to top speed, raked him to a stop outside the hitch rack, and gracefully combined jumping off his horse and enfolding his bride in his arms.

Finally the kiss was over, and Charley opened his eyes. His mouth fell open, distress showed clearly on his face, and he uttered words he would desperately regret. "What the hell? You have ruined my place!"

Evelyn couldn't believe her ears. She felt scorned, unloved, destroyed. Never in her life before had she felt so desolate. She turned and ran into the bunk house. She certainly didn't want to be around when Charley saw the inside of the cabin if he was so upset with just the outside. Her marriage was over, and she just hoped he would help her to get out of here. She didn't know if she would be able to walk so far. Bathed in tears, sobbing in loud jerky shudders she was unable to control, she stood in the dark dugout with her face to the wall.

Charley had never before faced anything like this in his life. His heart felt like it had been wrenched from his body by a huge bruising hand. He felt the blood drain from his face and his legs were not obeying him, although he willed them to hold him up. He sank to the ground, unaware his horse had already left to go back to Red Rock. What had he done? The only thing he had ever had in his hard life that he couldn't get along without was Evelyn. She was his life and now he had lost her! He could never win her back he knew. He knew this, because if anybody disapproved of him or hurt him, he just rode away. He didn't need them anyway. He had carried this tough, defensive shell for so long that he sincerely believed he didn't need anybody. He also believed that nobody needed him.

Finally, Charley was able to stand up. The sound of Evelyn's anguished sobs had ended. He knew he might as well face the destruction he had caused, so he trudged to the bunk house. He lit the kerosene lamp, and saw Evelyn standing small and stooped with her face to the wall. Not daring to touch her, he stood so near he could feel the heat from her body. His voice was faint, and full of pain as he said, "Evelyn, I'm sorry. I was surprised. I haven't learned to share my world yet. I wish I had learned in time, because I love you so much I believe I will die when you leave me. I know it is too late, but I have to tell you that I like what you did. The place feels like a home now. I wish I had helped you. I wish we could have fixed up the inside of the cabin, too. Can you ever forgive me?"

Evelyn turned slowly around. "I already did fix up the inside. I was so proud of what I had done. I forgot that everything is yours, and nothing is mine. I fixed a stew. It's on the stove. Will you ride out of here with me and help me take my stuff tomorrow?" She brushed past him, and walked quickly to the cabin. She was just putting the stew pot on the table when Charley came through the door. His eyes were round as a child's, filled with astonishment, and his mouth hung open in shock. He blurted out, "It is beautiful in here. I have never been in such a pretty house. How did you do this?" Without thinking, he grabbed her in a huge hug and whirled her around. Self consciously, he began to release her, when he realized her arms were around his neck, and soft tears were falling down her smiling face. Could it be that she would not leave him? Could it be that he still wanted her?

11

Wild Horse Camp

CHARLEY FINALLY HAD TO MAKE A DECISION about a tough problem. He had to ask Evelyn to stay at horse camp with him while he broke the four head that were tied up waiting for him at Red Rock. It was either that or he had to tell her he would be gone for a couple of weeks and leave her alone at the cabin. She would be the first woman ever at the camp, let alone to live there and it would be tough for her. On the other hand, she might leave him if she had to stay alone, especially so soon after the near-wreck of their marriage they had just survived. He got up the courage to ask her, and her answer was, "I want to be with you, wherever that happens to be." He decided to just let her find out for herself about horse camp rather than trying to explain it.

They packed enough grub for two people for two weeks, minus fresh meat which they would get once they were in camp. They packed their bedroll and bare necessities and the few things that Charley needed to work with the horses, put food out for the chickens, and rode off leading two big, gentle pack horses. They spent the night with Uncle Hy Mantle at Red Rock. After breakfast, Hy loaded a hind leg of a deer in one of the panniers and smiled at a nod of thanks from Charley. The four broncs which had been tied to logs for three days now were tired, thirsty, and ready to follow another horse, so Charley watered them all, then tied them to two big gentle horses he was going to lead. He gave the lead rope of the pack horse to Evelyn. He promised Hy he would send his horse back to him just as soon as he had led the broncs to the pasture.

The ride was short as the crow flies, but seemed never ending to Evelyn. They clip-clopped over extensive rock floors, slid down steep dirt banks, and jumped down off ledge rocks. They got beaten by trees, scorched by the brilliant sun, and whipped by a steady cold wind. The pack horse making his laborious way jerked her arm until it ached in its socket. At times she was hard-put to keep from being jerked backward off her horse and at times feared the pack horse would run up alongside her and crowd her and her horse off the narrow stone pathway to tumble into the canyon below. Her lips became dried, then cracked, then bleeding. Every muscle ached, she was thirsty and tired, and still they picked their tortuous way farther into the sandstone wilderness of buttes and canyons.

At last Charley stopped above one last ledge of rock where the dim trail led down a short jump-off through a crevice between two converging cliffs. He said, "That pinyon flat down there is where the horses will be pastured. This is the only way out, so we'll get down there, then you can get off and stretch your legs a little while I throw up a brush gate here so that the horses can't come back through. Evelyn was glad to slide off her horse, but was so stiff she doubted she could ever get back on again. Charley blocked off the crevice with some dead trees laying nearby, then got some old tin cans that were stashed in a small dry cave and tied them to the poles. Now the horses were in a natural stone corral from which they could not escape. The rattling cans would frighten them out of any attempt to break down the barrier and go back out he way they came in.

Evelyn was feeling better by now, and Charley held her horse close to a large rock where she mounted easily. They led the horses alongside a shallow slab rock gully where Charley told her that there was plenty of water in the pot holes. They came near to the sheer drop of the rim into the Bear River, and Evelyn became fearful the horses were going to carry them over the edge. Charley pulled up in front of a large pinyon tree with outstretched gnarled lower limbs, and told Evelyn they would be tying the horses up here while he showed her horse camp.

Evelyn was curious and excited about the romantic camp-out they were going to have. Her enthusiasm wavered as they approached the low opening of a cave whose large frowning mouth revealed nothing but darkness within. The doorstep was a fairly wide shelf of continuous flat smooth sandstone which very shortly dropped into thin air at the canyon rim. At one end of the cave mouth was a gnarled half-dead pinyon tree with a myriad of branches twisting their way in every direction about eye height. Hanging onto a limb above a large, flat boulder at the foot of the tree was a small broken chunk of mirror. Between the tree and the cave was a fire pit of stones, and a long smooth stick she recognized as a pot hook, was leaned against the tree trunk. A little way from the fire pit, between the fire and the canyon rim, was a huge log.

She was sure Charley had a silly smirk on his face when he said, "This is the kitchen. Come on and I will show you our bedroom now." They stepped into the shadowy cave, and Evelyn was surprised to find it not dark at all, but quite well lit from the bright sun outside. Two mounds of dry cedar limbs on a flattened place in the soft sand floor showed where two bedrolls had laid in the past. Charley swept his hand toward the spot and said, "I'll cut some fresh, soft cedar branches and pile them deep for the softest, sweetest smelling bed you ever shut your eyes in."

Next Charley walked to a little shelf of rock in the back of the cave and pulled out a gunny sack, which he handed to Evelyn and indicated she should take it outside. Then he went to a place inside the dry cave just a short way from the outside fire ring and filled his arms with already-cut kindling wood, and a strip of cedar bark. He laid this all beside the fire ring. He returned for an armload of larger chunks of wood and laid them beside the kindling, and told Evelyn to dump the gunny sack. It produced some really beat up, but serviceable items. There was a water bucket with an improvised rope handle and a bean pot with a lid that had been beaten to fit, but would have to be fitted again this time. There was a cockeyed coffee pot with a wire bale, and last but not least, a decrepit enamel wash basin with numerous little curls of cloth at various places in it to stop up leaks.

Charley told her to start supper while he took care of the horses. I'll bring the panniers of supplies over here," he said. "There is a good deep pot hole right over there where you can get water." Evelyn gulped down some good Red Rock Ranch water from one of the canvas water bags and looked over the job she had to do. She barely knew how to cook on a stove, let alone on a fire outside on some rocks. Nonetheless, she rubbed the cedar bark into a fluffy ball, gently stacked a little kindling on it, on top of which she created a minia-ture tepee out of the larger sticks. With a single match she lit it, and it blazed to life instantly. With a grateful gesture to the canyon rim, she seized the bucket and went for water. She found the pot hole all right, but the water was about six feet deep in a sandstone pit with no way for her to reach it! She returned to camp and took her lariat rope and walked back to the water hole. She looped the rope through the rope handle on the bucket and expertly low-ered it into the water, then flipped it on its side to dip some water. She raised it, and spent the next ten minutes scrubbing the bucket with clean sand. Satisfied it was clean, she rinsed it, drew a full bucket and carried it back to camp.

The shadows were getting long, indicating darkness was near, and Charley still hadn't returned, so she prepared to cook supper. She made some pancakes and fried strips of meat she cut from the deer leg. She had just finished when Charley came into camp, shoulders drooping from exhaustion. His face nearly burst apart in a wide-mouthed grin followed by a shout that echoed back and forth from the canyon walls below as he saw supper prepared and everything in order. He gave Evelyn a huge bear hug and kiss and said, "Let's just set down on the bullshit log and eat the best grub I ever saw." Evelyn was pleased at his approval, but hastened to tell him not to call the log by that name; maybe "conversation log" would be better. Charley said, "It shore does sound better, and we have to be sure to tell old Hy it is a conversation log."

Charley was tired and it was too dark to make the wonderful bed he had promised for Evelyn, so they just rolled out their bed on the soft sand and slept soundly in their cave home. Evelyn woke to clear, brilliant daylight and found Charley already up. He had the fire built, and was shaving in front of the tiny mirror tied in the pinyon tree. The night before, Evelyn had cleaned dried beans and put them in the pot to soak overnight. He had put the pot of beans on the fire to cook slowly. When he finished shaving, he fried up some salt pork, made pancakes, and poured Evelyn a cup of coffee where she was seated on the "conversation" log. As they ate he told her all the troubles he had had with the horses last night. First he had unpacked the big horses, tied the broncs to one, and led the big horses to water in the slab rock pot holes. One bronc had spooked, fallen down and scared the other three who had also fallen down. One had fallen with his head in a pot hole full of water and another had fallen on top of him. The big horse to which they were tied to was too off balance to pull them out, so Charley had quickly cut the rope from the big horse, then mounting his saddle horse, had roped the flailing hind legs of the horse laying on top, and pulled him off the drowning horse. They were all too stirred up to take a good drink, so they should be really thirsty this morning. He had tied the broncs to heavy logs they couldn't drag and thus panic themselves and run off the cliff. He had taken Hy's horse outside the gate and turned him loose so he could go home, and turned their saddle horses loose to graze on the flat.

Near camp was a small round corral built with logs and brush within a circle of trimmed living pinyon trees. This was where Charley worked with the four wild horses for two weeks. Charley cut feathery juniper limbs and piled them high for their bed, which was every bit as wonderful as he had predicted. Evelyn could help very little with the horses, but became a very good camp cook. She would wander for hours on the benches above the pinyon flat where Charley worked, exploring the numerous caves and overhangs for signs of Indian habitation in the distant past. She found lots of piles of flint of numerous colors and textures. These piles had been left centuries ago at the spots where flint workers had labored over making arrowheads, scrapers, awls and spear heads. At natural game trails into the pot holes she found many pieces of arrowheads. Occasionally she would find a whole one, which would bring a shriek of victory to Charley's ears in the corral below. In one rather large cave near the potholes she found a large red rock that was deeply dished from grinding corn. It was leaned up against the wall of the cave, and placed neatly on top of it was a red grinding stone worn smooth, and just the right size to be held in a strong hand to grind corn in the dished out stone. It seemed silently waiting where it had been left in readiness for the return of its owner. Also in this cave Evelyn found pieces of burned ash and charcoal, along with two large flint scrapers lying on a shelf of rock.

Juniper is clean burning wood that makes good coals, so Evelyn searched for thick solid limbs, some dead and clinging to living trees, others lying on the ground. These she pushed over the ledge into the flat below. Later she would gather them into camp where Charley would cut the big pieces into firewood. She broke up the small branches herself and stacked them for kindling. As the broncs progressed toward graduation, Charley would ride them out on the bench and drag large logs with them. He was always in need of new corral and gate material. Pinyon logs were usually what he used. On very cold nights they would build a hot fire of pinyon wood. It made black, sooty smoke, so they didn't like to use it, but it made a much hotter fire than cedar.

The pot hole water didn't taste as good as spring water, but at least Evelyn was glad it was winter so nothing was living in it. She found it left her hair shining and soft. She would heat the water to shampoo her hair, but she liked the icy bite of the cold water to rinse her hair.

The young horses were becoming cultured gentlemen under Charley's expert care. Each was very special in its own way, and was treated in such a way as to develop his talents. One was a single-footer, a special gait that a horse was born with. However, it took time to develop the gait. It also took skill on the part of the rider to develop the natural talent of the horse to its maximum. The fast, sure-footed, smooth gait would make the horse coveted by every rancher in the country. Only one of the young horses had this particular gait, as Charley had known he would. You see, in the country there lived two wild mares who produced the finest colts in the world around. One was named Pearl and lived in Pearl Park, a high valley on the west end of the north face of Blue Mountain named after her. Pearl's colts were nearly all single-footers. The other mare was named Martha. She lived in the basin, in the area named after her, Martha's Hole, at Martha's Peak, which was at the head of Hells canyon, in the center of the north face of Blue Mountain. Martha's colts were equally as fine as Pearl's, but were not gaited. All the mountainside between Martha's Peak and Pearl Park was full of wild horses. Fine stallions were slipped into their midst to ensure good stock. Pearl's and Martha's colts were so prized by the ranchers that each year the colts were "given" to a wild horse wrangler as his turn came up. Of course it had to be someone whose range land supported the horses, and who participated in trapping them. This year it had been Charley's turn to get Pearl's colt. It was a gelding and it was a singlefooter! Life was good! All these broncs would get a good solid start here at horse camp, but Charley would spend the winter polishing them to perfection. He would sell them in the spring when the work started and good horses were most in demand.

Hy rode in one day with half a deer, which saved Charley the trouble of hunting. Hy hung around a couple of days and Evelyn enjoyed listening to the yarns they spun. She finally gave up trying to get him to wash his hands, shave, and wash the tobacco juice and gravy from his whiskers. Once she asked him when he took a bath. He said, "Every spring." He had brought them some fresh eggs from the hens he kept around his place and they tasted heavenly. He had also brought her some watercress from under the ice in the little pond in front of his cabin. He explained, "I don't eat this rabbit food, but I hear'n you like it." She did. Despite his personal hygiene, Evelyn felt a little lonely when the old man rode off; she liked him and could tell he liked her. She just hoped she could always be in an airy cave or outside in the fresh air when she was around him.

Finally Charley said that tomorrow they would break camp. The grass was gone, and the broncs were all gentle and broke. They stored wood and the stash of "kitchen" items in the cave. One last evening they sat close together on the "conversation" log. Charley put their feelings rather well when he said, "I am so happy here with you I hate going back to civilization." Charley proudly took the lead on Pearl's son as they rode out of the horse camp next day. Evelyn rode behind the string of gentled horses as they wound their way from their education center back to the ranch in Hells Canyon. She was excited about going home, and smug in her thoughts of what a good wife she had become.

12

The First Winter, 1926-27

FTER BEING AT HORSE CAMP FOR TWO WEEKS it was very exciting for Evelyn and Charley to be coming home. It was almost dark when they arrived, so Evelyn quickly tied up her horse and ran to the shelter that served as a chicken house to see how her chickens had fared. She found them perched contentedly on the rails provided inside the chicken house. Apparently they had found enough to eat and had gone to the creek for water, because they looked healthy. Hoping for eggs, she checked the nests, but there were none. Suddenly she realized what the faint foul odor was that she had smelled when she entered the chicken house. A thieving skunk had been living off her eggs! Furious, she stomped back to the horses and told Charley she wanted to learn how to shoot right away.

After unpacking, Charley locked the milk cow in the corral and turned the horses out to pasture. Inside, Charley lit the kerosene lamp and was headed for the stove to get it started when Evelyn called attention to their new bed. True to his promise, Busby had delivered the mattress. There it was on the rawhide bed frame, clean, thick and new. There were even two clean white sheets folded on top of the mattress and a pair of clean new white feather pillows. A note from Buzz said, "Congratulations. I wish you much happiness. The sheets and pillows are from Thede and Pearl." There was no explanation of how he got it there on a horse. After supper Evelyn made up the bed and they crawled under the covers, savoring the luxury of it all.

Charley found Evelyn unwilling to stay at home any time he was going to be out riding on the range. Together, they rode hard finding and gathering the herd bulls from the rough range land. At the same time, they gathered steers that were now a year old and brought them to the ranch as well. They drove the bulls east onto the bench at the head of Hells Canyon a couple of miles, where they drove them into the river canyon at Hardings Hole. Here the river did elongated loops through the sandstone cliffs, leaving lush river bottom pastures at every crossing. They drove the bulls deep into the canyon, forcing them over the icy banks from river bottom to river bottom, at last leaving them on the farthest good sized pasture down the river. The ice along the banks of the river would keep the bulls from coming back onto the range during the winter months and getting at the cows before it was time. When they ate up the grass in each pasture, they would brace the icy banks some sunny afternoon and cross up to the next pasture where the forage was lush. The tricky part would be for Charley to leave them in this easy living environment, yet correctly guess the exact time he could still drive them out of the canyon before the river became too swollen by spring runoff to get them out.

It was almost Thanksgiving. Charley usually spent it with neighbors, as most single cowboys in the country did. The ranch women expected visitors and looked forward to them riding in. The really good cooks always got more than their share of guests. It was a time to share the harvest, cook their best for some really appreciative eaters, and catch up on the news before the long winter set in. Charley suggested they ride over to the Chews. Evelyn was all for it, but insisted they take something. Jerky wouldn't do and fish wouldn't keep. They finally decided to ride up to Quaker Spring and get a mess of blue grouse. The day before Thanksgiving was brisk but sunny and Charley saddled two good horses, a bronc that needed work for himself and the new single-footer for Evelyn. He had become very gentle and since the first part of the day would be a hard ride up the mountain, Charley felt he could be trusted.

Evelyn learned to shoot in order to protect her home from predators.

Evelyn was thrilled and decided early in the day to change the name of this wonderful horse to Sunshine. Charley's name for him was SOB. It was a day of fun. They took along a frying pan and cooked one grouse for their lunch. The quaking aspens were full of the fat young birds and Charley shot seven of them in a very short time. They cleaned them, packed a little snow around them in flour sacks, and rode home, all before dark.

Thanksgiving morning they left early, greatly anticipating the day. A smiling flock of Chews greeted them when they rode into the Pool Creek Ranch. Mrs. Chew was thrilled to get the grouse. She had a fresh pork leg and a huge stuffed turkey already roasting in the oven. The house smelled heavenly. Evelyn had expected to help her bake pies, but saw bulging mincemeat and golden pumpkin pies already set out to cool. Yeast rolls were rising to be baked at the last minute. Rial burst into the kitchen, grinning, and said, "Charley, we thought you might be over, so Mother made your favorite—Son-of-a-bitch-in-a-sack!" Horrified, Evelyn just stared. Mrs. Chew put her arm around her, and said, "Come see." She lifted the lid off a steaming kettle. Inside was a small cloth bag resting above the water line on a rack. The lovely aroma of dark rich pudding like Evelyn remembered from her childhood came from the sack. Mrs. Chew said, "Yes, it is suet pudding and I'm making a hard sauce to serve over it. Charley and my kids love it."

The fascinating Chew family was mostly all home, so it was a day of warm friendship and tall tales. Everyone ate all they could possibly eat, then ate again late in the day. Charley said they really must go home, but he had drunk too much chokecherry wine, so the Chews put him to bed and turned his horses out to pasture. Evelyn was pleased with the chance to spend more time with all these women, and made the best of the chance by visiting until the sky turned pink in the east.

Back at Castle Park Charley began making preparations to wean the calves from their mothers. Evelyn had developed into a good rider now and was a lot of help in gathering the cows and calves from the range, and separating them at the corrals. The mother cows were put above a fence at the second grove of trees in Hells Canyon. The calves were shut into the corral. She found it impossible to sleep for a couple of days, because the bawling of the mothers for their babies and the calves for their mothers was continuous and anguished. She consoled herself by spending a great deal of time in the corral with the calves offering them cottonseed cake and buckets of water. She felt relieved and fulfilled as each one learned that the taste was good and forgot their yearning for mother's milk. The mothers gradually drifted back to the range and soon the calves were let out during the day to eat grass. Shortly, the calves were put on the north side of the river in Castle Park. Charley broke a trail in the ice where it was thin and sanded it where it was thick to give them safe passage across the river to the warm bed grounds and plentiful grass.

At Christmas time Evelyn was very lonesome for her family, so they rode out to Hayden to spend Christmas with her folks. She visited all her high school friends and showed off her new husband. They stayed until New Years day, then started home.

They returned by way of Jensen to pick up their mail. Evelyn wanted to go to Vernal, to visit Thede and Pearl, so they got a ride there. She had asked Pearl to look for a good used sewing machine and lo and behold, Pearl had found one. It was in perfect condition and in a beautifully carved cabinet. Pearl had stocked the drawers with needles, thread, oil, and a stack of cloth. She showed Evelyn how to use the machine and smiled happily to see her young friend so eager and excited. She also gave Evelyn a crochet book and some yarn. She knew how long and lonely the winter was going to be for Evelyn in that canyon.

When they returned to Jensen, Marcus Jensen said he had a Jersey heifer he wanted to show them and both Charley and Evelyn fell in love with the sweet-faced little gray Jersey. She had graceful little horns that curved over her brows, and loved to be scratched and petted. They bought her, and Marcus assured them she would come fresh in April.

So now Charley had a wife, a Jersey cow and a sewing machine to get over Blue Mountain and home on a cold January day. Luckily there wasn't much snow. He packed the sewing machine carefully in a pannier and stuffed gunny sacks all around it. He loaded the other pannier with an equal amount of weight and hooked the panniers over the pack saddle. The pack horse rolled his eyes and lunged as the lash ropes tightened around his belly. Evelyn was jumping up and down in anguish at the thought of any harm coming to her sewing machine. So often Charley's pack horses laid down with their loads, crushing everything. She wished he would use gentle pack horses. The worst was yet to come. They turned the cabinet upside down, with its feet up in the air, and lashed it on top of the load. The horse's eyes were rolling back in its head as it looked at the dangerous

The only way to reach the Mantle home in the canyons far below, was by horseback. Supplies were brought in by pack horse.

looking thing on his back. Marcus had the horse's head snubbed to his saddle horn and Charley mounted his horse and squeezed up on the other side of him. They rode off with the pack horse sandwiched between them. Finally he accepted his load and they brought him back. Charley snubbed him close to his horse, Evelyn mounted, and Marcus drove the little Jersey cow in front of her. The caravan started off, Charley, pack horse with sewing machine, milk cow, and wife. Marcus nearly fell off his horse laughing at the taming of Charley Mantle.

It was a very slow, trying trip. Several times Evelyn had to dismount and lead the little cow when she got tired and tried to sneak off the trail to rest. Charley had to be extra careful not to let the pack horse bash into rocks or trees. They made it as far as Chews and spent the night there. Charley tried to ignore the snickers and snide remarks.

The next morning after a big breakfast Mrs. Chew caught her horse and went with them. She wanted to be sure Evelyn got her sewing machine set up properly and the cow settled into a better home than the wild range milk cow needed. How glad Evelyn was to get home. She had enjoyed the trip, but boy, was it ever hard on you to go to town from their new home!

Around the middle of January Evelyn started feeling sick. Her stomach was upset and she had dizzy spells. After a week of this Charley became very worried, and took her to Grandma Chew to see if maybe she could do something for her. After ten minutes of questioning, Mrs. Chew laughed until tears rolled down her cheeks and told Charley he was going to be a father. Charley and Evelyn were elated. When she got home, Evelyn had morning sickness for only a short time, then was back to her old busy self.

The winter was long and lonely. Evelyn found Jers, as they called the little cow, to be very affectionate and amiable. She fed her corn stalks and talked to her every day. She shelled corn for the chickens to keep them laying. Evelyn loved her sewing machine and found herself becoming very good at sewing. She made simple things with it at first, like aprons and smocks. She used up all the material Pearl had given her and couldn't wait to get out to buy some more.

Charley kept busy, too. With a large handful of hair pulled from the tails of the horses he'd trained, Charley would use his other hand to pull out five or so strands at a time and lay them neatly in a pile of long straight hairs. When he had a good sized bundle he would start another one. Finally he would be ready to start twisting the hairs into ropes. Whoever happened to be hanging around visiting would get put to work at this point. Charley would tie some hairs firmly around a hook on an apparatus known as the hair-twister that was nailed to a cedar tree about two hundred yards up the canyon from the house and which was called the hair-twister tree. The hair twister had four hooks on the front of it and ran on cogs when the handle on the back of it was turned. The helper would turn the handle and Charley would feed out hair. Slowly, a small rope of twisted hair started forming. Charley would back down along down the trail while his partner relentlessly turned the handle, making a tightly twisted string that needed lots of tension to keep it from kinking. When Charley reached the pole fence about fifty yards past the house he stopped and tied off the rope. He yelled for his partner to lock the handle and come to him. He would give the partner a strong, smooth stick about an inch in diameter and tie the loose end to another stick just like it. Then his partner would back off a ways, keeping the string tight and Charley would back up carefully all the way to the hair-twister. The important thing was for both men to keep the string very tight so it wouldn't unravel. At the hair twister tree Charley would tie his end to a hook. Then Charley would twist while his partner held the other end tight. They would double this two strand rope back just as they had the first, and continue doing the same thing until they had a rope of as many strands as they wanted. A six-strand rope was usually used for tying horses up, so it was the largest and strongest. The rope called a Mccarty, which secured a hackamore on the head of a bronc, was usually four strands so it could be tied and knotted easily. They tied off the ends of the ropes with rawhide thongs.

Charley also cut up miles of rawhide. He would soak a dry cow hide until it was soft and pliable, then cut it in long strips. He would stretch the strips between two trees or posts until they were as thin as he dared stretch them. He would let them dry, then scrape off the hair and roughness from the strips. Again, wetting the strips he would embed the points of two sharp knives about a quarter-inch apart on a bench. Then he would sit on the bench and carefully draw the strips of rawhide through the knives to make perfectly matched long strips of rawhide. Again, he would stretch the strips to dry, then form them into big rolls. He was an expert braider and would later braid these strips into hackamore bozells, ropes, fancy knots, chair seats, etc.

One of Evelyn's winter projects was to clean up Charley's language. Now that they were going to have a baby he had to set a better example. All the cowboys spoke respectfully in front of her, and only swore a lot when among themselves, so she knew it was possible. She explained to him that the child would be around him sometimes when she wasn't, so he would be responsible for what kind of language the child heard and learned. He tried, and did pretty well except when he got around the livestock. He just needed to cuss or he couldn't do his work.

A cowboy who passed through and spent the night with them brought the surprising news that Wellen had married. He had married a girl named Lorraine Fisher. The cowboy understood she came from a ranch in New Mexico and allowed that she was pretty and could ride like a man. Charley was shocked. Wellen had a violent temper and it had been made much worse by his sickness. Charley just couldn't imagine him married. He was happy his brother had found somebody to be happy with, but was really anxious to see for himself.

13

Trapped and Pregnant, 1927

INALLY THE COLD, FRIGHTENING DAYS OF FEBRUARY came to an end. Charley always said that February was the worst month of the year on livestock. It had been dreary, nothing green showing, the trees without leaves, river frozen over, and hardly any visitors. Charley didn't let her ride much for fear of her horse falling on the ice. Nobody had brought in the mail and Charley had not gone out for it. Evelyn had written a long letter to her cousin, Eva telling her what she thought Eva could understand about her life and the exciting news that she was pregnant. She was very anxious to get the letter mailed, as she just had to tell Eva this news.

By March, Evelyn was thickening perceptibly in her waist. She craved food and had to be careful not to eat too much. She was sick of meat and biscuits, and knew that for the health of her baby she had to get some vegetables and fruit. One day she talked Charley into riding over to Chews with her to get some water cress from the beautiful deep pool in Pool Creek. How good it tasted and even better was the nice visit she had with the Chew girls and Mrs. Chew.

Evelyn had noticed that tiny shoots of green grass were showing. The rooster's comb had changed to a bright red and the combs of the hens were brightening up, too. One morning she was wakened by the joyful cackling of a hen, which could only mean that she had laid an egg. All the chickens, especially the rooster, rejoiced with her, making the canyon walls echo. Sure enough, there was an egg. She served it to Charley for breakfast in a grand manner.

The second week in March, Evelyn gathered all the tomato cans she had been saving. She pounded holes in the bottoms with a nail, and filled them with rich garden dirt. She carefully planted seeds of tomato, pepper, cabbage, and egg plant. She put the cans in a warm place along a wall of the cabin, and checked them every day to see if they had sprouted. Finally they did. Vegetables! Every day she put them out in the sun, and every night she brought them in. They grew healthy and strong.

One day Wellen and his new wife rode in and what a pleasant surprise that was. Evelyn and Lorraine liked each other instantly and visited endlessly.

Charley and Wellen were inseparable and talked of plowing and planting so they could get on with the more important business of horses and cattle. They talked of how to manage so as to make the most profit they possibly could from the horses this summer. Charley told Wellen he most likely couldn't spend much time on the mountain, as Evelyn was expecting a baby and couldn't ride much. Besides, she wanted to grow a bunch of vegetables. He told his brother that his dream was to have a successful cattle ranch. He had gone into debt and bought a bunch of cows two years ago. Along with what he already had it was a nice start.

By this time all the beef was used up or spoiled. The deer were poor and tasted like the rabbit brush they ate. The fish were starting to bite, but hard to catch with the river still so cold. They couldn't afford to butcher a yearling from their small herd. Next year they would have some chickens to eat, but now they couldn't spare any. They were pretty much back to jerky and eggs. On a visit to the Chews they had bought a sack of potatoes. Mrs. Chew had promised to teach Evelyn how to can meat so they wouldn't get in this fix every spring.

One morning around the last of March Charley found that Jers had calved. A beautiful little white calf was waving his tail vigorously as he sucked hungrily. Charley yelled for Evelyn to come look. She ran to the cow and hugged her and said, "Oh Jers, this is the beginning of a beautiful herd of milk cows. Charley said, "Afraid not—look again!" It was a bull calf, and Evelyn was so disappointed she almost cried. The truth was that in all the years they had Jers she never had a heifer calf to replace herself as a milk cow.

The milk was very sweet and good and the process of getting it peacefully compared to taking it away from an angry range cow was wonderful. Jers loved to be milked and coddled. She gave milk that raised a thick layer of cream on top when cooled in the cold spring water. Evelyn made butter and cottage cheese and there was plenty of milk for all their needs, as well as enough for the little bull calf to become fat and healthy. He was full of mischief and got into trouble all the time butting over buckets and scattering the chickens into squawking confusion.

In April Charley and Wellen rode into Hardings Hole and got the bulls out in anticipation of the high water that had already started and would soon make it impossible to cross the river. They drove the bulls out onto the bench, then east, driving them down the steep trail into Bull Canyon. They fenced them in and would leave them there until around the first of July when they would be put out with the cows.

Evelyn had to really be careful now, so she was riding Pat Lynch's horse, Laddie. After Pat had become old and gone to live in Lily Park, Laddie got homesick and came wandering down the river from Deer Lodge to the place he loved. He had been there several years and Charley let him stay there, out of respect to his friend Pat. But now he needed Laddie, and he knew old Pat would get a chuckle out of a pregnant woman riding his horse. Pat had loved his mother dearly, and had a tender heart for women. You could mount on either side of Laddie. He would let you walk him up to a rock to mount from. He would never leave camp, leaving you afoot, and was always easy to catch. His favorite place was the lower park, which was on the other side of the river, just down stream from Hospital Hill. Everyone started calling the little park Laddie Park after him.

All the cattle were moved out of the river bottoms so the grass could grow for winter feed. The grass was coming up good now and the cattle were put out on the benches. Calves started coming. The cows were out on Red Rock Bench and didn't need much care. They had grass and water aplenty. This gave Charley and Wellen a chance to get the ranch work done. They dug out the irrigation ditch and plowed a small garden area. Evelyn planted corn and potatoes. The plants she had started in pots would have to wait to be planted until all danger of frost was over. Charley plowed up a little field in a swale along the river and planted alfalfa. He figured the ground water would give it a start.

The young horses Charley had broke to sell, were kept in, along with Pacer, one gentle saddle horse, and of course Laddie. All the rest were turned out on Blue Mountain until needed. It was always important to keep as little livestock in the canyons as possible, because the winter feed had to be allowed to grow. A couple of ranchers showed up to buy horses. Charley made a hard decision. He had the young horse Evelyn called Sunshine, Pearl's colt. He was a single footer and a wonderful riding horse. He had been going to give him to Evelyn, but he was too young to be trusted with the baby coming. They really needed the money, so Charley finally sold him to one of the ranchers who wanted him so bad he was willing to pay a big sum for him.

The beginning of May the river turned muddy and started rising fast. The creek also started running muddy water from melting snow on Blue Mountain. The drinking water was ruined in the creek, so they dug a small well back along the bank of the creek. The water that filled it was clear and clean from filtering through the sand, and they could easily dip out the fresh water.

One day Charley left to take horses to sell on Blue Mountain, leaving Evelyn alone. She spent a hot, sweaty day, made more so by the warm wind. She finally got into bed and fell into a troubled sleep. In the middle of the night she awakened to a terrible racket. The walls of the canyon magnified a terrible roar that was like cannon firing. She leaped from bed to see if it was wind. No leaves were moving in the moonlit night. She realized that the roar was coming from the creek. Huge boulders were being hurled into the air and falling amongst other boulders. The black seething water was up to the banks of the creek, threatening to spill over. Bushes and trees were rushing by. If a big tree got lodged the creek would jump its banks and flood out the house and corrals.

Evelyn, still in her nightgown, ran to the corral and let out Jers and her calf and the horses. She drove them to the higher ground behind the house. Then she frantically started carrying all their possessions out of the two cabins. She took them just far enough to be on higher ground than the flood would reach. Her strength completely gone, she collapsed on top of the heap and sobbed miserably. When her house was gone, they could move into the granary, which was on high safe ground.

She was afraid to go around to the north side of Castle Rock, because if the creek broke over it would be impossible for her to get back. She must stay here where there were milk and eggs to exist on until Charley came home. Lying there quietly through the terrifying night, she prayed that her baby would not come. It was a very cold night, which was a blessing because it stopped the rapid melting on the head waters of the creek and the water level finally dropped within the banks.

Next morning Charley realized that the snow had melted enough to have caused a big flood in Hells canyon. Frantically, he rode down the mountain trail and found the canyon impassable. He watered his horse and turned him into an old brush and tree corral on the rim of the canyon above the homestead. Always when the creek flooded this was the only way to get home. He scrambled down the steep trail to the ledge above the creek. There was the old ladder that spanned the distance from the top of the ledge to the bank of the creek in front of the cabin. The ladder creaked and bent and swayed as he scrambled down it. The deafening sound of the raging creek was below him. He couldn't make his voice heard over the roar, so he had to run and search for Evelyn. Water had reached the door of the cabin, but no harm had been done. Evelyn was not inside. He finally found her sound asleep from exhaustion lying on gunny sacks of cottonseed cake on the shady side of the granary. He was sobbing with relief when he reached her.

Tom Blevins rode by to say that he had seen two wild cows with yearling calves still sucking their mothers on upper Red Rock. Charley had gathered the cows before and put them with the bulls, but obviously they had gone right back. He must gather them one final time about November. He would rope the yearlings and lock them up. He guessed he would have to shoot the cows because they were impossible to herd, even with other cattle. They would be good beef and he was pretty sure he could trade one to the doctor for delivering the baby.

One day Charley was riding along the trail beside the river at Laddie Park, headed home. It was toward the end of the spring runoff and piles of driftwood rested at every bend of the river. His eye chanced to notice one driftwood pile with something strange sticking out of it, something that resembled a human hand. Riding on, he couldn't get it out of his mind and finally turned back and forded the river to the drift pile. Sure enough, it was a human body caught and tangled among the driftwood, with one hand sticking straight up out of the debris.

Charley took down his lariat rope and lashed the body securely within the driftwood and anchored it with some heavy rocks, in case the river should rise again and carry the pile off before he could get help. He then trotted on home and told Evelyn what he had found and that he must get the sheriff to come and supervise getting the man out. He changed to a fresh horse and rode to get help as fast as the horse could manage.

He gathered up the sheriff and several other men and they made the long ride down into the canyons. Untangling the body from the drift pile, they lashed it onto a homemade skid and pulled it out of the river with a horse. Somebody recognized the corpse as a man named Burdet that had been working the gold mine in Hardings Hole. His fellow workers confirmed that he had gone for a swim a few days back and never returned.

The decision was made to bury him in Laddie Park. A grave was dug and he was buried in the blanket they had wrapped him in. His grave had no permanent marker. Evelyn had faithfully delivered food to the men

Drowned man buried in Laddie Park. The slip made of logs used to remove the body from the river is beside the grave.

while they worked, and when they were finished everybody spent the night in the bunk house. They left early the next morning after a big breakfast.

◆　◆　◆　◆　◆　◆

Rial heard that Evelyn was lonely and needed a friend so he brought her a sheep dog. Rial had been forced to remove the dog's front teeth because he was too rough with the sheep. He was smart and friendly and loyal to whatever his job might be. He had visited several times before and Evelyn and the dog were soul mates from the first. She named him Sport. They were never more than a step from each other. He wouldn't even go with the men to work cattle. His job was taking care of Evelyn.

Hells Canyon finally quit rampaging and became a peaceful creek once again. Thankfully, Evelyn moved their bed out of the hot cabin and out under the big Box Elder tree beside the spring. They covered it with a water and dust proof tarp so it stayed clean and dry. The sweet, cool night air was wonderful, and they both rested better. The night sounds of crickets and owls and small creatures lulled them to sleep. Sport slept on the ground by Evelyn's side of the bed.

Evelyn's folks were sick with worry, so they rode down to check on her. Evan and Charley repaired the dam, which had washed out after it turned a huge head of water out on the new garden, flooding it completely out. Evan replanted the garden. June was a little late for that, but they hoped it would grow fast. Evelyn's seedlings in the cans were strapping big healthy plants that would grow quickly.

Her parents insisted on taking Evelyn to the doctor. They rode out to their homestead on Blue Mountain, then drove their car to Vernal. The doctor said to come and plan to stay a month before the baby was due, which was probably in November. Evelyn arranged with Thede and Pearl to come stay with them the beginning of October.

Charley worried about all the scary tales the women were going to tell Evelyn of the worst childbirth they ever saw. He wished he could spare her that. He, too, was afraid, since his own mother had died in childbirth. He picked up Pacer at Fullers' and met Evelyn in Jensen to take her home. It was an easier route to ride home by Pool Creek and besides he wanted to stop by and see Mrs. Chew.

Mrs. Chew was full of good advice and comfort, as he had known she would be. She traded saddles with Evelyn. Hers had a low horn and a long seat that would fit her figure better. She said, "Don't lift, don't walk too much since your veins have a tendency to bulge anyway. Eat vegetables, dried fruit, drink milk. Don't worry about getting fat. You need to be in good shape so you have lots of milk. You will lose weight fast enough, what with the life you lead and nursing a big baby. Stay home—don't go to Blue Mountain. It's too hard on you squatting, lifting, sleeping on the hard ground, bad diet. You could get kicked and jerked and bleed to death." That was her only warning of anything bad that might happen. She gave Evelyn an old maternity apron to use as a pattern and some flour sacks.

Branding wasn't fun. The smell sickened Evelyn. At least they didn't dehorn the calves, so she didn't have to see that bloody operation. Only Jerse's calf lost his horns, because Charley said there was nothing meaner in the world than a Jersey bull. They drove the cattle onto Blue Mountain for the summer, and put the bulls out with the cows by the Fourth of July. Charley liked to have his calves come in April and May so there was plenty of grass for the mother cows to make lots of milk.

It was a long hot summer for Evelyn. She was clumsy and slow. The sewing, gardening, milking and keeping house was almost more than she could manage. Charley put a mean looking range bull in with Jers. Charley was not home all the time. He had taken in a lot of horses to break because this baby thing was starting to look expensive. Nobody had any money. Most purchases were made by trading. Lorraine stayed with Evelyn most of the summer. Grandpa Fuller made a cradle of wood for the baby. It was made to hang on the bottom of the bed, and when taken down and put on the floor it rocked. He promised to get it to them in plenty of time for the baby's arrival. Many people came by to visit and brought soft fluffy things.

When they came off the range, Charley culled the bulls. He cut off the barren cows and put them all into a pasture on the mountain to be sold. In

September they gathered the big-horned steers from Outlaw and trailed them to the pasture on the Mountain. Wellen and Lorraine trailed the whole herd to Rifle where they were sold. Charley hated to not go and worried that Wellen might not get as good a price as if he were there, but he just couldn't leave Evelyn.

Ed Lewis, one of Charley's friends, got together some cowboys and gathered wild horses for Charley and brought them to the ranch. Ed said they had made a good gather, and had castrated and jointed the tails on the two year old studs. He said there was a really fine bunch coming up. He had also brought Charley two beautiful young mares. "Charley it's time you started a little stud bunch of your own." he said. Ed promised to bring his big thoroughbred stud in the spring and leave him long enough to breed the mares. The mares had black hoofs and good heads, with big eyes, pretty necks and shoulders, and strong, straight legs with lots of muscle. Charley fell in love with them.

Helplessness and loneliness began to work on Evelyn. It would be twelve long, hard hours riding a horse over treacherous trails to get to a doctor. Could she live through that? She longed for her mother to take care of her. Carrying water and wood to wash and clean and cook made her body ache. This home was Paradise to her, but the price might be her life. How desperate she felt for a road to her door and a car.

14

Potch, 1927-28

SINCE SHE WOULDN'T BE ABLE TO COOK FOR A CROWD after the baby came, Evelyn cooked up a big Thanksgiving dinner. Evan and Julia Fuller, Wellen and Lorraine, along with Ed Lewis, joined Charley and Evelyn had a big turkey dinner with all the fixings. They even had squash pie with whipped cream heaped on top. Since Lorraine had helped cook, Charley and Wellen insisted on cleaning up after dinner.

On the day they rode out to Vernal and the hospital, Ed offered to stay around and feed the chickens, make hair ropes, and watch the place. Charley saddled Pacer with Mrs. Chew's big roomy saddle. Even though the baby was not due for another month, Evelyn could barely fit her bulging stomach into the saddle. If Pacer stumbled she was sure the baby would be crushed.

They dropped Sport off with Uncle Tom Blevins at Red Rock. The dog whined and howled as they left, but Evelyn commanded him to stay and he did. They rode up Sand Canyon, over Iron Springs Bench, then up and over Blue Mountain. Evelyn found that the hardest thing was getting off and on to relieve herself. At frequent rest stops she would lie down and rest a bit.

At dark they rode in to Grandma Haslem's place in Jensen. Her three sons, Joe, John, and Clyde were bean pole thin and over six feet tall. They had bony faces and spindly limbs. When they rushed out of the house shouting greetings and grinning their big friendly smiles Evelyn chuckled to herself. How, she wondered, could three such skinny boys have such a good looking sister, the only one with any meat on her bones. The boys took care of the horses and hustled Charley and Evelyn into the house. Joe and Charley had been childhood friends. Joe was an accomplished story teller and could mimic anybody. He entertained them with his yarns until bedtime. He waved his arms around so much, and crossed and uncrossed his long spindly legs that Evelyn found herself wondering if he ever tied himself in a knot.

The Haslems always got up before the chickens, so Charley and Evelyn ate a big breakfast and headed off to Vernal at an early hour. Thede and Pearl were eagerly awaiting their arrival. The doctor showed up soon after their arrival and checked Evelyn out. He told her to take it easy and have somebody come get him when he was needed. He was glad to accept Charley's offer of a beef in exchange for his services.

Tom Blevins standing beside his cabin at Red Rock.

They had barely arrived when the Mormon women started flocking in to do their part. They seemed to just swarm around Evelyn, who realized that she had been around nobody but Ed Lewis all summer, so it was natural that she felt swarmed by all these women. On the evening of October twelfth she ate a huge meal and went contentedly to bed. At two a.m. she was awakened by labor pains. Charley jumped into his clothes and ran to get Thede and Pearl. The car was ready, so they were soon on their way to the hospital.

When the doctor arrived, he took her into the delivery room, but despite his pleas, Charley was not allowed to follow. "I've delivered calves, colts, pups, why can't I deliver my own baby?" Charley asked. "No dice, you wait out here," said the doctor. Pacing, sweating and terrified, Charley waited through the hours. Then, just at daylight he heard the baby cry. There was no holding him then. He burst through the door then stood in awe at the sight of his baby son, all red and coated with the cheesy substance of birth, screaming from a tiny toothless mouth. He dropped to his knees at Evelyn's side and gently hugged her, as they both silently rejoiced at the gift of this tiny boy. They sent a telegram to the Fullers who arrived at noon from their home in Oak Creek.

Charles Evan Mantle was the name given the baby. He was born on October 13, 1927. Evelyn spent two days in the hospital, then rode to Pearl's house in the car, lying flat. She spent the next week in bed as was then the custom. The doctor visited and found her to be in fine shape. The women flocked around, all wanting to hold the baby. They taught Evelyn to crochet and brought snowy white materials and clear soft baby colored threads and made a quilted lining for the cradle at home. Evelyn started a crocheted edging around it, but Pearl had to finish it. They also crocheted a white outfit with frail blue lace.

Cowboy friends and army buddies dropped by. They all came tiptoeing in and most of them greeted Evelyn with, "How is that little pot-licker?" Before

Charles Jr. even got home he had been nicknamed "Potch." Evelyn enjoyed her time of rest. She enjoyed the company of the women who came to visit her, and listened intently to the good advice the experienced mothers gave her. Evelyn's mother cried bitter tears that she couldn't come help her daughter with the new baby. However, it just wasn't worth the risk because she had the dreaded tuberculosis.

Charley made a fast trip back to Blue Mountain to be sure the horses he had been breaking had all been returned to their owners, and payment had been received. Wellen and Lorraine, who were still at the Horse camp informed him that all the horses had been delivered, and payment received. Wellen turned Charley's half of the money over to him. Charley was greatly relieved to get the money, because a lot of people had been telling him all the expensive things a new baby would be needing.

On the big day Evelyn rode Pacer home. Charley carried Potch. The only reason he didn't put the baby in the pack pannier was that Evelyn wouldn't let him. They showed Potch off at every ranch and cabin on the way home. Then it was home at last! And how good it looked to the exhausted new parents. The Chew women rode over to arrange and organize and supervise what work needed to be done to organize the care of the baby. They told Evelyn what she could do and were very firm about what she should not do. They warned her if she worked too hard she wouldn't make enough milk for the baby. Wellen brought the little crib Grandpa Evan had made. Wellen said that the way the little pot-licker was growing, he knew he needed to bring it in before it snowed up for the winter.

Life was very hard. For the baby's bath Evelyn packed water, then wood to heat the water on the stove, then mixed it in the dishpan to bathe him. For washing clothes she carried water, heated it, and then scrubbed the clothes clean on a scrub board in a wash tub and draped the clothes over bushes to dry. The diapers seemed endless. She scraped the bad ones off, then put all the dirty ones in a bucket of water. She rinsed them out, then boiled them on the stove in lye soap. She rinsed and rinsed the diapers so baby wouldn't get a rash, then dried them in the sun.

Her hands became rough and raw from so much washing. She worked too hard, did not eat the proper food and her milk supply dropped. The baby was not getting enough to eat, so he sucked and chewed on her breasts until her nipples were so sore it brought tears to her eyes when he nursed. Ed Lewis had stayed on to help Charley through the fall work, so Charley was able to leave much of the ranch work for him to do. Charley took over the washing and cooking and insisted that Evelyn spend most of her time either sitting or lying down. He fixed potatoes and carrots and cabbage for her to eat, but refused to eat the stuff himself. He and Ed stuck pretty much to their old diet. In a surprisingly short time the baby was full and happy again. Evelyn healed up and the crisis was over. Charley and Ed cut and carried all the wood and water. They milked the cow and prepared special food for the chickens and kept them warm and cozy so they would lay. A good lesson had been learned about women's work.

A family fun time started to happen each evening. Charley would warm up the cabin, then strip Potch down to stark naked, and lay him on a blanket on the dirt floor. Charley and Evelyn would sit on the blanket with him. He would cry wildly, exercising every pore of his lungs. Then he would kick his legs and thrash his arms and smile and gurgle. He came to insist on this play time, and his doting parents looked forward to it, too.

It was a long winter. The snow was deep. The ice froze thick on the river. Charley had to chop a trail out of the ice each day for the weak and sick cattle he kept on Hospital Hill to be able to get a drink from the river. In late December he made a quick trip out to Jensen to get the mail and some Christmas supplies.

His sister, Nancy Mantle Ayers, wrote that she and her two boys would be out from California in the spring when school was out to help Evelyn, and spend the summer. That was good news. Evelyn enjoyed Nancy, and would welcome the companionship and above all, help with the work.

Evelyn sent a letter out with Charley to her cousin, Eva, in New York. This was the first of a lifetime of letters the two would exchange with each other all through their lives. Evelyn would be twenty-one on her birthday in February. She had a new baby, lived in a wild country with no roads. She had no car, lived in a dirt floor dirt roof cabin with no electricity or running water. She did her wash in a tub with a scrub board, and was married to a man she adored who saw nothing wrong with all that. Eva was the only one in the world she could share her true feelings of joy and despair with. Charley played endlessly with the baby. He was always around home. Evelyn would look back on this as the best year of her life.

15

New Parents, 1928

INALLY SIGNS OF SPRING BEGAN TO SHOW. Best of all, Jers had a fine new red and white bull calf, which meant they would soon be able to get milk from her again, rather than from the half wild Hereford they had milked for the past month. Jers now produced rich milk and cream. Potch liked the foamy warm milk from the bucket when it first arrived from the corral and drank eagerly from a cup.

One morning the canyons were filled with the sound of cracking and splintering ice. The ice in the river had begun breaking up and had jammed into a pile that formed a dam in the river, which was now backing up and filling its banks. Soon it would overflow and all the farm land would be washed away. Charley rode to Tom Blevins cabin and asked if he had any dynamite. He did, and he came back with Charley to help. It was dangerous work. Charley had to walk out on the tipsy ice layers to somewhere in the middle of the river to set the charge. At any moment it could all begin to move again, topple him into a hole and grind him to pieces. Cautiously, he made his way out onto the ice, praying that the great force of water dammed up behind it would not break through. Carefully he set the dynamite charge into a crevice, attached the cap, and gingerly returned as far as the length of fuse he strung behind him would reach toward shore. Still some distance from where he would be safe from the blast, he ran out of fuse.

Striking a match, he lit the fuse. Quickly turning around he retreated as fast as he could over the slippery, unstable ice. He had not quite reached shore when the explosion came. With a great boom, ice was thrown into the air and bombarded him as it fell. Unhurt, he scrambled on. Behind him he heard cracking and rumbling followed by a great crash as the water broke through the hole made by the blast. From safety on the bank he and Tom watched the great wall of water and ice roar off down the river. The water level of the river quickly returned to normal. Hells Canyon was flooding, too, and Tom opined that this damn desert country always had too much water or none at all.

Evelyn had few conveniences to help her through each day's chores. Occasionally, however, a given day would produce a pleasant surprise, as happened on the day Tom Blevins helped Charley break up the ice jam in the river. Upon learning that Evelyn had no real boiler to heat water, he proceeded, with Charley's help, to build her one out of a fifty-gallon oil barrel, with one side cut out. The makeshift boiler was then hung, with the opening on top, between two upright poles sunk in the ground. After dinner and a final cup of coffee, Tom played with the baby for a while, then went out and scrubbed it and after heating the oily barrel, he wiped it shiny clean with a gunny sack. This done, he and Charley carried buckets of water from the creek and filled it to the brim. They started a fire under it again, and in no time at all had a big boiler full of steaming hot water. Evelyn was elated, and hugged her old friend until he turned red.

Spring work was hard, and time in which to get it done was short. Evelyn planted the garden and stayed home washing diapers, bedding, clothes, and the baby. How tired out she was carrying that big baby. She missed riding with Charley and the freedom that gave her. She was also lonesome and desperately wished there was a road to her home so friends could come visit and she could go visit them. She longed for news of the outside world. She missed magazines and books to read. Most of all she wanted a house that had more light and was bigger and safe from floods.

One day in April Evelyn bundled up Potch and rode over to see Mrs. Chew. She was lonely, too, and very glad to see Evelyn and the baby. They had a good visit, and Evelyn was reassured to know that she was normal being lonely. They laughed about how the men always had another man around to visit with, and they never had another woman.

Mrs. Chew was midwife and doctor to everybody in the ranch country. She took her unofficial position seriously and shared her knowledge and skills as best she could. She told Evelyn all about the various illnesses with which she might have to deal, ranging from colic and fevers to vomiting, choking, rashes and sunburn. Treatments included mustard plasters and various antidotes. It was a very good beginning to all the knowledge Evelyn could see she was going to need in this life she had chosen. She soaked up every scrap of information given her.

One day three men came walking up from the river. The obvious leader was short, powerfully built, had red hair, bright rosy cheeks and smiling blue eyes. He introduced himself as Bus Hatch. They had come down the swollen, dangerous river from Deer lodge in a wooden rowboat. Evelyn immediately liked him and asked them to sit down and visit until Charley came home. When Charley arrived there was a great back slapping, wrestling, joking and rowdy greeting between old friends. Bus Invited Charley and Evelyn to join them next day for a dutch oven fish fry across the river. To be invited out to supper was a most welcome occasion for Evelyn. Riding across the swollen river in the boat with her baby was scary, but she knew it was safe. She had heard many times what an expert boatman Bus was. He was already rather a legend. The men had caught a big mess of catfish. Bus rolled them in corn meal and fried them in a big Dutch oven. In another oven he made golden brown biscuits. He had even brought along apples and a big butter cake for desert. They visited until far into the night. Bus rowed them back across the river.

Bus and Evelyn formed a special friendship in that short time. During the years ahead they would spend many happy hours together. When he made a trip down the river he always tried to spend one night of the trip in a comfortable bed at the Mantle Ranch. The next trip down the river Bus delivered a big pressure cooker. Evelyn had asked him to see if he could get her one so she could can vegetables and meat.

With Wellen and Loraine away in New Mexico, it was a very lonely place, but Evelyn's spirits soared when the two of them returned that spring. Finally the snow was almost gone on Blue Mountain and the flooding in Hells Canyon settled down. Evelyn's parents rode in when they returned to their homestead on Blue Mountain for the summer. Evan had come as early as he could so as to help with the spring work. Charley made a deal with him to return in the fall to save Laddie Park from flooding away by building a strong cribbing at the head of the Park where the high water had started a channel down through the park. One more spring of high water and it was likely the whole park would wash away. In return, Charley would help Evan plow up the lower end of the park and plant corn, which he could irrigate out of the river. The income from a good corn crop would sure help the Fullers out, so Evan happily agreed.

Friends dropped in to see the new baby and visit. Evelyn was embarrassed that she had no meat but jerky to serve them. To her guests, though, it seemed that she set a very bountiful table. The chickens were laying all the eggs they could possibly use and Jers was giving lots of milk, so she had butter, buttermilk, cottage cheese and thick cream. The garden was producing lettuce, radishes and spinach. Asparagus could be found in special places along the river bank. The rhubarb growing along the ditch made delicious pies.

Charley rode to Jensen on the first of June to pick up Nancy and her two boys, Tab and Herb. He took the lead with their three horses behind him. The boys could hardly wait to see the baby and swim in the river. Nancy begged to go by way of Hells Canyon so she could ride the beautiful trail off Martha's Peak once again. That meant they had to take an extra day, but Charley was glad to spend the night at the horse camp and see how Wellen was doing. He had been pretty sure his sister would want to come this way to visit Wellen, so had warned Evelyn they might be an extra day and not to worry.

Charley drove home the new bull he had purchased in Jensen last fall. The little boys were excited to be "real cowboys on a cattle drive." They worked hard the two days keeping the bull out of the brush and on the trail. They were so tired when they finally got to the ranch that they were nearly asleep on their horses.

Evelyn had a big garden planted, which required a lot of irrigating, but it rewarded her with a bountiful crop, including lettuce, radishes, and spinach. She didn't have to worry so much about the baby, who was crawling every place now, because Sport had taken personal responsibility for him. He guarded him constantly and if Potch crawled in the wrong direction he would block his path, and even push him over with his nose if all else failed.

Evelyn and Nancy hurried through their work so they could take short rides, relax and visit, or explore caves and hunt for arrowheads. Charley took the two boys with him much of the time. The bad news was that Nancy could only stay for the month of June, as she had to get back to California.

Shorty Chambers was helping Charley that summer. Shorty was a short, slight, bow legged man with one leg shorter than the other. He was always clean and tidy and impeccably dressed. He wore high heel cowboy boots, and took great pride in his small feet. Charley had small feet, too, and they spent time making fun of other people's big feet. It mattered not that both of them had such bad feet they could hardly walk. One or the other, when a person's name came up would say, "that bastard's feet are this long," indicating with a wide spreading of hands and just the right wrinkling of eyebrows to express disgust. He was not much for playing with babies or milking the cow, or hoeing the garden. He resented Charley being domesticated, and sniped a lot at Evelyn. As was her way, though, she won him over and he came to enjoy being with her whenever he had a little time. He was an excellent cook and he showed her some cooking tricks, carried water and wood for her, and loved to hear her stories of New York. Little Potch was a total fascination to him, but Potch's occasional dirty diaper and constant drooling as he cut new teeth revolted him. He held him in his lap only if he had a saddle blanket over his lap. He made Potch some little chaps with buckskin fringes and promised to make him some woolly sheepskin chaps, too.

The branding was done, the cows shoved up on the mountain, and the bulls turned out; they were to summer on Clark Feltch's place. Charley and Evelyn decided the baby should go, too and Evelyn would just ride down and water the garden every few days. Potch was eight

Shorty Chambers.

months old now, so could sit up and was easier to carry on the horse with her. That meant Jers also had to go to the mountain. The gentle little cow didn't do well with all the horses, the rocky ground and no shade or comfort, but they resolved the problem by taking her over to the Fuller homestead, from where the milk was carried.

Evelyn rode Laddie down the steep mountain, holding Potch in front of her every three days to water the garden, but the routine was telling on her. She grew thin and worn out. Her body was over-stressed with the heavy work load and making milk for Potch. She was determined to nurse him until he was one year old. Charley had no choice but to break horses. They had to have the money. In late July Evelyn's father said, "I got a lot to do at the ranch, Evelyn. Will you go stay with me? Evelyn didn't want to leave Charley, but this just wasn't working, so she accepted her father's generous offer. The day before they were leaving Marcus Jensen showed up with a pregnant cat in a gunny sack for Potch. Sport was the only one who didn't want the cat, but as it turned out she reduced his work load considerably by helping entertain the baby. They set out for home with the cat and Jers and Sport. How relieved Evelyn was to get home and stay there.

Potch was trying to walk, and was crawling terribly fast. Shorty said, "Tie him up, and just let the little feller exercise on a rope or he's gonna drown in the river." Charley was so lonesome that Wellen finally protested that Charley wasn't holding up his end of the deal with the horses and was so moon-eyed he might as well go on home. A spark of concern kindled in Charley at the mean way Wellen said this. As he thought about it, he remembered some other sharp remarks Wellen had made lately, and he was having fits of anger and abuse with the horses.

So Charley did spend most of his time down in the canyon with his family. He wasn't free to go ride in every rodeo around the country as he once had. It was just hard to get around much with a wife and baby, and garden, and a bunch of chickens. His old bachelor friends teased him and didn't come around much any more. He found himself content, though, and loved to be with his baby and wife. He even helped Evelyn can vegetables in her shiny new pressure cooker.

Charley and Evan cut tall trees from the mountain side and used green broncs to drag them to the upper end of Laddie Park where the river was beginning to make a channel down the middle of the little park. They lashed the logs together with cable and dynamited out a cavern in the ledge upriver to secure the cable. They built and reinforced a thick bank of boulders behind the logs. When they had the "cribbing," as they called the logs, securely fastened in place to resist the beating they would receive each spring, their work was still not finished. Charley sent for Wellen to bring more green broncs down from camp. The three men dragged every dead tree they could find and wedged them behind the logs. They even pushed dead trees off Red Rock Bench, then dragged them across the river to be a part of the mighty crib. They piled rocks on top of the trees and were finished at last! Every day Evelyn rode

Evelyn and baby Potch ready for a ride.

Laddie down with Potch perched in front of her on the saddle. She brought them food and made coffee for them. Usually they would all take a swim in the cool river while they rested.

Ranchers who had left their young horses with the Mantle boys to be trained would have been horrified had they known the indignities their horses suffered that summer. Charley thought "Them squatter farmer bastards is the ones ought to be getting these horses, not ranchers." The horses ended their training by plowing the bottom end of Laddie Park, then harrowing it and pulling a little homemade ditcher Evan invented.

Both handles broke out of their one-horse plow. Evan cut two strong limbs from the birch grove. He chose limbs that had just the right bend in them to make a good plow handle. He peeled and shaped them with the ax, pounded them into the handle guides, and plowed on. The plow became very dull, but the closest grinding wheel was at Chews, and besides they had plenty of horse power to pull the dull one. They made what they called a 'sorta ditch' to get water to the field. It would need improving for the long term, but for now it served the purpose. When they finished planting the field they were very proud of their work and waited excitedly for their corn crop to get growing.

16

Survival, 1928-29

HE KITTENS ARRIVED and soon their eyes were open. Potch grunted mightily as he lugged around arms full of black and white kittens. The
mother cat let him play with them as long as he didn't hurt them. If
they complained she grabbed them one by one and hid them. Evelyn would
scold and punish Potch for being mean to the kittens, but he would finally
have his privileges restored. He learned to be gentle. The kittens were a great
help to the family because they kept Potch occupied and everyone could get
their work done.

Evan and Charley built a rock and cedar crib along the creek to keep it in
its banks when it flooded. They built it where the creek hit the ledge head-on
a couple of hundred yards above the house. The sharp change in direction
there caused a backwash of the powerful flood waters that always threatened
to re-channel the creek through the house and corrals.

They built a second crib to reinforce the bank by the dam. The creek was very
narrow at this point and the bank had been washing away a little more each spring
and would soon would have washed out all the chokecherry, elderberry, and squaw
brush that held the bank firm. The two men enjoyed working together and Charley
learned a great deal from Evan about constructing things and about farming as well.
Evan was constantly entertained by Charley's unquenchable humor and amazing
memory from which he dredged up endless stories.

Evelyn sent them out to get a fat buckskin. They made a day of it and came
back with the biggest, fattest deer they could find from the side of Blue
Mountain. Evelyn cut up and canned almost the whole thing. She also had
Charley and Evan catch and kill chickens. They plucked them, only with the
promise of pie in payment. Evelyn also canned the chickens. She just wasn't
going to be caught with no meat again in the spring. They labeled all that meat
and cleaned out the shelves in the cellar to store it.

Evan stayed on to help as long as he could, but finally had to get back on
the mountain and get ready to move off before the snows came, as he could
not make a year around living farming their homestead. He had work in the
coal mines in Oak Creek for the winter. It was so very quiet and lonely for
Evelyn after her father left.

Evelyn, her father, Evan Fuller, Charley and Potch.

Evelyn felt very discouraged. There was so much to do just to survive. Getting and storing food, and building and improving shelter were her daily concerns. Potch was walking, but still needed to be carried a lot, and was a really big heavy baby. The kittens were a great help, because they kept him occupied. However, in the wink of an eye he would toddle off and have to be hunted down. She always started the search by running to the river, as it was her constant fear he would drown. Sport always stayed with him and would bark when called, indicating their location. Evelyn developed a distinctive call that carried clear and far through the canyons. It meant "Come now!" Everyone would come quickly, because she was saying time to eat, help needed, rider coming, baby lost, horses out, etc.

About Thanksgiving time Evelyn found herself feeling sick a lot. At first she feared she might have stomach worms, or worse, but soon recognized the pattern. She was pregnant again! Tears flowed like a river and fear wrenched at her as she thought of the hard time coming. She was burdened with a heavy baby barely walking. There was food to grow, clothes to sew, water to carry, and she would have to do it alone. She could foresee never again having the chance to be with Charley. He had to be away tending the cattle and horses, while she had to remain alone.Potch was fourteen months old now. Charley and Evelyn hoped with all their might he would be through with diapers soon. Christmas for Potch brought a box from Eva all the way from New York. It was a small enamel potty made like a cup, with a big handle. Charley called it his coffee cup. Potch was very possessive of it, and carried it around. He screamed and turned red when his Daddy teased him by taking his cup. Out of pure love for the potty he finally let himself be trained.

A bobcat moved into the neighborhood and one by one caught all the kittens. Only mama cat was left. One late afternoon Evelyn lay in wait and shot the bobcat just at dusk. She was hugely relieved, because her chickens would have been next on his menu. They were beginning to lay much needed eggs as spring came and food was scarce that time of year. The fish weren't biting yet, the deer tasted like rabbit brush and they simply couldn't afford to eat a beef. She must have the eggs for Potch and her unborn child. Charley skinned the bobcat and salted the hide. Ed Lewis tanned it with the hair on, and Potch had a furry mat for his playtime each evening.

17

Pat, 1929-30

CHARLEY STAYED AT HOME AS MUCH AS HE COULD and was always home at night, even through the spring floods. Evelyn rode with him occasionally just to get out of the house. He rode gentle horses so he could carry Potch. Finally in June Evelyn had to stop riding. She had never felt more desolate in her life. She couldn't go up on Blue Mountain, or even over to see the Chews.

As summer came on, Charley was gone most of the time. The season started out hot and keeping everything watered required a lot of hard work and as a consequence, she was sick a lot. She and Potch were there alone at the ranch. The milk cow's calf was now big and active and milking the cow became a nightmare for her. She couldn't afford to get hurt because Potch needed her. She would bleed to death if the baby started to come early from some blow or fall. How she longed for Charley to stay home.

Then wonderful news arrived in the mail! Nancy and the boys were coming in July to spend the summer and help out. Survival alone had become Evelyn's obsession. In her overworked, weakened and almost helpless condition the sparkle had left her eyes, her cheeks were pale, and she was losing hope. Nancy's arrival changed all that. She organized the house, prepared meals, put Evelyn to bed out under the cool tree by the spring and she and the boys took over complete care of Potch. Evelyn soon became her optimistic self again and slowly regained her strength.

One day Nancy and Evelyn were alerted by Sport that somebody was coming. In rode Joe Haslem and a woman. He greeted them with, "godammit, I just had to come show off my new wife, Ruth. I ordered her out of a catalog and damned if I don't believe she's a keeper." Beside him rode a dark, rather unremarkable woman who didn't sit a horse very well, and looked confused and exhausted. Nancy ran to her horse and held it while Joe helped her climb down. When she spoke Nancy and Evelyn were dumbfounded. She spoke with a Boston accent in a low, cultured voice. Her speech was proper and precise. The question was, what was this woman doing with the likes of Joe? They speculated that she must have come to look him over and would be moving on. Joe was obviously moon-eyed over her, and did his very best to keep his language cleaned up when around her.

Joe and Ruth stayed for dinner and they had a very nice visit. Ruth was a complete city girl, and way out of her element, but seemed devoted to Joe and determined to adapt to his life style. Joe told Evelyn she looked to him like she was "gonna pop that kid out any minute." He begged her to come out to Jensen and stay with his mother so she could be near the doctor. Ruth couldn't believe this woman planned to ride out on a horse in her condition and insisted that she wanted to help, too.

Charley rode down to check on his family every other day. They decided that he should come for Evelyn on the twentieth of August. Nancy said she could stay until the end of September, but would have to have some help. Charley said probably Uncle Hy could come stay with her, but she told him there was no way that dirty old man would be allowed around a new baby. One way or another, Charley said she would definitely have help. Evelyn insisted, however, that Potch go with her and that Pearl would take care of him for her.

On August fourteenth Charley decided to get Evelyn earlier than planned. Next morning at daybreak, before it got too hot Evelyn was mounted on Laddie and they started off on the long ride to Jensen. The forty-mile ride was miserable but uneventful. From Jensen a car took them on to Thede's at Vernal. Potch was so tired and sore from the long ride that he wailed uncontrollably. Evelyn wished she could do the same thing. After a good supper and a night's sleep everybody felt better. The doctor came and after examining Evelyn told her that she had cut it a little short this time, that the baby was going to come any time now. Pearl took Evelyn to town the next day and they bought diapers, along with a few clothes and supplies the baby would need. They also bought Potch some new shoes.

On August 27, 1929 a healthy baby boy was born and they named him Thomas Patrick. Twenty-two month-old Potch was amazed at this tiny human, and wanted to carry him, kiss him, feed him, and generally made a pest of himself in the process. Evelyn lay flat in bed for one week, after which the doctor said she could get up and around now, but not to do any lifting or pulling and was to limit the time she spent on her feet for at least two weeks. The doctor warned her to remain at Pearl's and rest for at least three weeks. Slowly, her strength returned and by the last week in September she felt she could make the trip home. Thede drove her and the two babies to Blue Mountain where Charley met them with horses to finish the trip.

Guy MacNearlin, an old cowboy who roamed the country, was at the ranch helping Nancy. The land was dry and winter feed for the cattle was going to be short. Guy was a gentle, friendly man without whose help, Nancy and Evelyn could never have gotten through that first week with a new baby, as Charley was still at the horse camp.

They harvested everything possible from the garden and stored it away. The potatoes had produced well, and Guy dug a pit below frost level to store them in, then fashioned a cover. Armed with a shopping list from Evelyn, Guy took pack horses out to Vernal to get winter supplies. Charley had sold some horses, so there was enough money to get what they needed. He had also shipped a few steers, but they weren't very fat, so he sold only what he absolutely had to.

When Nancy and her boys left at the end of summer, Evelyn felt like her life line had been ripped away from her. Guy calmed her down by sticking close, helping with the work, and visiting like a woman friend. How she appreciated him! He would softly say, "Now Missus, you just take it easy, I'll do that. You need to make lots of milk for that little boy."

Potch was as good as a two-year old could be with Pat, but had to be watched all the time that he didn't hurt him. He imitated Guy down to the very way he walked with a slight limp, to the way he wore his hat. Guy was short a thumb on one hand and Potch would pull and bend at his thumb trying to make it look like Guy's. Pat was a sweet, good natured baby.

It looked to Charley like a drought was coming on, so he bought all the cottonseed cake to be had in Vernal. In November Clark Feltch and Charley packed cottonseed cake in by way of Serviceberry Gap. They packed it on a string of burros and broncs. The unwilling horses' panniers were packed with sacks of cake. More sacks were piled on top, then covered with a heavy tarp that wouldn't get ripped up in the serviceberry brush. Finally they tied all the snorting horses head-to-tail. Clark then mounted his big horse and dallied up. He dragged the pack hoses kicking and snorting down the mountain until their feet finally got so sore they had to straighten up and walk instead of causing trouble. Then Charley turned loose the string of burros who had also been packed to capacity. They were tied together in a string and calmly followed the horses down the rocky trail. Charley brought up the rear.

There was hardly any snow that winter, but feed was so short that Charley had to move the cattle around a lot to keep them in grass. He fed the cottonseed cake conservatively, and it did get him by until the green grass started to show in the spring. There was plenty of cake left over for the even worse times Charley figured were coming. Snowfall in the mountains at the headwaters of the Yampa was light, so at least they wouldn't have to worry about the river flooding for any extended amount of time.

18

Moving to New Mexico,
1930-32

PRING CAME EARLY IN 1930. There was no runoff in Hells Canyon, so they planted the garden extra early, knowing it would be hard to keep it alive and producing. Charley and Guy repaired the dam in the creek, to make sure no water could escape and they cleaned the ditch to the garden as well. That was about all Charley had time to do around the ranch, because Guy had to go back to his own place for the summer, and there wasn't anybody else around to help him with the livestock.

One day Wellen and Lorraine showed up with the announcement that they were staying for the summer and would help with anything at all. Lorraine looked unusually thin and nervous to Evelyn. She didn't say what the trouble was and Evelyn thought she was just working too hard. The two couples had a wonderful time together. Lorraine couldn't keep her hands off baby Pat. He responded with hugs and coos and wet kisses. Not to be outdone, Potch demanded equal time and also gave her hugs and kisses. He loved to have her tickle him so he could scream and run. Wellen, too, played with the two "little men" as he called them.

Ed Fisher, Lorraine's father, came riding in one day. He was an old friend of Charley's from their army days and was now a rancher in Seligman, Arizona. Lorraine had grown up on his ranch and had become an accomplished cowboy. Ed had gotten himself a real estate license, so he knew all about all the ranches around. He set Wellen and Lorraine up as managers on the old White ranch outside Regina, New Mexico shortly after they married. They really loved the White Ranch, but they just couldn't get Charley's ranch out of their minds. The Whites wanted to trade off their ranch for one that fit them better and a couple of years ago Charley had expressed some interest in making such a trade and Ed was here to talk business.

Wellen had been discharged from the army in 1922 with complete medical disability, one which made it impossible for him to father children. Since he and Lorraine would not be having any children they could easily adjust to conditions on the Mantle Ranch, such as no roads, for example. On the other hand, Charley realized that the ranch was just too tough on Evelyn, what with

Best friends Evelyn and Lorraine Mantle.

no roads, no conveniences, and a rapidly growing family. The boys would soon be old enough to start school, and there was not a school within twenty miles. As a young man Charley had worked one winter in the rugged cattle country around Regina and kind of liked it. Wellen had also told him how the ranch lay and how it operated and Charley felt it was just right for them.

It was so nice for Evelyn to have a woman friend and she and Lorraine became fast friends. Charley, also, thought Wellen was a very lucky man to have found her. He adored Lorraine and Wellen, and had one of the happiest summers and winters of his life having them with him. His life as a child had been completely devoid of any family closeness. They stayed on through the summer of 1930.

In late September, Wellen helped Charley gather and move all the cattle to Ashley Creek. Ashley Creek, near Jensen, is where Charley's Uncle Hy lived. Charley had made a deal with him to winter the cattle there. He didn't have any help for the winter and the drouth had made pasture so short the cattle could not survive in the canyons. More important than that, he had a four-year-old, a toddler, and a wife who would be needing help through the winter.

While the men moved the livestock Evelyn and Lorraine packed up the belongings they would need for the winter. They carried the chickens in gunny sacks and left them with Mrs. Chew, along with some grain to feed them. Moving day came and they were quite a procession riding the long trail to Jensen. Two women, one with a year old boy on her horse with her and a four year old on his own horse. They led two pack horses and drove a Jersey milk cow and her big calf with the help of an old dog, who kept the cow on the trail. The mama cat was in a gunny sack tied on top of a pack horse. Potch went to

Evelyn and Wellen, preparing to ride twenty miles to vote. November 4, 1930.

sleep on his horse so Lorraine lifted him to her horse and carried him the rest of the way.

Hy welcomed them heartily and told them to just come on in the house and make themselves at home. Evelyn was somewhat prepared for what the house would look like. Lorraine, however, grabbed the two little boys and went running back out the door. She stood in the yard helplessly throwing up and voicing her total disgust. "My little boys just can't live here," she moaned. Evelyn hugged her, and in a low voice said, "Raine, I have to live here or go back to the canyon and live alone. Charley has to be here with the cattle. I don't think I could take care of these boys alone." They camped out in the yard for the night.

The two women took the boys to Vernal and left them with Pearl and returned bringing lye soap, kerosene, ammonia, and Dutch Cleanser, plus a new broom and a bag of rags Pearl had given them. They dragged every last thing outside into the yard and spread it in the sun. They emptied the ashes from the stoves, swept the walls, ceilings and floors. They heated water, added plenty of lye soap, and scrubbed every inch of the old frame two-story house from roof to floor. They even scrubbed the bed frames and springs, and furniture. Then they went back over it and scrubbed every inch of it with kerosene to kill the fleas and lice and bed bugs. They joked that it was a good thing they didn't smoke, and nobody else had better do so, either if they didn't want the house to go up in smoke.

Another night they camped and cooked and slept in the yard, far away from Hy's household stuff. They wouldn't let him go back in the house to sleep, either. The next day they heated up a barrel of water, added a generous supply of lye soap and washed all of Hy's bedding, his clothes, hats, boots, and anything else that had come out of that filthy house. They washed the windows inside and out with ammonia and polished them until they shined.

Uncle Hy Mantle in front of his house with nephews Potch and Pat Mantle.

They even made Hy himself take a bath with lots of lye soap. Wellen and Charley were the wardens for this project. First they cut off the eight old long underwear collars from around his neck. He never bothered with the collars after the underwear rotted off each spring. They figured it had been eight years since his last bath. The two young men especially enjoyed being sure he washed his hair and mustache and ears. He was mostly good humored about it, but at one point the women heard him put up a howl that "If God hada wanted men to take baths he'da put fins on em!" Finally he stood before his tormentors, scrubbed and combed and in freshly washed clothes. Grinning, he stuck a big wad of chewing tobacco in his mouth and said, "I'm gonna chew this 'baccy afore you wenches wash it, too.

They heated yet another boiler of water and scrubbed every pot, pan, utensil and dish in the house. They giggled as they washed the stove poker and ash shovel. They even emptied out the flour and cornmeal, sugar and salt into different containers and washed the sacks and cans they had been in. Everybody, even Tom, helped move everything back into the house and put things in their places. They camped outside one more night to give the house a chance to air out and the kerosene fumes to disappear. They set the legs of all the beds in lids full of Kerosene to prevent future bugs from crawling into the beds.

Finally, the next day they moved in. It was really quite comfortable, with much more room than they were used to in their little crowded cabin. Potch was so intrigued by the board floor that he marched and stomped until his little body was wet with sweat. Charley hung the hind quarter of a fat buck in the barn. Evelyn put the vegetables she had brought in bins and tubs and stored them in a cool, dark place. Hy cocked a wary eye at the vegetables and announced, "Don't expect me to eat any of them damn things."

After they were all set-tled in, Lorraine and Wellen left. The parting was a little tense because Wellen, increasingly touchy these days, thought Evelyn had insulted him and was angry with her. Wellen and Lorraine planned on doing some travelling. Wellen was restless and unhappy and wanted to see some new country. They parted from the horses they had ridden all summer with almost as much regret as they felt at leaving the family they loved. They boarded the bus with their saddles, and waved goodbye. They planned on buying a car in Denver after Wellen got his checkup at Fitzsimmons. Pat wanted to go with Lorraine, and cried inconsolably when she left.

Charley rented pasture in nearby fields, bought a

Lorraine Mantle with her beloved nephews, Potch and Pat.

little hay, and fed cottonseed cake to the cattle, who made it through the win-ter in fine shape. Hy was the happiest he had ever been. He truly loved the family, and was glad to be a part of it. He played with the little boys endlessly. He bought a little saddle from a neighbor for Potch, who now rode every day. He and Charley also taught the little boy to rope and chew tobacco and cuss, much to Evelyn's chagrin. Pat was a tag-along but really didn't have long enough legs to manage in the snow. Mostly they pulled him behind them on a barrel lid wherever they went. Evelyn fixed vegetables every meal and Hy, even though he complained, ate a big share of them. She would put a skillet of fried meat on the table and let people help themselves. Hy would cut a big piece of homemade bread and wallow it in the meat drippings in the bottom of the pan. He would say, "Gotta wallop my dodger." Peas were a problem for him—they kept falling off his knife he ate with. He said, "If God would a meant men to eat peas he woulda made em flat."

Evelyn's biggest problem with Hy was to make him stop chewing his tobacco and spitting on the floor. She offered him tomato cans to spit in, but he just wouldn't do it. After her threats of withholding pie, he finally took his spitting outside.

Evelyn loved the chance to be with other women. She fit into the social life of the little community except for the church activities. Charley would not allow her to participate in the Mormon church. She knitted, crocheted, exchanged recipes, and quilted with them whenever she found time and Charley enjoyed visiting with all his childhood friends. Evelyn wouldn't let them cuss and chew in the house, so they would gather outside, whittling and swapping yarns, mostly of childhood mischief. Joe Haslem claimed that they went to grade school in a sod cabin. He and Charley would go around back, on the side with no window so the teacher couldn't see them and try to pee a hole through the dirt wall. They finally got busted before they got the job done because the teacher got suspicious about the huge amounts of water they kept drinking and upon investigation discovered their work site.

The winter of 1930-1931, Bryan, (Charley and Wellen's youngest brother), was in Regina running the ranch. Their brother Joe was also there with him. Wellen and Lorraine figured the two of them could handle the ranch and went on a trip. It turned out to be a terrible winter. Snow piled up to thirty-eight inches and cattle died by the dozens. Bryan was exhausted and discouraged. In the spring of 1931 Charley and his family returned to the ranch in the canyon. Joe figured Bryan needed a rest and sent him to Colorado to spend the summer with Charley and perhaps visit the Hackings in Vernal. The Hacking family had taken him into their home and raised him after his parents died. Joe said he would take care of the place until fall when Bryan returned. Joe was not well himself, but the quiet ranch life seemed to be helping him. He was able to keep things running until Bryan got back.

In June, Wellen sent a post card from New York, saying they were headed for eastern Canada. He said the farmers were all broke and that 20,000 veterans were in Washington D.C. causing a lot of trouble. They wanted to get the bonuses promised to them for World War I service, but it didn't look like they were going to get it. Wellen reported that the marchers were all broke and hungry. The whole nation was wallowing in the Great Depression.

With the dawn of spring on Blue Mountain hoards of Mormon crickets hatched out. They were shiny black or brown, flightless creatures about two inches long. They made a high pitched, menacing chirping sound that filled the air. They ate the grass off the range and everything else.. They formed flocks of maybe a half-mile diameter each. All in that flock moved relentlessly in one direction. They climbed up and over anything in their path, devouring it. Hitch racks were left with skeletons of saddles and pack equipment left around them that had been eaten. Boots, clothes, hides, foliage, and even bark off trees...anything in their path was destroyed and a barren land remained behind them. Each band moved in a relentless path until all in their path had been eaten.

Charley knew that soon his cattle would be out of feed as the crickets swept across Blue Mountain. He was checking his range one day to see when the inevitable move of his cattle to the bench and canyon part of his range would be necessary when he came upon a disaster in the making. A big band of Mormon crickets was headed toward the north rim of the mountain at Martha's Peak. They would come down the north side of Blue Mountain, spread out and eat all his range if they weren't diverted, but he had a plan!

Wheeling his horse around Charley rode like a man possessed of the devil around to all the cabins near enough that his horse could make the circle. At each place he asked for help and that they bring kerosene, matches and any-thing they had to clang together to make noise. With amazing speed people answered his call and rode to the flock of crickets. Charley told them to circle the sides and back of the band of crickets and drive them into the narrow confines of the cliff walls of upper Hells Canyon. Some brush fires had to be set along the east side to change the direction of the crickets, and they were driven onward from behind by the clanking of tin on tin and the shouts of the ranchers Finally the massive band of crickets was funnelled within the confin-ing cliffs of the canyon and the steep natural descent lured them rapidly on.

Meantime, Charley changed horses and rode as fast as he could to the homestead. There he told Evelyn and Bryan of the crickets and his plans for them. Evelyn and Bryan gathered up kerosene, rags, axes and noise makers and took them to the foot of the mountain where Hells Canyon breaks out of the mountain. There Charley had assembled the extra men who were not needed after the crickets had been driven within the canyon walls. With lariats,they dragged dry sagebrush and cedar trees into rows on either side of the creek where the crickets would want to spread out onto the benches when they emerged.

Just in time they finished as the first of the chattering band of crickets burst from the rocky canyon. The men trotted their horses down the row of brush sprinkling it with kerosine as they went. Each section was set on fire as the lead crickets arrived and the noise of pots and pans and buckets and yelling people behind drove them onward. For about a mile and a half the determined crew manipulated the crickets until finally they were once again within the confines of the walls of Hells Canyon. Their clattering voices echoed in the canyon walls to make a deafening, ominous roar. Now a few people could drive them and the rest rode their reluctant horses through the crickets and on down to the mouth of Hells Canyon where they would have another 200 yards to drive them through open country to their destiny. The flock of crickets was tiring and hungry, as it had been a long day and the sun was setting. Relentlessly the men and women clanged their noise makers and tried to make their hoarse voices shout as they forced the now very long string of crickets onward. A line of fire guarded the open sides once again.

Victory! The first of the vanquished Mormon crickets were forced into the flooding Yampa River. The river was running so high that it swept the crickets into the center. Evelyn reported that there was a black line of crickets riding the crest of the Yampa River as far as you could see as darkness fell over the canyon. By firelight the straggling crickets were herded into the river and the exhausted herders shouted and danced in victory. The destruction of the crickets was complete. No other flock would ever come over the mountain and into Charley and Evelyn's paradise until much later in history.

Bryan enjoyed his vacation. He became particularly attached to Charley's two little boys. He had never been recognized much by Charley as a child, so he really enjoyed Charley's friendship and approval that summer. The whole Mantle family looked up to Charley as the best stock man in the world and Bryan felt privileged to be learning at his side. In addition to working for Charley, Bryan got a job working for the state of Colorado fighting Mormon Crickets. He still had not received twenty dollars of the money due him from the state when he had to return to New Mexico. That money would have bought him a new set of clothes and some new boots, all of which he needed, so he was uneasy about leaving before collecting. He had been a big help to both Charley and Evelyn that summer. They were sad when he had to leave and the kids missed him, too.

In July, Evelyn realized that she was pregnant once again. The baby would arrive sometime next March. Her only hope was that the ranch exchange between their ranch and the White ranch would take place, and she could live in a real house with a road up to the door. Otherwise she didn't think she could survive another baby.

Wellen had always been very good to Bryan; he considered him and Lorraine his only real family. Bryan was proud to return to Regina as the trusted manager of the ranch. Lorraine and Wellen had promised that they would be back that winter.

Lorraine corresponded regularly with Evelyn. She was lonesome and wanted to go home. The traveling was very wearing on her. As summer progressed Wellen had been having fits of rage, along with uncontrollable attacks of nervousness and unrest.

Late in the summer Charley came upon the tracks of a shod horse, driving a cow and calf. It was on his grazing land and nobody had any business there, especially driving any livestock. He followed the tracks, and smelled smoke coming from the thick cedar trees ahead. Suspecting the worst he proceeded quietly, and came upon a neighbor who had roped the calf, tied it down, and was branding it with his own brand. Choosing a punishment to fit the crime, Charley tied his own branding iron, which was a worn-thin horseshoe bent into a circle, into the end of his lariat rope. He allowed the man to mount his horse, then Charley took after him swinging the branding iron so swiftly around and around through the air that it made a whistling sound. The two horses and men flew through the trees, into the sagebrush flats, over gullies and rocks, with the flashing branding iron biting into the flesh of the fleeing man. When he considered the lesson well taught Charley stopped the chase. The neighbor went to the Sheriff in Craig and filed suit against Charley. As a result, Charley had to appear in court. A date in December was set for trial. He could be sentenced to a jail term, as well as fined if found guilty. He was at a loss as to what he would do to provide for his family in case that happened. Much to his relief, when Charley showed up for trial the neighbor had left the country, and the charges were dismissed.

On his way home Charley found Guy MacNearlin and asked him to come work for him that winter. Guy agreed to do that and said he would show up before Christmas. He said he would have to get on back to his own place the minute spring broke, though, because he had some cows to calve out.

In November, 1932 Lorraine and Wellen returned to their ranch in Regina. Lorraine wrote Evelyn that Wellen had shown improvement for about two months after they got home, but then became even worse. He was drinking heavily and was explosive. He had lost all interest in riding and caring for the livestock. She and Bryan had to do all that. In January small patches of hair began falling out on his face and he became sicker. She feared he would become violent, and blamed herself for "being too dumb" to calm him down when he was in one of these moods.

Bryan was Lorraine's dependable hole card in getting all the work done. Joe left for California. He could see that nothing good was going to come from Wellen's hellish moods and he just couldn't stand the strain. He himself was not well and needed an operation. His money was frozen in the bank and he couldn't get to it. The depression had everyone in the area in such terrible financial shape that they were desperate. Bryan wrote that they watched their backs at all times because they felt that some of the people might get desperate enough to do them harm and take their food and money. Wellen's disability check of fifty-six dollars per month from the government was about all that got them by. The hard economic times, combined with Wellen's illness and drinking made for a tough life.

Disaster, 1933

HARLEY WAS THIRTY-NINE AND EVELYN BARELY TWENTY-SIX when a tragedy happened that would destroy their family, rock their marriage, and change their lives forever. Letters between the tortured souls involved tell of the heartbreak they felt.

In January, 1933, Ed Fisher wrote Charley that he had worked out the details of the ranch exchange and would come to Colorado in July, 1933, to close the deal. Charley and Evelyn felt a mixture of sweet regret and elation at the news. They loved their canyon home, but felt that they just must move to provide a better life for themselves and the children. Accordingly, plans were made to move in September following the exchange.

The previous fall came the first of a series of letters that gradually revealed an unfolding tragedy. On November 27, 1932, Lorraine wrote to Evelyn and Charley, bringing them up to date on family matters. She and Wellen had returned on the first of November. She also reported that Joe had gone to California two weeks ago. She thought the summer season had helped his condition. Lorraine also expressed concern that Evelyn might have gotten sick again. And she and Wellen were glad to have Bryan's help. We "...sure can depend on him," Lorraine added.

In January, Lorraine wrote again, saying that a horse had fallen on Bryan who was laid-up in bed with a badly wrenched back and that the hair was coming off Wellen's face in little patches. His condition was deteriorating. A month later Charley and Evelyn learned that Wellen took no interest in the stock or much of anything else. "He is crazy to get out," Lorraine told them, "but he is just as well satisfied here as he will ever be anywhere. Poor restless devil. I've never known any person who got as little of pleasure out of life as he does." But the troubling news about Wellen was not without its lighter moments. He now had his head shaved and Lorraine thought him a funny sight. "He doesn't exactly appreciate it when I laugh at him but oh—how funny. That little round head on top of those big broad shoulders. Just picture it for yourself."

Meanwhile, at the Mantle ranch things were getting tense. The new baby was due in a couple of weeks, and on March 9, 1933, Charley saddled up to take Evelyn out to Vernal to Pearl's house. He left the ranch in the care of an old cowboy friend of his, but he and Evelyn weren't brave enough to leave the little boys with him. So Charley put them on a horse with Evelyn and led a pack horse loaded with things they would need for about three weeks. Evelyn was huge, and looked like the baby might come any minute. She really hoped the doctor wasn't wrong about the delivery date.

They rode out of Red Rock Canyon and across the bench to Sand Canyon. They had barely started up Sand Canyon when suddenly Evelyn's horse stumbled and caught himself sharply. She cried out, and Charley carefully helped her off. She lay in the shade of a cedar tree being as still as she could. The pains started, and she knew there was no stopping the birth. Charley helped her to remount and they turned toward the Chew ranch. It was only a couple of miles, but seemed like ten to Evelyn. Her water broke about half way there. Charley gave his best cattle herding yell as they came close to the ranch house, and by the time they rode around the last jutting ledge and the house came in view they saw Mrs. Chew and Rial running to meet them. They grabbed the boys off their horse and led Evelyn's horse to the door of the house.

Mrs. Chew had feared this would happen as Evelyn's time drew nearer. Charley and Rial carried Evelyn into the house and placed her on the bed. Water was already hot on the stove and the bed had clean sheets. The pain was continuous now and the squalling baby arrived just thirty minutes later. It was a healthy baby girl with a head full of wild black hair. Rial and Charley both cried joyful tears. Not only was Evelyn safe, but they had both wanted a baby girl very badly. Mrs. Chew told Evelyn they both were so excited and happy that nobody would have guessed which one was the father. The two little boys were so awe struck they were speechless.

Evelyn didn't bleed excessively as everyone feared. Mrs. Chew soon had her cleaned and comfortable. She closed the curtains and door and left her to sleep away her total exhaustion. Rial had prepared a big meal by then and everybody ate hungrily. While Rial had been cooking Charley had gone out and unsaddled the horses and turned them out to pasture. The baby grew hungry and cried insistently. Potch and Pat thought she sounded like a kitten. As the baby nursed, Charley and Evelyn checked with each other again to see if they still agreed that her name would be Lorraine Evelyn. They hadn't discussed it with Lorraine, but they loved the name and loved Lorraine and were sure she would be pleased to have the baby named after her. Lorraine Evelyn Mantle was born on March 9, 1933.

The word went out all over the ranch country that baby Lorraine had been born at Pool Creek and Rial had been the midwife. Charley and the boys went home after three days. Mrs. Chew wouldn't think of letting Evelyn out of bed for a week, and cared for her tenderly. Through the long nights she comforted and tended the baby. Evelyn became strong and felt well again. She was anxious to get home to Charley and the boys.

As soon as they could, Evelyn and Charley wrote letters to family members telling them about Lorraine. Charley had a badly injured leg from a horse falling on him early in the winter, and had trouble getting around. When Guy had to leave it left Charley and Evelyn hard pressed to get everything done.

Meanwhile, the situation at the ranch in New Mexico was worsening. Lorraine's letters had made them aware that things were not good with Wellen and that he was very sick. What they did not know was that only fourteen days after the birth of their baby girl, Wellen died. Lorraine contacted Joe Haslem by telegram on March 24 and he rode in with the death notice. The horror of it was described in letters from Lorraine and Bryan.

On March 30, 1933, Lorraine wrote to Charley with the dreadful news.

My dear Brother Charley,

Oh God Charlie if I could just see you and tell you instead of trying to put it on paper. But I must try to tell you.

For two months after we came home Wellen just seemed so contented and looked so well. Then after Xmas he started drinking and seemed to me he just had something just driving him. Always before I could seem to quiet him and talk him out of his terrible moods.

Toward the last, everything I did was wrong.

Bryan never crossed him—just humored him like a child—and it seemed he felt every one was against him. The only thought was to get rid of me. He plotted every time he could get Bryan out of my hearing to knock me in the head. When Bryan was here he didn't touch me, but every time he felt we were alone, he would abuse me in a way no one can know but me. Then when those spells would pass how sorry he would be. I have known since Xmas that a terrible change had hold of him and I felt in time it must end in tragedy.

Then a week before he died he had a sort of stroke after which he was never the same. George (my brother) and his wife came by on their way to (unreadable). He seemed so pleased when they came and he visited with them and the last terrible night he told Bryan he was going to Cuba and get poison to give all three of us. He then had several others they would "get" and go on to Old Mexico. That seemed to be the only time he threatened Bryan just when he said what he'd do if he didn't stay with him. (All this I didn't know until afterward.)

When they came to the table I knew he was worked up to a terrible state but that if I just didn't cross him his mind would clear again. He just raved about every one and said "I'll leave my mark in this country" and smile a twisted grin at Bryan. Then he'd say "I've fought these S . . . alone alone alone" and just glare at me with eyes I've never seen in any human's head before. They were just like big pieces of watery glass bulging out of his head. Bryan went to the kitchen to pour some tea and something in Wellen seemed to snap— he lunged at me grabbing me by the throat with a fork in his hand. I screamed and George grabbed him by the arm he was holding over me. He seemed to have the strength of a demon. He threw George off and against the wall like he were a child.

Bryan shot him. He fell without a sound—never knew what hit him. Bryan knew that Wellen meant Kill and that he couldn't be stopped once he had started.

Everything seems a blank for a while after, but I can remember Bryan was the only cool one in the group. They went to Cuba and brought the ex-senator (Wellen always talked so much about) John Young, the Doctor and another man. The next day an inquest was held. There were forty men here (not Mex). Not one person thru it all but felt there was only one thing to be done and Bryan did it.

We buried him the next day. I put the clothes on him he liked the best—had everything at the grave as he would have had—just a few words and a song he liked. The coffin was nice and some pretty flowers. He looked so quiet and peaceful after the terrible unrest and nervousness that had been hold of him for the past weeks.

If I could feel that just my life was saved I'd know it was all wrong—for today if I could just be with him I could ask for nothing else. But I was just one on a long list his poor broken mind wanted to "get." If he had gotten away from here he would have left a trail of blood and been shot like a cornered coyote—maybe suffered hours. He always feared death but my poor Pallie never suffered—never knew he was going out.

Oh God! Charley why did it all have to happen this way. He was still just young but now he is gone and I am alone—just drifting along because some power greater than my own desires keeps me behind. He was everything to me and in just a flash it was all snatched away from me.

Thru it all Bryan just stood like a man and looked at all square in the face. I don't think you cared for Bryan, but I only wish you could have seen the boy thru it all. At the trial in Bernalillo on the witness stand I'll never forget him. He looked every man in the eye and said, "Men I did a terrible thing—I had to kill my own brother and I loved him." He just held up good until it was all over but now he just seems broken. Every time he sees any of Wellen's things he can't stand it.

If, while Wellen lived, they had ever quarrelled or he had been harsh in any way with Wellen I just couldn't feel as I do, but he humored him in every way—waited on Wellen and never once seemed to resent anything.

At the end of the trial the Attorney for the State made a good talk and throughout it all he carried the thought that according to all evidence it couldn't have been otherwise. He said in his mind and that of the court

Bryan had done a beautiful deed and that it was not my Boy who had been killed but just his body with a poor sick deranged mind.

Everyone has been kind to us and now I just want to stay away alone and not see anyone.

It seems I have been hours and hours trying to write this to you and no doubt it all seems so confused and muddled up that you can hardly glean any sense from all of it. I haven't the strength to write another letter to Nancy, but just send this one I have written on to her, for I surely want her to know all about it.

Charley if I could just see you and tell it all to you instead of this jumbled letter. The one relief I had was when I had your letter about Evelyn and the baby and knew she was all right before the wire got to you. I sent the word to Haslems and felt they would get word to you immediately.

Just a week today he went, and Charley I never knew one could live so long in just one week.

How I would love to see all of you and that dear little baby and boys. Oh Charley, write to me—both of you.

Love, Your little sister, Lorraine

Two clippings from the Cuba, New Mexico newspaper of March 24 were enclosed with Lorraine's letter.

Fatal Shooting Climaxes Row Between Brothers

A quarrel which started at the supper table led to the fatal shooting last night of Wellen Mantle, 38 (36), allegedly by his brother, Bryan, at the Mantle ranch, 12 miles north of here. The brother surrendered to J. T. Young, United States commissioner, following the shooting and was held pending an inquest which was called for late today.

Members of the family said Bryan shot in self defense when his brother sprang back from the table and threatened to kill his wife, his brother, Mrs. Mantle's brother and a sister-in-law. Bryan struggled with his brother and in the course of the struggle shot him, he told the commissioner.

Man Who Killed Brother Faints In Court When Case Is Dropped

(Condensed) As the attorney started the review, Bryan Mantle began to cry, then fell off his chair in a faint. Mrs. Mantle fainted a few moments later.

Testimony of Bryan Mantle, Mrs. Wellen Mantle, and the latter's brother and sister-in[law, Mr. and Mrs. George Fisher, was substantially the same as to the slaying.

Wellen Mantle had made statements before supper that he was going to kill his wife, the brother and several other persons, it was testified. At the supper table he suddenly seized his wife and Bryan shot in defense of her, himself and the Fishers, according to testimony.

John F. Young and Dr. A. Gillespie of Cuba were other witnesses.

A coroner's jury sitting at Regina last Friday also held the shooting justified.

On March 31, Charley heard Bryan's account of what had happened.

Dear Charley,

I can't hardly make myself believe that what I am going to tell you is possible. O God, Charley it seems just like a dream to me. But I had to kill Wellen.

Now Charley, I no you have never cared any thing for me. So I can't help how you feel toward me over this. Wellen was the only one of my people that ever gave me a word of encouragement. O God, I feel like that my only friend is gone so nothing matters to me now. But all I want to ask is for you to do all you possibly can for Lorraine. No one will ever no what she has gone through to stay with Wellen. Charley you have no idea what those last weeks have done to Lorraine. She is just a shadow. She just had to drag herself around to wait on him but never once did I hear complain and at the last we just had to tear her away from him. She just new she could help him. We can't do anything with her. She says she says there isn't anything left for her to live for because Wellen was everything she had. Thru all of it the only way we could keep her on her feet was for the Dr. to keep her full of dope. We can't get any food down her. Just a little milk and she never sleeps a minute without medicine.

Now Charley I no if anyone can do any thing with her it is you and Evelyn. She feel you were more to Wellen than any one and of course you no how she loves them little boys especially her little Pat.

She always was so high on your judgement some of her friends have rote her other letters for her. But she said she must get strength enough to rite one letter to you if it was the very last thing she ever done. She has been to days trying rite it to you folks. The only spark of interest she has seemed to have was when your letter came about the baby. She got this letter the day after we had buried Wellen. She seemed to brighten up just a little this morning and said to me if we could just see our little boys and the new baby Raine.

Well Charley I just can't set here any longer to rite. I cant explain how I feel. Bryan

Nancy, always the worrier for everybody, was beside herself. Her husband was out of work and they were flat broke so she couldn't do anything to help anybody. On March 25, 1933, she wrote to Evelyn from Stockton, California.

Dear Jobbie Long ere this I guess you have heard of poor Rains sorrow. The telegraph operator said—"It's a death message" and oh my heart went cold. I felt sure some one had been careless and you had passed on with my baby. Every day I have looked for a letter from Vernal or Jensen from you so maybe you miscounted but do let me know when you feel well enough to write.

I am sitting here just helpless as far as Lorraine is concerned I have no way of getting there and I guess there would be no way to help her if I was. She has been so good to him I just hope she can realize it was for the best and not grieve and go into ill health again. Joe said she looked pretty good last fall.

I have heard nothing from Lena. I do not think the earthquake hurt Pasadena. Please have Charley write as soon as you are O.K. Love, Nancy

Two days later, Nancy wrote again to both Evelyn and Lorraine.

Dear Evelyn and Lorraine, How glad I am that you are safe and sound. I had hoped that you would get no farther than your own bed this time for a Dr. is of no use only in case something goes wrong and very little good then. Two of our young mothers have died here under the best of professional care. No one know why. And I think that trip back is far worse on you than the birth would be so I am just so pleased about it all and happy for you and I know Lorraine will be delighted. She has worried so about you.

The little jaunt from Mrs. Chew's will be nothing compared to your auto ride from Jensen up and you know Lorraine may have inherited her father's jinks for autos too and the bottom fall out, and on a horse I'm sure she is safe. Bless her black head—how I would love to see her. Tab is tickled pink. I think he feels better about her than he did about the boys. Thinks maybe a girl wont be too close to Charley I guess. Won't Potch be able to be the man now with a female around for a guy to have to wait upon. Dear little Pat how cute he must be by now.

I am waiting to hear from poor Lorraine. I just hope she keeps up. She was doing so well Joe said when he left there. Maybe she can get hold of herself real well—I hope so.

Write again soon. Love, Nancy

On April 15 Charley left the ranch to go to Regina and get Lorraine and bring her back to the ranch. Her agonized letter had torn at his heart. He wanted to go see Wellen's grave and see if there were any loose ends that needed to be tied up. Although Ed Fisher was handling the real estate transaction, he felt he had to see Whites to be sure they still wanted to trade ranches. After the hard winter he and Evelyn surely hoped so. He knew he could never forgive Bryan for shooting Wellen, but for Lorraine's sake he was determined to be civil to Bryan. Then he hoped never to see him again. The Powers boy from Bare Valley had come to look after the ranch in his absence.

When he arrived he could hardly believe that the emaciated, hollow eyed woman who threw her arms around him sobbing could be their beautiful Lorraine. Bryan was off tending the cattle on another part of the ranch and he was glad of that. The gloom that hung over the place was almost unbearable. He went to the cemetery to see Wellen's grave. It was an ugly barren place, but then he supposed all cemeteries were. An old acquaintance approached him on the street and asked him if he would have a drink with him.

After some embarrassed shuffling of feet the man said, "Charley, I think you ought to look into Wellen's death. That young guy livin' out there and the wife was awful friendly. After he was killed they just put him in a box and buried him the next day. There wasn't an autopsy and no undertaker. Nobody knew about the burryn' 'till it was all over. It just don't look right to me."

Charley inquired around and found that several people thought there was a love triangle going on between Lorraine and Bryan. Charley had never trusted women. He thought all women were just out to use somebody, so it was easy for him to turn on Lorraine. In his tortured, grieving mind he came to believe that Lorraine had tempted and lured the young unworldly Bryan to fall in love with her. Then she had conspired with him to murder Wellen and make it look like self defense. He believed her motive was Wellen's monthly disability check of fifty-six dollars. He concluded that they had set Wellen up, killed him, then stuck him in a box and buried him like a dog, just as the man had thought.

Charley got the address of the hospital in St. Petersburg, Florida where Wellen had been declared eligible for disability insurance and the name and address of the issuing officer. He got a death certificate, and went home without telling anyone his suspicions. If what he believed was true, his life would not be safe if he started asking too many questions. He went home.

When he got home he was grim and hard faced. He told Evelyn what he had found. She was angry with him and asked how he could think such a thing of Lorraine. Hadn't she written letters telling of Wellen's worsening condition and violent moods? Hadn't he seen it himself? Charley flew into a rage and she feared he was going to strike her. He seethed with hatred and condemnation for all women. He said no woman should ever be trusted as they were just all conniving whores and added that under no circumstances ever was she to mention the name of Lorraine again. He said no baby of his would ever have that name and so the baby was temporarily without a name.

His rage was so fearful that Evelyn gathered her children and took them from the house. She told the boys to take care of the baby and keep her quiet until she got back. She returned to the house to find Charley drinking the last of a bottle of whiskey and nearly passed out. Stealthily she gathered all the guns and took them out and hid them, then she gathered enough blankets to keep the kids warm for the night and spent the night in the granary with the door braced shut.

When Charley awoke at first light of dawn he found himself alone and hung over. His family was gone. He searched everywhere for them and finally heard the baby crying in the granary. Evelyn wouldn't let him in until she was sure that he was back in his right mind. He said how sorry he was, but they both knew it would never be the same again between them. She had lost her complete trust in him, and he had lost his respect for her because she was a woman.

Charley's suspicions were further strengthened when he received a letter from J. Hensen at the Veterans Hospital, St. Petersburg, Florida, dated May 10, 1933.

In answer to your letter in regard to Wellen's will, it was made several years ago, either 1929 or '30 and left everything to his wife unconditionally. If he made another or any changes in that one he never said anything to me about it. I have not seen him since about 1928 but corresponded with him regularly until the last few years since both of us have been travelling a lot. Of course I have expected him to go any time for years for no one knows better than I how the poor fellow suffered but it was quite a shock. His health I know was decidedly worse the few months before his death but that kind of an end is always a shock.

I would appreciate hearing from you as to any . . . as we were very close friends and I am the last one of our "old gang" at Fitzsimmons in Denver. Very Sincerely, J. Henson

Meanwhile, Lorraine, knowing nothing of Charley's suspicions or investigation wrote to Charley and Evelyn on May 25, 1933.

Dearest Folks, At last I will drive myself to write a flew lines. I think of you every day and wonder how the baby is—wish I could have her and the boys to hold every long night!

Don't know when I'll get to see you. Hope sometime this summer. Lots of red tape to go thru but things are getting straightened out.

Two months today since we buried poor Wellen and god it seems like two years. If any one had ever told me time would drag as long I'd never believed.

Can't write any sense but I want to know how you all are so much.

I have a middle aged American woman here with me. She is so good. I've been gone so much and she keeps everything going good.

Why don't you write. Please do. I love you all so much.
Kisses for my babies. Your Raine

Nancy thought the whole horrible thing was over when she wrote to Evelyn on June 20.

Dear Jobbie, Thanks for the nice long letter. Indeed you are right September will be here before you can get all your packing done, and I do not envy you your job of moving but how glad I'll be when I know you are out. That's a glorious old place but so hard on both Charley and you. Its going to take a long time for Potch and Pat to forget it (tho I know they love it), for our kids still think of it as the only place in the world. . . . Write often to Lorraine. I know she must get pretty lonely down there.
Love, Nancy

Charley wrote to Nancy telling her what he suspected. He told her of his plan to quietly gather all the evidence and then bring the culprits to justice. He asked for her help. Nancy was frightened and angry and responded to Evelyn on July 6, expressing her concerns and fears.

Jobbie, Charley is all wet and lets drop this thing or Joe and I'll both be crazy. It nearly did me up and it shook Joe all to pieces again worse than his (*blast?*) I have never ever told Herb or Poncho and Tab and I'll kill the person that does. It will do no good to stir this up. Joe said that boy was crazy when he left. Joe told me he didn't see how Rain and Bryan could stand it He got out just as soon as they got home and told me then how things stood and they wrote him all winter here and Wellen kept getting worse and worse.
 It cost Joe a heap of dough to save Wellen from one scrape and he knows all about it. Please don't let Charley write Joe for he is a darn sick fellow as it is and his money is all tied up in the bank and he can't get a cent. He walked from Los Angeles to Arizona and a friend is staking him to grub until his bank opens again. He gave me the last $15 he had and I didn't know then or I wouldn't have taken it. So for the good of all Charley must cool off and forget it or we will all suffer and I've been through all I can stand so call him off for once and all. Lots of love, Nancy

P.S. A fellow ran amuck here and killed 3 people and it took 3 cops to kill him. They were ordered to turn loose with guns on site and they did. So you can see for yourself. I made it my business to question a nurse here for the insane. She has been there for 20 years with insane people and she told me of the strength they have and you'd hardly believe her.

On the same day, Nancy also wrote to Charley:

Dear Charley: As you know I have always relied on your judgment in everything but I think you are dead wrong this time.

I asked them to spare you the shock of this affair for I thought you had worries enough. They telegraphed me and they telegraphed Joe and a man wrote Joe about it and he wrote me and I asked him again to spare you. It nearly drove him over and it did more to me than I can tell so now for every child's sake yours and mine let the dead rest. It would do no good and I did not ever tell Herb or my boys and I'll kill anyone who does. They have enough to live down as it is.

Now just get a little cold thinking in your head. Suppose your suspicions could be proven. You couldn't bring that boy back. You know and I know that sooner or later he was bound to have done some terrible thing and he was insane. Joe said he was crazy as a loon when he left there.

Yes I'll come over just as soon as Hy can send me the money. Love, Nancy

Charley threw her letter aside and said, "Crazy damn woman. She is so afraid that no-good husband of hers will quit her over the scandal that she won't do anything." So he wrote to his sister, Lena, who he hadn't even seen or talked to in years, soliciting her help.

Lena responded from Pasadena, California on October 3rd.

"Dear Brother Charley—

Did you go down there when you received word and how did you first suspect his wife and Bryan? I understand how you feel about keeping your plan secret. I realize in this day and age life is considered nothing. So I will wait until I hear all you want to tell me about the whole affair. Jack (her husband) just told me she will receive a $30 pension also from the government as a widow—and another thing she will come in for Wellen's share of Uncle Miner's estate. I want to cooperate with you because Wellen was good to me and we owe him that much as his own people. Don't be long in writing. Sincerely, Lena"

P. S. If it can be proven that she had any connection with poor Wellen's death all money from the government will be held up else stopped as they are pretty touchy.

♦ ♦ ♦ ♦ ♦ ♦

The only joy Charley had was in his children. Over the summer Potch and Pat finally learned to not call their little sister by the name of Raine. They didn't understand, but obeyed their parents. Everyone said she was growing like a weed, so they began chanting "Queed the weed." Evelyn refined the name to Queeda, and everyone accepted that as her name. Her birth was not registered for two years after she was born, so they registered her as Queeda Evelyn Mantle, born at Pool Creek Colorado.

During the summer an artist named Jack Herndon came into the canyon. He was on special assignment as the travelling artist for the *Chicago Tribune*. His article was to be on the wild and beautiful west. He was intrigued by this family that lived the true West every day. Charley was the best possible subject he had found for the cowboy image, too. Jack asked if he could paint Charley's picture with the canyons as the background. Reluctant, but flattered, Charley posed for the picture. He posed in his white shirt and black scarf, chaps, hat and big spurs, leaning against a hitching rack. In the background was the Crows Nest high on the pink and yellow sheer-faced cliff of the north side of the Yampa River as it disappeared off to the west. He did a glorious job of capturing the color and grandeur of the canyon, and also of his cowboy subject. The article he wrote and his pictures were later published in the *Chicago Tribune*. He painted a portrait of Charley that day and a small painting of the canyon. They were magnificent. He gave them to Charley and Evelyn as a gift they treasured all their lives. Jack Herndon a short time later painted the famous face on the bar room floor in Central City, Colorado.

The misery and aftershock of Wellen's death just went on and on. Lives were ruined and futures shattered. Charley told Evelyn that there would be no more talk of moving to New Mexico. This place was plenty good enough and if she didn't like it she could leave with the baby girl, but the boys were staying. She was crushed to have to give up her dream of moving to some place with a road to it. Mostly she was crushed at the harshness toward her that had come over Charley. She wondered what they would do for schools. Potch was six in October and Pat was four. Bryan wrote:

On November 6, Bryan wrote to Charley and Evelyn from Lapoint, Utah.

I would like to see you all. Them two little men and the little girl baby. I would sure like to have all of them little folks in my arms. It seems like ten years since I saw or heard them little men. Everything seems so still and lonesome not to hear them little men telling their wild stories.

Charley I don't know just what the hell to do. I have trouble with my old spine all the time since I came back. I am down most all the time. I sold my saddle and went to Vernal and got my teeth out—thought that would help my rheumatism some, but don't seems to do any good. I'm here at Hackings am down most all the time and there gettin very badly burnt on me. I sure wish I could sell this note and go to Salt Lake City and get the dam thing pulled back in place or take poison or do something. I'm no good to anyone or

Artist Herndon Davis painting Charley Mantle's portrait.

myself the way I am. O God I wish I could get out of everybody's way. Seems like the hole dam world is against me. I would sure like to save up and invest into the future but god damed if I no whether to try to go on or not.

Well Charley and Evelyn I sure would like to hear from you to know just how you feel towards me. I've got to where I don't care much about anything or anybody but would hate to have you folks turn me down. I tried to treat you right. Well just suit yourselves about answering this but if you feel like it I would certainly love to hear from you. Best luck to you all. B. Mantle

By now, Lorraine knew what Charley suspected and on a Christmas card, postmarked December 19, 1933, Cuba, New Mexico, expressed her sadness. "Charlie and Evelyn, Why can't you find just some little word to write to me. I lost everything—have I lost you too and my little fellows. Are you certain you are right?

Kiss my Baby Pat for me any way. I know he loved me. Lorraine"

20

Drought and Hope

VELYN FELT THE AGONY of Lorraine and the entire family, but was powerless to help. And it was best she not express any opinions either or her own family would be torn asunder. Charley was like a raging bull, but it seemed that gradually his mind was calming somewhat. By turns he cried and cursed and descended into deep brooding silences. Evelyn was afraid for herself and the children, but even more afraid for Charley. She stayed close beside him, making every effort to console him. It certainly seemed best if he never saw any of his brothers again. Evelyn gathered all the letters and newspaper clippings that made any reference to the terrible tragedy and stored them away in a secret place where they would never be seen again during the lifetime of any of the people involved.

The post office at Youghall was discontinued so the Mantle's mail service was now Youghall Rural Route out of Elk Springs. Evelyn had written a letter to Eva in December, but it had been lost. They could only hope the service improved.

Despite the sorrow that touched their lives, Christmas was a fun and renewing time for the family. Santa Claus came bringing pretty beads and popcorn strings to the tiny tree sitting on the wood box. Charley had gone to Elk Springs for a few things and thoughtful Eva had sent a huge box, filled to the brim with treasures. All the tiny extra spaces were filled with nuts and candy. For Charley there were cigars, hankies and matches. For Evelyn pillow tops, stuffing, dish cloths, a wire dish scrubbier, needles, pins, and envelopes. For Queeda a towel, little pink nities, a cap, and a rattle that whistled. The boys got a $1 bill from Eva's folks for their savings, a spinning top that whistled as it spun, pocket knives and a sharpening stone, along with coloring books, crayons and pencils.

Their 12 x 12-foot one room home was a busy place. Queeda was walking some and into everything, whistling through her rattle and cutting eight teeth all at once. The top spun on the stove, floor, bed, table and even on people. The boys sharpened their knives daily, but Charley dulled them on the sly. Always methodical and orderly, Evelyn liked to keep up with her children's height and weight. She began a yearly practice of standing the children against the center post in the cabin and carving a notch at their height. Then she would carve the name and date beside it. Charley called it the Bear Pole. Weights were harder, because all she had was a fifty-pound spring scale you held up high while what you were weighing swung from a hook on the bottom.

Evelyn liked her children clean. The dirt floor of the cabin was covered with rugs because the children, especially the baby, were on it all the time. Evelyn spent endless hours cutting and ripping old clothes she scavenged from anywhere she could get them. She washed and cut them into strips and braided them into nice heavy rugs. She even spiral cut old socks, darned holes and all, and braided rugs from them. Her most precious possession was her sewing machine, as she had to make all the kids' clothes from old clothes and pieces of cloth.

There was never enough time for Evelyn to make a new dress for herself. Since it seemed she was pregnant most of the time she wore full aprons over her old clothes, which had to be slashed and trimmed to fit her swollen stomach. She carefully saved a pair of jeans and a nice shirt for the rare times when she got to go where people were.

It was a wonderful surprise when one day Evelyn's friend Mrs. Powers from Bear Valley rode down and spent five wonderful days with her. Mrs. Powers was very good at handwork, like knitting, crocheting, and embroidery. Evelyn had expressed great eagerness to learn how to do all this, so she had come to teach her. Evelyn was an eager student, and learned these precious skills during the visit. The livestock were doing well, and the radio predicted prices were going up. Charley and Evelyn made plans to buy her a home, on a road! Potch was six and needed to start school in September. They both believed strongly in education and it never was a consideration that their children would not go to school.

Evelyn's winter in a one room cabin with a husband, two young boys and a baby not yet one, or weaned, or diaper trained; with no running water, gas, or electricity, had left her overworked, lonely, and depressed. She couldn't control her yearning for a new house and wrote her cousin," I'm glad you are getting located in such a nice spot. I'd give a lot if I could say 'wait until my next letter for my new address'. But since living so tucked up as I have I'm afraid I'd become lost in some one of the rooms and have to send out a distress signal." She told Eva she had started a new quilt, called The Modern Tulip, and asked her to please send some varied colored fabrics for it if she got the chance. How she missed woman talk. Letters exchanged with her dear Eva helped some, but it wasn't nearly enough.

Their one contact with the world was a battery operated radio that worked poorly inside these canyon walls. They too enjoyed the world's fascination with Mae West, but many of Evelyn's and Charley's favorite programs had been discontinued. Even worse, the battery was so weak they could only listen to the radio sparingly. How she longed for the snow on Blue Mountain to melt so they could bring in fresh food and a new battery and precious magazines for something to read.

Charley finally made it out for the mail. He returned with a big box from her folks of Easter goodies and a new house dress. Her spirits were a little lifted by this contact. The trees were beginning to show signs of spring, which helped. A letter from Charley's sister Nancy in Jensen at Uncle Hy's made Evelyn's heart race. Nancy suggested Charley and Evelyn come to Jensen for a visit, and she would keep the children while they hunted for a home. It sounded so tempting, but Evelyn knew she couldn't do that.

Mail was always fun, as Evelyn wrote lots of letters and received as many in return. The three cent stamp was an extravagance she indulged herself with.

Two of the milk cows were about to calve. The generous supply of milk, cream and cheese would be so very welcome. Milk mixed with the chicken feed always made the hens start laying earlier, too. Also, the two baby calves would instantly become the little boy's playmates. They would ride them, teach them to lead, and it would fill their days with fun. Also, they would be outside more! A mother always hoped for that! However, memories of the terrible floods in Hells Canyon, and the assurance they would begin again soon haunted her nights and days.

Charley had to decide how he was going to tend his cattle and also help take care of his wife and three children. The floods in Hells Canyon always complicated his life, because he couldn't ride out through the canyon when it flooded and had to leave his horses on the other side of the creek if he needed to get out. Yet the farming had to be done with a horse and that one horse, at least, had to stay on the same side of the creek as the house and garden. If the cows crossed the creek and then a flood came, they were separated from their calves. Feed was scarce, as it looked like a real drought was coming on. Cattle prices went down, food was scarce, and the nation was still reeling from the Depression. His little Paradise was nearly self-supporting, but it would take some figuring.

About this time, Nancy fell desperately ill and had to go into the hospital in Vernal. Evelyn brought her two boys to the ranch to care for them. They brought the measles and the three Mantle children soon caught them, too. Queeda was the first to become sick. Evelyn thought it was a bad chest cold. When she got a fever Evelyn gave her Castor oil. The fever persisted, so Evelyn brewed up some of the foul tasting sage tea people used to break a fever. Sagebrush contains Quinine, and during World War I doctors had found that quinine was good for breaking the raging fever of malaria. The fever broke and much to Evelyn's relief Queeda broke out in glowing spots.

Cooking and tending five children, all voracious eaters and at least one with the measles at all times, was a full time job for Evelyn. However, in addition she fought for the very life of her garden. The drought was in full effect. The creek was so low that the water had to be dammed up during each day to get enough water to turn out to irrigate her garden. She watered as dusk fell, putting every drop of precious water on the garden. Then she again closed off the ditch so the water from the spring would collect in the dam during the night. Each morning before the sun could creep down the cliffs to scorch and kill her garden she gave every bit of the

Potch and Pat with a giant whitefish, which is now a protected species.

stored water to the garden. The boys even helped a bit. Frogs would make holes in the earthen dam, letting her precious water escape. The little boys were more than happy to spend endless hours giggling and digging a frog out of the slimy mud and finishing him off. She washed clothes and bathed the kids in the river. God was good to her she thought as she saw the blessed fruit trees producing fruit, the garden producing vegetables, and the cows providing milk. This little paradise in the canyon also gave food that preserved the very life of many of their friends and neighbors during the terrible drought.

Charley went to Browns Park to see if he could buy a place he had heard was for sale. They simply had to move from their beloved canyon home so they could put their children in school. He found it was leased out until next year. However, they were going to be in big trouble very soon because the kids just had to go to school. In 1915, Dinosaur Monument had been established on a site near Jensen, where an impressive quantity of petrified dinosaur remains had been discovered. Word was going around that there canyon home was to become a national park and they hated to let it go until they found out there was to be an enlargement of the original monument. By moving to Browns Park they could still use this ranch for grazing and it would make a nice spread.

Evelyn explained to Eva, who was a teacher, what they had found out about schools for their kids. The taxes were down as people made less, thereby affecting the schools. Most schools now could afford only five months per session, with two sessions, one summer, the other winter, both usually with the same teacher. One teacher she knew was paid eighty dollars a month, with living quarters and wood furnished. This teacher had Bear Valley School, with four pupils, along with the Three Springs School with two pupils. In Browns Park there were twenty-nine children of school age, but not all of them went to school. There were three schools in Browns Park, one with two pupils and one with one pupil. They would like to consolidate under one teacher and add a couple of years of high school. Decision time for the boys' schooling was fast drawing near.

Mormon Crickets were thick again, devouring what forage there was. They stayed more on the mountain than on the benches and almost not at all on the river bottoms. By mid-August the drought had become so bad that the family had to take the milk cows and horses and move up the river about five miles to Hardings Hole. There had been a gold mining operation in Hardings Hole years before in the park they chose to live in. It was a lovely wide park on both sides of the river where the river began a series of sharp hairpin bends between the canyon walls.

A barely discernible rocky trail began at the canyon rim and wound among the cedar and pinyon trees, descending steeply from the sagebrush flats above the canyon rim to the river bottom. They camped there, along the river bank on the north side of the river, living and cooking outside on a campfire. There was an old dugout here, but it was too grim to live in. In case of intense wind or an electrical storm they could retreat to the overhanging cliff about 100 yards from their camp. The grass was lush here, which was a joyful sight in itself. The cows gave lots of milk, and the horses stayed strong and healthy for the hard work Charley had to do, moving and tending the range cattle closely to keep them alive through the terrible drought.

Every other day Evelyn would put the two boys on one horse, and she would carry the baby on another, and ride the five miles home to water and weed the garden and can and preserve the harvest. She canned fifty quarts of choke cherries she and the boys picked along the river bottoms. By mid-August she had already canned twelve quarts of green beans, had a three-gallon crock and a fifteen-gallon keg of pickles in brine, and had already sealed sixteen quarts of dill pickles. She would start on the tomatoes next. Pat was five this August and Potch would be seven in October. The boys were a big help to her, picking and washing vegetables, stuffing jars, and a million chores their small legs would run to do. Evelyn was always careful to teach her children how to do everything, but she never let them get too tired and always saw to it that they had lots of time to play and putter. They spent a lot of their time in the melon patch. Neighbors would ride to the ranch, and Evelyn would fill their buckets and sacks with vegetables. Her garden was the talk of the country.

As a result of a near accident that haunted her the rest of her life, Evelyn learned that one of their favorite old faithful, gentle kid horses was night blind. Sometimes it would be after dark when she returned to camp down the steep trail. One night the familiar sound of the boys' horse's hoofs clicking on the rocks behind, stopped abruptly. Panicked, she couldn't turn her horse around on the narrow trail, so she jumped off, and holding the baby in her arms ran back up the trail, stumbling in the darkness. She found the horse trembling on the edge of a fifty-foot abyss, with the two boys crouched on his back, urging him on in the total darkness that no human eye could penetrate.

Ordinarily, horses can see very well in the dark, but this horse, being night blind, had missed a turn. Luckily he sensed danger underfoot and stopped dead still in spite of the urging of his little riders. After that Evelyn always started back to camp well before dark.

The river was only knee deep, even in places where it was usually deep enough to swim a horse. Fish died by the hundreds as their food and oxygen was used up. The small spring from which they drew water for camp was a tiny seep. Evelyn cooked with the river water, washed clothes, and gave baths in it. She hoarded the trickle of sweet spring water in containers and kept it and the milk cool by storing it deep under a damp overhang in the cliff.

There in the primitive camp Evelyn started piecing another quilt, and anxiously awaited a box of cloth pieces Eva was sending her. Charley was away a great deal of the time. He had to fight for the life of each head of cattle they owned. He moved some of them daily to any scrap of feed and drink of water he could find along the mountain side and in the box canyons and pot holes. Deer were dying, along with rabbits and coyotes. The government had sent buyers into the country to give assistance to failing ranchers by buying up cattle for four dollars to twenty dollars per head. This helped ranchers by giving them at least this small sum as an alternative to their cattle starving and getting nothing.

Charley wasn't selling his! When a cow died he took her calf and kept it alive on milk from the milk cows. He saved some of the lush river bottoms for winter, and was determined to make it through. By spring they would know where they stood. They saved every leaf and stalk of corn and grain for winter feed for the cows and saddle horses. Cabbage, beets, and tops, as well as anything green except tomato vines from the garden was saved. It fell to Evelyn to ride out the twenty miles to Youghall, then catch a ride to Elk Springs for the mail. It was a journey she only made a couple of times during the summer and fall. One gully she had to cross was solid granite and shale, washed jagged and deep by a flood from the year before. She worried always about the one misstep the horse might make that would leave her three tiny children without a mother in this bitter land.

That fall Charley hunted deer off the remotest river bottoms for jerky. They were the only ones with enough flesh left on them to eat. If a bad winter came no deer would survive at all and neither would the cattle. Charley and Evelyn knew that they could get their family comfortably through the winter on canned vegetables, potatoes, jerky, chokecherries and milk. They hoped they could buy a sack of flour, a can of lard, a little salt, and a sack of cottonseed cake for the milk cow, as well.

Along in October Evelyn started having wrenching stomach cramps. By November she had blood in her stool and was startlingly thin. She also feared she was pregnant again and must get to a doctor!

Getting together a Christmas package for Eva was fun. She sent her the predominantly lilac quilt top she had made during the summer, along with small gifts she had made for Eva's daughter, Barbara. She enclosed a small sack of jerky with instructions on how to prepare it, and a small jar of chokecherry

jelly. Charley rigged up a pack horse for her to lead to bring back supplies and
mail and also to carry Queeda and Evelyn's meager supplies for the trip. Off she
rode to Elk Springs. From there she caught a ride into Craig and made the
dreaded trip to the doctor.

Yes, she was pregnant and yes, she also had a bad ulcer. The ulcer was dangerous, but could be treated with diet and rest. She and Queeda stayed with her
parents for two weeks. Her folks were busy most of the time, but she got to be
with her dad quite a bit and went to Hayden to visit her friends there. She
enjoyed showing off her daughter, and hearing her father brag to his friends,
about what a whopper Queeda was for being only twenty-months old.

The doctor had told her to rest and not worry, but that was impossible.
She worried about her husband and two little boys all alone and about her
own health. If she should die she would leave three orphans and a husband
who had already suffered too much in his life. Even if she got the ulcer under
control, she had already lost her strength to the point that she couldn't cope
with the move they were contemplating and the urgent need of schooling for
the children. She felt ignorant and careless to have become pregnant again and
took all the blame on herself. What chance did yet another child have in her
incompetent hands?

A ray of hope shone through. One day the sheriff looked her up. He was
a good friend and had heard of her despair. He told her that the Yampa
Canyon and the north side of Blue Mountain was going to be made into a
national park. By the end of next year, the government was going to build a
road right down Hells Canyon to the river. He had heard it wouldn't affect
their grazing rights. If that was true, the road would go right by their doorstep
and there would not be any need to move from their beloved canyon ranch.
She couldn't wait to share this hope with Charley. Perhaps the news would
serve as a tonic for Charley, who still seethed over what he regarded as the
murder of his brother.

A thin, gaunt faced woman of twenty-seven, two months pregnant, holding a baby of twenty months on the horse in front of her and leading a heavy-
laden pack horse rode alone down the steep, rocky, slick trail off the east end
of Blue Mountain and wended her weary way through the sage brush flats and
craggy cedar draws to her home in the canyon. Her heart was pounding, and
her stomach wrenched with anxiety as she struggled to keep herself from thinking of all the bad things that could have happened to her family during her
two week absence.

A dog barking joyfully was the first to spot her, then two dirty, screaming
and laughing little boys came running from the cliff side where they had been
playing in the soft sand. She quickly dismounted and let the horses find their
own way to the corral while she gave hugs and shed tears of joy. Hard but
gentle hands grabbed her and she was smothered into the arms of a tall,
bewhiskered and thin, dirty man in a sweaty hat. Charley and Evelyn clung to
each other while tears coursed down their faces and silly murmurings of love
filled each other's ears.

The boys had been keeping house while Charley worked outside. It took Evelyn a week of scrubbing to clean up everybody and everything. How good her meals tasted to them after batching for two weeks! Even the animals were glad to have her back making their home run smoothly again. Relief washed through her as Charley came through with his usual good humor and reassurance when Evelyn told him about the new baby on the way. He said, "We will need a big house, for it looks like we will have twelve." He couldn't wait for another little girl to arrive.

A government man from Vernal had ridden in and told Charley the same thing Evelyn had heard about the road coming in next year. They always dreaded giving up their canyon, but did not like the hardship that went with not having a road or school. The money it would take to buy another ranch could be used to make this one perfect if they could have a road. They made plans on the hope they would be so fortunate as to come through the winter all right. They would begin improving the place in the spring. They would build a house of about six rooms on the hill behind the cabin, against the cliff. It would be out of the danger from the floods. The logs would be about twenty feet long cut off the side of Roundtop Mountain and snaked by horses down to the canyon to dry. Evelyn pondered over the placement of windows and rooms to take full advantage of the light from the south and west.

How lovely it would be after the dark little cabin! Evelyn even started dreaming about a few pieces of furniture she could polish to a gleam. After they got the grounds prepared around the new house they would install a pump and plant a lawn, trees, etc. They decided that Evelyn would move to Bear Valley for the winter with the kids. They would go to school there until they could get a school house built in the canyon and a teacher arranged for.

21

Lonnie, 1935

HE EXCITEMENT OF A NEW HOUSE sustained Evelyn through January. Her ulcer had responded well to rest, good food, and a more contented life. The cattle, too, were doing well due to Charley's constant vigilance to make certain they were on good feed and fresh water. In each of the river pastures in the canyon he sanded the river ice to provide them a safe trail to a drinking hole.

They cleared brush and would start moving the corrals when spring broke. Charley started searching for a "powder man" who could dynamite out the foundation for the new house and a space to set it firmly against the high cliff that would be the back wall. They also wanted large spaces blasted into the cliff for a storage cellar, a chicken house, and a shed by the corrals. These would be sheltered, warm places, as the cliff received lots of daytime sun. They planned on a pump to bring water from the creek into their house and to water a lawn. They even visualized a weeping willow tree by the new house. They knew the house would not be finished this year, but hoped to at least get the logs up, the roof on, and the first floor in by that time.

An old lady from four or five miles up the river had died last fall, and Evelyn made a deal with the daughter to buy her mother's big cook stove. It was a Majestic, with a warming oven, a reservoir, and an eight lid heating area, plus plenty more space for simmering and warming on its surface. Her old stove had just four lids, no extra space or reservoir, and was getting old and burned out. She hoped to find a way to get the new stove home before canning season. It occurred to her that maybe it could be delivered by boat down the river in the spring. Charley had bought a boat from the same family that had the stove, and Jens, the owner, would deliver the boat down the river in the spring.

One day, they received word that their dear friend, Shorty Chambers, was near death from a ruptured appendix. The doctors had given him but two days to live. Right at that time a government veterinarian came to their place. He and an assistant were going through the country testing all range and dairy cattle for tuberculosis. His assistant said he had heard that Shorty was still alive one week after the operation and had a chance to make it. They were much relieved, since there was no way they could go to him. The veterinarian had further good news: their cattle were free of tuberculosis. If they had been infected, every single head of their precious cattle would have had to be slaughtered and buried and that would have been the end of the Mantle Ranch.

There was such a shortage of feed that they had to preserve the strength of the horses every possible way. Charley needed every ounce of the horses' strength to tend the cattle. They didn't even dare to ride them out to get the mail. Finally, on April 22 someone brought their mail. The letters whisked Evelyn away to a magical world. For a while, she was far away from the cramped cabin with the dirt floor, no running water and no electricity, pregnant, with three children to care for; with starving livestock, and her husband soon to be boating the swollen river, while Hells Canyon would soon endanger home and family and livelihood with raging floods. Wonderful letters!

May finally arrived. Evelyn had to make whatever clothes the family had out of old clothes people gave her and that Eva sent her. She was getting heavy and slow with the baby inside her. Carrying water from the spring, heating it over wood she carried, then scrubbing the clothes clean over a washboard in a metal tub was difficult and tiring. Then there were the meals to prepare. The bright side was that May had brought green grass for the livestock, as well as wild greens like dandelions and lamb's quarter to pick and eat for the family. Now there were plenty of eggs from the chickens and new calves from the milk cows, so milk and butter, cream and cheese were plentiful again.

But meat was scarce this time of year. The deer tasted like the rabbit brush they ate. They couldn't butcher a beef because it would spoil before they could eat it all. What meat they did have was the meat she had canned the summer before, and occasionally they had fish. She was careful that each child had eggs in their diet every day and a vegetable. In the mornings she prepared Jo Dandy, a cracked wheat cereal, or Mothers Oats, with plenty of milk and cream. Charley was the most difficult to make eat his vegetables, but usually did eat them to please her. She made light bread twice a week, and kept a sour dough jug behind the stove to make pancakes and biscuits.

By April 22 the river started to rise and Hells Canyon flooded for three days. This meant the water was very dirty and they had to invent a flue off a ledge to catch rain water to wash in. The wind was blowing constantly, so they took advantage of it to burn the brush and matted grass off the river bottoms so new healthy grass could grow. Charley took Potch and Pat with him and they seeded pasture grasses and clover in all the burned areas. The spring rains would bring it up quickly.

The muslin lining on the ceilings of the cabins was dirty, and needed to be washed and then put back up. Evelyn fretted about it, but finally decided to wait until she came home after the baby was born. She was afraid she might fall. The radio battery was dead. During any resting she did, Evelyn read the *Pathfinder*, to which she subscribed.

By the first of May the side of Blue Mountain was still covered with snow, but they needed supplies badly, so Charley rode out. Evelyn was expecting to spend about a month out when the baby was due, and was discouraged at the prospects for her garden. Mice were eating her seedlings in the hot bed, and while she was gone she doubted that Charley would have time to take care of the kids, the cattle, and the garden. She would need to can for the winter ahead, but it looked doubtful there would be vegetables in the garden and the time to can them before fall. Also, school would begin for the boys in the fall, and that meant moving to Bear Valley.

While Charley was in Vernal he checked with the doctor. The baby was due about July 7 rather than in June as the doctor in Craig had told her. So, on June 12 Evelyn was still at home. Her father had been with her since the last week in May and was helping them in trying to get the new house started. He was also standing by to take care of his little girl. He had brought his car as far as he could, which was ten miles from the house at Johnson Draw and had walked the rest of the way. The plan was that Evelyn would only have to ride a horse ten miles when she went out to have the baby. She would ride the rest of the way "in style" as she put it, in the car.

Charley planned to raft the rough lumber for the house down the river when the high water was over about the first of July. Evan and another man were up on the north face of Roundtop cutting logs for the house. They already had logs for a new chicken house and Evelyn was delighting in deciding on what kind of chickens to get. She believed she would like to get two dozen white leghorn hens this fall, along with a white Wyandotte rooster. The Leghorns are the best layers, but the Wyandotte would produce more meat. The combination should be perfect. She was anxious to get rid of the Rhode Island Reds she had now, because they hung around the door all the time. Her chickens ran free, and fended for themselves on plentiful worms, bugs and seeds. They drank from the creek. The only places off limits were her garden and right in front of the door. Gathering eggs was like an Easter egg hunt every day, as each hen chose her own place to make her own nest. The boys loved to hunt for nests. They would hear a hen cackling to announce she had laid an egg and they would run and check the area around her for her nest. If they found it they would triumphantly bring the eggs home to Mama. Only in the winter were the chickens locked up in the warm chicken house and food provided for them. Even then on sunny days they were let out. Charley and Evelyn both believed in every living thing having its freedom.

A CCC camp of about 300 young men had been set up in Elk Springs. This was a work program set up by the government during these hard times to provide work and room and board for men who needed jobs. Job foremen were sent out with a group who would live in tents at a job site until it was completed. They built dams, trails, roads, and did other projects in the area for a small wage and keep. This crew had been sent into the country to fight the Mormon crickets that were devouring every blade of vegetation in their path across northwestern Colorado. They were also going to clean up the prairie dogs, which had become a plague on the range lands. Charley and Evelyn hoped that they would also build the road into their canyon ranch.

Charley and Potch were gathering the cattle from the benches, branding the calves and driving the cattle to summer pasture on the mountain. Potch was eight years old, and doing the work of a man. Charley came home with a story that caused Evelyn's heart to lurch. Potch (now eight) and Charley, were rounding up the saddle horses, who were fat and sassy from the winter's rest. Potch's horse ran away with him, joining the bunch. He couldn't get him stopped for a mile or more, running wild-eyed, jumping tall brush, crashing through ravines and over rocks. Charley finally overtook him, separated Potch's horse from the bunch and got him stopped. He was Charley's right-hand man and jealously guarded his position, revelling in the praise and bragging to all the other cowboys. At this young age he developed an arrogant swagger and great disdain for lesser cowboys. He didn't like to do any woman's work, which was any kind of work you didn't do on a horse.

Pat was needed at home, and willingly took care of Queeda and his mother. He, too, became an expert cowboy at the tender young age of six. However, his way was gentle with everything. He gathered the milk cows on his horse, careful not to run them. He milked the cows, tended the chickens, weeded the garden, carried water, and helped his mother out with cooking and washing. He studied and practiced everything he did until he could do it perfectly. He practiced roping from the time he could walk and could catch anything he went after. The rooster raised such a ruckus at getting roped that it got him in trouble with his mother, so he only roped him out of ear shot of the house. Little sister, Queeda would toddle past him and get roped as long as he asked her to, but he got in trouble there, too, if he accidentally put a rope burn on her. The milk cow calves were good subjects, but he lost his rope quite often when they ran off with it on them. He was sure he would only get one rope in his lifetime, because this was his Dad's old one, so he always got it back even if he had to chase the calf until it gave up from exhaustion and laid down.

As summer progressed, the heat became stifling. Evelyn was miserable. Finally, on June 26 she rode out the ten miles to Johnson where her Dad's car was. Charley and the boys stayed home to look after things and followed later. They camped the night there and the next day Evan drove her to Bear Valley to the Powers' ranch, near where the Youghal post office had been. From there they planned to go to Vernal, where she would have the baby in the hospital with her doctor in attendance. Disappointing news awaited them, however, as an epidemic of chicken pox had hit Vernal, Utah. The family Evelyn had arranged to stay with had sick children. She got to thinking that the CCC camp just eighteen miles away would surely have a doctor. So she asked a friend to get hold of the doctor and see if he would come to Bear Valley to deliver her baby. He sent word that he would.

"Auntie" Powers, a grand old lady who lived in Bear Valley insisted Evelyn stay there and none too soon! Labor began about 3:00 a.m. on July 1. Charley had left the night before to ride to Rifle on business. Mrs. Powers sent a boy who lived nearby racing to overtake him. Horse lathered and spent, he overtook Charley at Skull Creek. They got a car and drove to Elk Springs for the doctor. He arrived about 10:00 a.m. and at noon, a healthy eight pound boy was born. They had always assumed it would be a girl, but joyfully accepted the beautiful baby boy. Charley named him Lonnie, but they couldn't decide on a middle name yet. They later gave him the middle name Miner after one of Charley's favorite uncles who had helped raise him after his parents died. Lonnie Miner Mantle was born on July 1, 1935 in Bear Valley, Colorado.

Mrs. Powers took good care of Evelyn and the baby and Queeda. On the twelfth of July the new mother got out of bed for the first time and felt well rested. There had been many visitors who helped pass the long days and Evelyn was eternally grateful for all the care her friends had given her, but she was homesick and lonesome for her family.

While in Bear Valley Evelyn worked on an exciting project. Due to lack of students, the school in Bear Valley had been closed. But by building a school house, the Mantles could have the school moved to their ranch. Great Day! they wouldn't have to move to Bear Valley for the winter and live on the bleak, cold mountain in a shack, to put their kids in school. The superintendent of schools was authorized to give them the desks, books and supplies from the abandoned school in Bear Valley. The district would pay a teacher eighty dollars per month for an eight month term. The secretary of the Bear Valley District School moved away and Evelyn was appointed secretary. She joyfully accepted the position, as it would give her the ability to set up the school and requisition supplies.

Evelyn, carrying the baby in front of her and Queeda riding with Grandpa Evan, arrived safely home. She was thrilled to discover that all the logs for the new house were cut and stacked, ready to be brought home by sled as soon as there was snow. She found that the men had already brought home logs for a chicken house, which would be built against the cliff behind the cabin, just east of the site for their new house. Evelyn told them to plan on building a school house, instead, with the logs.

As soon as she was able Evelyn, carrying baby Lonnie on the saddle in front of her, rode out to Jensen and made a deal with a school teacher to come in and teach at their new school. Ruth Haslem had been a school teacher in New Jersey and had come west to marry Joe. They had two sons, one five and a half, the other three. She would teach her oldest, Sam, along with Potch and Pat. It was decided that she should start on Labor Day. The school house wouldn't be finished yet, so she would board with Mantles and live and teach in the dugout bunk house. Just as soon as the school house was finished, she and the boys would move into it, and set up a class area on one end. Of course Joe couldn't be with them much, because he had his own ranch to run.

On October 30, Charley arrived home with winter supplies for the family. He had packed them in on three unruly, untamed horses, so supplies were a little shaken up. Next he was taking the "gentler now" horses back out to pack in supplies for the teacher and the school.

Joe Haslem came to help build the school house. Evan was supposed to go to Oak Creek to start work in the coal mines, but arranged to start late so he could help, too. Besides, he enjoyed being with his daughter and four grandchildren. By November twelfth they had the school house almost built. It was fourteen by twenty feet, with a big window in the front and another on the

Schoolhouse the Mantles built in Hells Canyon. The back wall is the south face of Castle Rock.

west side. The back wall was the cliff. A skylight in the roof helped light it and a small stove in the corner warmed it. It was furnished with rough hand made benches and stools. They chinked and dobbed the walls and made it warm and cozy.

About Thanksgiving, Charley victoriously drove a team and wagon to the front door. He was greeted with all the excitement and honor of a conquering hero. He had brought in the first wagon to ever reach the ranch. He had bought the wagon, loaded up with a harrow, a heating stove, and all the desks and supplies for the school and headed for home. He had made a road so he could pass as he came west from Johnson Draw, which was the end of the road ten miles to the east. He tipped over twice, but didn't smash anything up too badly. The important thing was that he got the wagon and everything in it to the school house. The wagon would sure be handy to haul hay, cedar posts, fire wood, logs, rocks and building supplies. The question was, would the snorting saddle horses, the bawling cows, squawking chickens and barking dog ever get used to this ominous looking contraption.

The CCC crews had returned to Elk Springs without doing any road work, much to the disappointment of the Mantles. However, with the road blazed by the first wagon, their determination to have a road was even stronger and for this young couple nothing seemed impossible.

The school supplies were very quickly put into the school house and the room was organized into a classroom on the west end, and living quarters for Ruth and her boys on the east end. The school desks were a wonderful surprise and made a big hit with the kids. They were made of wood and black scrolled iron, constructed with a seat in the front that folded up. Built into the back of each seat was a desk with a top that lifted up so each student's supplies could be stored in his own desk. There was even a place for an ink bottle to fit in a hole in the desk top, and a groove along the top to keep your pen in. The feet of the seat-desks were bolted to boards, making two desks per row, with the extra seat in front for recitation or visitors. The package of supplies produced enough pencils and crayons and tablets that each student could have his own. Potch and Pat had never owned anything that was their very own before, and were in a state of giggling delight. At last the Hells Canyon School was ready!

Evelyn had been cooking and doing laundry for the teacher and her two boys, and was looking forward to them doing their own now that they would be moving into the school house to live. Ruth, who had been sleeping with five children in the bunkhouse, was just as glad to have a little privacy.

Christmas came and all were snug and happy. They had the radio working again, and the news was disturbing. There was talk of war. Having lived through one world war, they both understood what the consequences would be from another. One Man's Family was their favorite radio program, and they allowed themselves the luxury of listening to it. They just hoped the battery would last until the next time they went to town, which would not be until spring.

Evelyn became the barber for the family and all the cowboys who dropped by. She had become such a good cook that several cowboys dropped by for a meal whenever they were nearby. Many visited just because they needed a warm home to be a part of for a while in their lonely lives.

With the new year Evelyn wrote her cousin, "Well a New Year. Our old one was great—a new and lovely baby—debts all paid and a nest egg for our house. Greater farming outlook for next summer and all well and happy. Hope 1936 will be as great and that I can have a feeling of comfort and well being next January first."

22

Hells Canyon Rages, 1936

HE WINTER WORE ON, and heavy snow storms piled up huge drifts on Blue Mountain. It was obvious that the drought had ended at last. Charley was excited as he anticipated all the grass that would be coming up on the pasture lands due to the good moisture. However, Evelyn reminded him that huge floods were likely in Hells Canyon when the snow melted in the spring.

The children loved school and were progressing well. Ruth's husband, Joe, came to visit as often as he could leave his ranch. He was a big help with the chores around the ranch. He helped Charley and Evelyn build the long-awaited chicken house. They built it as a semi-dugout with the cliff for a back wall. It would be warm and cozy, and they put a chimney in the dirt roof to vent it. It even had a window in it to let some light in during the cold winter days. They found boards in the driftwood piles along the river and made a row of boxes for nests, elevated off the ground. They cut long slender poles from the grove of birches at the Lower Park from which to make a roost for the chickens. They lashed the poles between two slender logs, and leaned the structure against the wall, making a comfy perch for the chickens off the ground. A small hole was cut in the door to allow passage of a hen while keeping out large predators and the cold.

Ruth's youngest boy, Jack, was only one year older than Queeda, so they had a great time playing together. Lonnie was a healthy, good natured baby and laughed and squealed at their antics and was their favorite toy.

The Jersey cow Charley had bought several years ago, hoping to raise milk cows from, had only bull calves. It was obvious from the size of his family that they needed more milk, so in early March he rode to Vernal and purchased five beautiful yearling Jersey heifers. He drove them home, and as with any animal around the Mantles, they soon became great pets. Potch and Pat soon had them leading and when their parents weren't looking they rode them. One day Evelyn caught them in the act when they were even riding the poor things with spurs, for which they received a switching.

Ruth was a tough disciplinarian and gave her four students a good year of learning. School was in session every day but Sunday in order to get in the required number of days in the shortest possible time. They had only one day off

124

Ready for the wild horse chase. Notice that horses are ground-tied. Against the cliff is the school-house and root cellar.

at Thanksgiving and again at Christmas. How sweet it was when their reward came in the form of getting out early in the spring. The kids all jerked off their shoes and socks and shirts and ran screaming with joy to celebrate their freedom. Joe came for Ruth and they bade farewell to the Mantle family.

Spring came and the frantic plowing and planting began. The house plans were complete and they hoped to get started building right after the cattle got shoved up on Blue Mountain for the summer. The snow had begun melting on Blue Mountain and Hells Canyon ran a little more water each day. Charley had left one morning and would be camped out overnight while he gathered the cattle off the river bottoms at Harding's Hold. That night Evelyn was wakened by a terrible roaring of water and crashing of careening boulders as they were thrown high into the air by the rushing water of the creek. She leaped from her bed and rushed outside in her night gown. Horrified, she saw that a trickle of water from the overflowing creek had started a path a few feet in front of the cabin, and it was increasing rapidly. Terrified, she grabbed up the baby, and dragging Queeda with her, ran to the bunk house to wake the boys. Half dragging the sleepy children she had time only to snatch a quilt off the bed and climb to the higher ground behind the house before the trickle of water in front of the house grew in size until it reached the door of the cabin. The thunder of the terrible flood was amplified by the canyon walls.

After seeing that the children were safe in the school, Evelyn ran to the corral and opened the gates so the milk cows and calves could save themselves. The night was pitch black and the ominous rumblings of the flood continued on through the night. Evelyn knew of a ledge nearby where she could get them all another twenty feet higher. She visualized the entire canyon floor covered with raging water, and remained ready to go to the ledge when necessary.

When dawn finally came, the water level gradually receded as the coolness of the night slowed the rapid melting of the snow on the mountain. A survey of the damage found the dirt floor of her home a mass of mud, and the contents of the cabin touching the floor soaked. The corrals had been washed clean and many posts and rails were broken, leaving the corrals useless. Her garden, freshly plowed and ready for planting was washed out. The dam in the creek was gone. The ditches were all filled with rocks and debris.

She gasped when she saw the reason for the flooding in front of the house. A huge cottonwood tree had been uprooted upstream and carried down the creek. Where the creek made a sharp bend, causing the huge amount of water in the creek to rush headlong into the cliff, the tree had lodged. Other debris and rocks had caught in the tree, making an obstacle that diverted the water into a new route in front of the house. Had the water not abated it would have flooded away the house. Evelyn knew there was only a short time to remove the tree before the snow melt on the mountain resumed and the flood started raging anew.

Charley whooped and whipped the cattle out of the river bottoms. Ordinarily, he never ran his cattle, but this was different. He had two huge worries. He had seen the snow turn brilliant on the mountain, which meant it was melting fast. Today was his last possible chance to get the cattle out, as the river would be rising. Yesterday by dark he had cleared them out of the upper pastures of Hardings Hole and Bull Canyon. This morning by daybreak he was already below the cattle, on one of the most distant parks down the river from Harding's Hole. The only way out was up the river. As soon as he could see them he began frantically pushing them up the river. As he crossed them onto the south shore of the river in Hardings Hole he heard the ice cracking and groaning as the river rose. His horse was lathered and exhausted. The panting cattle laid down to rest on the first dry land they hit. It had been a very close call for man, horse, and cattle.

Charley let his horse rest just long enough to get his wind back, then set off to attend to his second worry. To save the horse's strength, he led him up the grueling climb out of the river. Then he mounted and raced to Hells Canyon. As he feared, the water was already high and he could see marks from the incredible flood of the night before. His fears rose. He knew it would be slow and perhaps deadly to try and ride down the canyon, so he forced his horse to cross the muddy stream and scramble out the west side of the canyon, then north to the rim overlooking the house. He turned his horse loose then climbed down the steep, ledged up deer trail off the rim to the bench below. Breathless, he looked down upon the destruction of the flood from the night before, and the new channel that had carried water last night. He scrambled down the long, limber ladder and sprinted to the house, mentally counting children and wife and pets.

There was no time for a tearful reunion. Evelyn quickly told Charley about the lodged tree, then handed him the dynamite, fuse and caps she had gotten out of the cache in the cliff. She was relieved that he was here to do the blasting, because she never had before. As with everything in her life, she was going to do it because it needed to be done. They raced to the tree and she showed Charley where she had used an axe to cut a deep notch in the underside of the tree over a nest of boulders. It was placed so that if it worked, a hole would be blasted in the middle of the debris, making a break for the water to pass through and force a bigger and bigger hole, until hopefully the whole mess would go on down the creek.

The creek was rising fast. There would be only one chance to explode the dynamite and save their home. Charley laid the dynamite on a square of tarp to keep it dry and nudged it into the deep notch. He carefully laid down the cap and a short fuse. Striking a match he held it to the fuse. The match blew out. Water was licking at the tarp. He struck another match. It took. Tiny sparks sputtered as the fire crawled down the fuse, but Charley didn't see it. He was scrambling as fast as he could up the bank. He barely reached the top and threw himself behind a tree trunk and covered his head when the blast went off. Being so close under the overhanging cliff, a big charge and not buried deep enough to muffle the sound, the blast was a real ear splitter. The sound knocked everyone within one hundred yards off their feet, and hurled splinters and rocks so hard against the overhang that they flew back out over the area like shrapnel. Intimidated, Charley finally peeked out of his cover to behold a perfect, wide channel restored in the creek. The tree had been broken in two and hurled aside and was ready to ride the flood to the river.

The victory was sweet, yet bitter, because they knew they were in for another night and probably several more of the raging flood. At least they were all together and out of danger! Even with Charley home, Evelyn continued to have nightmares every night about the floods.

The river swelled and overflowed its banks from all the spring runoff. When it finally receded some, Charley crossed in his boat and found that the river had over flowed into the field they had prepared in Laddie Park, making trenches where it washed through the top layer of soil. It would have to be leveled again, so would take even more work to plow and plant the corn crop this year, but Charley doggedly stuck to his plans. At least the new crib had held and his new boat had gotten him across the river.

The garden had also suffered. The overflowing creek had nearly ruined it. Evelyn asked if there was any possible way they could move the garden to the same side of the creek as the house. She chose a place just around on the north side of Castle Rock. After considerable study they decided how to do it. The cowboys who stopped by for Evelyn's good cookin' didn't get off with just chopping a little wood that spring. They were handed a shovel, axe and a crowbar, and sent to clear land and shovel a ditch from the dam in the creek to the new garden site. It was already pretty level, well sloped for irrigating and the soil was a deep sandy loam. These cowboys even suffered the indignity of guiding a horse and plow through the virgin soil time and again until it was soft and fine. There was a lot of cussing and whining to save face and protect their reputation, but secretly the homeless cowboys loved the life here. The grub was great, they had a clean bunk house to sleep in, and four of the sweetest little kids they had ever seen to play with. Guy MacNearlin even changed Lonnie's diapers, but Shorty just said, "I'd rather be shot by a sheepherder." Nonetheless, Shorty tenderly held Lonnie and sang songs of the range to him. How glad Evelyn was that the baby didn't understand the words of these songs. These cowboys even stooped so low as to milk the cows, feed the chickens, carry water, and wash dishes. One of Evelyn's favorite memories was of Guy washing dishes and Shorty drying, while Shorty berated Guy for not getting the dishes clean, and Guy responding with abuse of Shorty about not having enough to do or he wouldn't have time to bellyache.

The garden was beautiful and everybody so proud of it that Ed just hopped on his horse one day and went to town and bought wire to fence it with to keep out the cows and horses and deer. Evelyn was thrilled. Then the men prepared the field and planted the corn in the lower park. They repaired the corrals just enough to do the branding in. New posts would have to be cut and put in to repair it right, but there just wasn't enough time to do that now. When May arrived the friends had stayed as long as they could. Ed and Shorty had to get back to their cattle and Guy to his horses. They said fond goodbyes and promised to return. Potch and Pat ran up the canyon with their heroes as far as their flying little legs could carry them, then climbed on a high rock and waved as long as they could see them.

As a result of the flood, plans for the house were canceled until a new location could be chosen. Evelyn wanted desperately to get her family out of Hells Canyon, away from the danger of the floods. She began searching for a place. It would have to be on the north side of Castle Rock. That would be simple, since the long narrow cliff ended far enough from the creek to make a road around it, which could then run east along its north face. Along the cliff, the land was barely higher than the banks of the river, but about a half-mile along the cliff the terrain rose a good fifty feet from the river bottom. There it formed a bench, with a still higher bench that continued to rise up to where the cliffs formed a huge bowl that seemed to hold the canyon bottom in its protecting hands. She chose a spot on this first bench, about a half mile from her garden on the west and two hundred yards from the river. Charley didn't like the location because it didn't have any water and it would be a long way to carry it. Evelyn's eyes were pleading, however, and she reminded him that their old plans had included the installation of a pump. It looked to her like they could dig a well to no more than the thirty feet to the level of the river, pump it into a storage tank, and have all the water they needed. Knowing she would never again live on the low ground where she so feared the floods, Charley finally reluctantly agreed to the location.

Charley and the two boys gathered the cattle and drove them down Hells Canyon to the corrals. How happy and proud the two little boys were as they rode along with their lariat ropes ready, spurs and hats in place, breathing in the stifling dust through their cracking lips. How they loved the sound of the cattle lowing and the frantic bawling of the calves. And how happy they were to be cowboys out here, helping their Dad, the greatest of all cowboys. They branded calves and started the cattle up the trail to the mountain. The cattle knew the routine well and were eager to get to the cool mountain range land. Some had already gone up, and their calves would have to be branded later, by which time they would be big and wild and a challenge to brand.

Evelyn washed, cooked and sewed. She irrigated the garden and tended the toddler and the baby. Soon she would pick and pickle and can along with all that. Charley had bought her a twenty-seven quart pressure cooker, so canning vegetables and meat was easier and the product safer. She had ordered a canner from the Montgomery Ward catalog, too. It consisted of quart tin cans lined with something gold colored They came with the bottom already in them, and a raw edged lid. An apparatus that looked like a huge can opener was screwed down tight on a table. It held the filled can and the lid and crimped them together, so accurate it almost never failed. After sealing, Evelyn put them in her pressure cooker for the required time. The cans were reusable, as the crimper also cut off the old rim, making it ready to crimp again. Canning meats was much easier and quicker now. She had so much to do and was continually exhausted. She was very thin and hollow eyed. Lonnie was still nursing, but luckily he was drinking from a cup, so didn't need so much from her now.

As soon as the cattle were out on pasture, Charley and the boys returned and took over some of Evelyn's burdens. She rested and ate enough to restore her strength and energy. Charley irrigated the hay fields and by mid-June it was ready to harvest. He bought a mowing machine and had it delivered to Johnson. It had steel wheels so he knew it couldn't be pulled all the way by horses. So he hitched up the wagon and made the grueling trip to Johnson. It was a two day job, but he loaded the machine on the wagon and hauled it to the head of Hells Canyon, then hitched the horses to it and carefully pulled it home.

Charley oiled the six-foot sickle and greased all the wheels. After hitching it up, he drove the mower across the rocky bed of the creek and into the field. All was well until he lowered the sickle and pushed the stick forward to engaged the teeth. They made a terrible clatter as they passed back and forth over the bar below, literally chewing apart the stalks and laying them down behind in a neat row. Henry and Dugan, the big white horse team, thought something was after them and charged off across the field with the noisy machine. With great effort, while perched precariously on the tongue, Charley managed to yank back the stick and disengage the teeth. With the unfamiliar noise over the horses calmed quickly. The sickle needed some teeth replaced, but there wasn't much damage done. Charley hitched the team to the mower again. This time he got Potch to ride along beside them with Dugan's head dallied to his saddle horn. When the mower started up the terrible clatter again all Dugan could do was roll his eyes and snort. Soon, however, both horses came to understand that there was no danger, and the mowing began in earnest. The whole family had come out to watch the marvelous machine and were not disappointed. Charley finished the whole field early in the day. The hot sun would have it dried by tomorrow noon.

Next day Charley found the hay dry enough to stack and hitched a hay rack he had made up to the wagon. With slender poles he had extended the sides of the wagon far out beyond the box. The poles were close enough together, with frequent cross pieces on which to pile the long stems of hay on top of them. First, he and the two boys made rows of the hay with their pitch-forks. It was grueling work in the hot sun, and the little boys became exhausted. Charley all at once threw down his pitchfork and said, "Let's go swimmin." They were near the river, and it didn't take them long to strip off their clothes and hit the freezing water. The river was still running high, so Charley watched the boys carefully and cautioned them to not go too far into the current. Soon their teeth were chattering from the cold, and they crawled out and lay in the hot sand on the bank. One more dip and they were ready to go back to work.

They finished putting the hay in long rows a wagon's width apart. Then, driving the team from on the ground while he walked along, Charley drove them between the long rows of hay. Soon the team learned the routine and Charley never had to touch the reins. They would stop and Charley and the two boys would pitch the hay that lay alongside the wagon up on the top of the load. Then he would say "Git up Dugan," and the horses would pull slowly forward. When he said "Whoa" they would stop dead in their tracks. As the stack grew taller Pat couldn't throw hay high enough any more so he got on top of the load as the "tromper." His job was to jump on the corners and edges to mash the hay down so it wouldn't slide off. His little feet flew and he jumped and jumped until he was too exhausted to jump any more. By that time the wagon was stacked so high that Potch couldn't even reach it. Pat felt like the king of the mountain viewing the world from up here, but he sure was tired of haying. Potch was staggering from exhaustion, too. They had both given all they had to give. Charley helped Potch up on the wagon, then climbed up himself. The sun had sunk behind the Crows Nest and the field was in shadow now. They drove the swaying mountain of hay across the rocky creek, hoping and praying it wouldn't slip off. Then they did a triumphant pass by the front door of the cabin, the boys shouting and giggling at their Mother and sister. Queeda had a screaming, stomping fit until her mother finally handed her up to Charley to continue the triumphant ride. They pulled the load into the stack yard above the corrals. Since they still had the cows to milk, chickens to feed, wood to gather for the night, and supper to eat before dark Charley parked the load of hay and unhitched. Each boy was tossed giggling up on a sweaty horse, where he held onto the haimes for the ride to the creek. Queeda had another fit and earned a ride behind Pat on Dugan. At the creek they un-harnessed the horses, hung up the harnesses in the boxelder tree and led the horses down the bank to water. An old coffee can was left there just for this purpose. The horse's galded shoulders and lathered necks and backs were bathed and rubbed. How they loved it, and stood perfectly still so as not to give anybody any reason to quit. Afterward they rolled in the soft dry dirt to "scratch" their backs, and trotted off to the green pasture.

The next day they would unload the hay, making a perfectly shaped haystack, tromping it as they progressed to make it waterproof. It had to be big enough at the bottom to accommodate all the hay yet to come without getting too high to reach. Charley was thinking seriously about a horse drawn rake he had seen that put the dried hay in rows. That would sure cut down on the hand work. He would have to wait until he shipped the beefs this fall to see if he had enough money. Before the rake would come Evelyn's Maytag washing machine that ran off a gas engine. He had seen one at Thede's house his last trip out. He grinned to himself as he wondered what a cowboy was doing with all these machines.

Charley told a friend that Evelyn was raising all kinds of hell about those damn chickens now that she had a chicken house. She had found some laying hens through a friend and made a deal for them. There were twenty-four Leg Horn pullets and a Wyandotte rooster. The corn in the lower park was doing great so there would be plenty of winter feed for them.

Finally Charley decided he just as well get it over with. His old friend, Walter Goldsmith, had stopped by just to visit and said he'd go with him to get the chickens. They rode out to Vernal and got pretty drunk that night, but early the next morning went out and gathered up the chickens. The lady who owned the chickens had to use a firm hand to get them to put only three chickens in each gunny sack so they wouldn't smother. Her foolishness meant that they had to borrow a pack horse, because they couldn't manage nine sacks on their saddle horses. She also saw to it that the poor chickens were right side up in the sacks.

They could hardly endure the shame of cowboys hauling chickens. They struck off for home, stopping on Blue Mountain for buckskin and biscuits at a friend's cabin. The chickens just stayed loaded. After a snort or two of whiskey just to be neighborly they resumed their journey. They trotted some, which quieted the chickens. Then they walked and slid the horses down the steep trail off the mountain into Hells Canyon.

They stopped at Rat Spring to water the horses and refresh themselves with a drink or two of whiskey. The chickens were quiet so Walt finally said, "Charley, don't you think we better water them chickens?" Charley allowed they was probably dry as hell and could use a drink. They unloaded the sacks and started dumping out the chickens. Some could stagger, others just lay and blinked their eyes. Walt allowed they sure wasn't gonna' drink without some help, so they filled their hats with water and poured it on the chickens. It worked like a miracle. Their squawks were mere raspy groans, but they did stand up. Then the boys took them and stuck their heads down in the water. They drank until they felt good enough to stagger around. Deciding to let the herd rest awhile there on water the two men loosened their cinches, then sat with their backs against a cedar tree for a little social hour. The sun set and the chickens flew into the trees to roost for the night. When Walt and Charley decided it was time to re-sack them they couldn't be reached. After some serious consultation they decided the only thing to do was shoot them down. Drawing their six-shooters, they shot wildly into the trees, bringing three chickens down before they ran out of bullets. What to do! They sacked up the three they had and rode home.

Evelyn was furious with them for bringing home only three of the twenty-five chickens she had ordered, and those dead. The culprits were too drunk to question so she just pushed them over, covered them up, turned loose their horses, cleaned the three chickens, and went to bed. Next morning, under intense questioning Charley and Walt remembered getting as far as Rat Spring with all the chickens.

Evelyn left Charley to watch the children and she and Walt rode back to Rat Spring. There were the chickens contentedly searching for grasshoppers and worms for breakfast. With a gentle "chick, chick, chick" she called the chickens to her, and with the help of grain from her pocket caught them one by one while Walt put them in the sacks. One hen was missing, and they guessed it had been a passing coyote's breakfast. With her twenty hens and one rooster in her possession, Evelyn rode home with a smile on her face.

After the incident with the chickens Charley's old buddies could see a change in him. He was very moderate in his drinking, and almost never strapped his pistol on any more. They snickered behind his back about being hen-pecked.

23

The Orchard, 1936-37

RUTH HASLEM WAS RETURNING IN OCTOBER to teach again and the boys were excited about school. However, one day in late August Joe rode in to give them the devastating news that Ruth was not coming back after all. Evelyn took the baby and rode out to Youghall to see what she could do about getting another teacher at this late date. Upon arrival at the county superintendent's office in Craig she was told that all the registered teachers already had schools. The superintendent told her there was one slim chance. They drove out to the home of Inderselia Snyder. She was a beloved teacher who had taught at many schools in the district and had chosen to retire. The superintendent told her of the Mantle school and also of a new family who had moved into Bear Valley who had two school-age boys. There was no school for them. After a long discussion Mrs. Snyder offered to teach the Bear Valley school if the Mantles would move up there with their two boys. Evelyn readily agreed, willing to do almost anything to get her children an education.

Evelyn rode home with the news and they sadly began preparing to move to Bear valley, some twenty miles away, for the winter. In October they took enough belongings for the winter, and driving the milk cow in front of them, rode to the Powers ranch in Bear Valley, where they were welcomed with open arms. Potch and Pat had never walked on a board floor before, so they stomped and jumped and marched endlessly to hear the strange sound under their feet.

The Mantles were going to live in the teacher's quarters beside the school. Mrs. Snyder would live in a partitioned off part of the class room. The other family, Miles and Lona Robinson and their two boys, Neil and Wade, lived just over the hill. They helped prepare the school. The building was in sad disrepair and required a lot of work to be made liveable. Even at that it would be a desperately cold place to spend the winter. There was a small shed for the cow, and they bought hay from the Powers. When the school house was ready they sent word and Mrs. Snyder arrived with teaching supplies and moved in, ready to begin classes the following day. Her little students, Potch, Pat, Neil and Wade were speechless with anticipation.

School went well. Charley came as often as he could to stay with his family, but the livestock at home needed his attention most of the time. The Robinsons supplied an abundance of chopped wood for Mrs. Snyder and the

School in Bear Valley. L-R: Queeda, Wade Robinson, Pat, Mrs. Snyder, Neil Robinson, Potch, Evelyn, Lonnie.

Mantles supplied her food. Charley would bring fresh meat every time he came, and finally, fearful of not being able to make the trip through the deep drifts, hung half a beef under the shed for the winter. The milk cow was pampered and fed and in return she provided plenty of milk. The snow fell so deep that they made a tunnel through it from the door of the teacher's quarters to the door of the school house. Charley was hard put to keep the cattle at home alive, so he seldom was able to be with them. He was losing the precious time he treasured with his children. Evelyn worried constantly that he would try to make the trip and be frozen in a drift.

Lonnie learned to walk by pulling and pushing Queeda in a wagon over the board floor. She was ruthless and sometimes when she didn't want to ride herself she made him pull Pansy, her doll. All the kids liked to rock Lonnie in the rocking chair on the nice smooth wood floor.

By going to school six days a week, with the only days off being Sundays, Thanksgiving and Christmas, the required number of school days was completed in April, and school was let out. Evelyn and Mrs. Snyder had become fast friends and there were tears on both their cheeks as they hugged goodbye. Evelyn could not express just how grateful she was to Mrs. Snyder for the sacrifice she had made to come to this dreadful place to teach her children.

What a happy day it was when the family was reunited in their snug little house! They hoped never to have to spend another winter on that cold, miserable mountain. Evelyn rode out in June and arranged for a teacher who would arrive in the fall. Her name was Miss McFadden, a spinster lady. She had taught other schools in the district, so the superintendent felt sure she was capable.

*Henry and Dougan hitched to a Fresno, as the new field and orchard are leveled in
Castle Park.*

Uncle Tom Blevins, at the Red Rock Ranch, had a horse drawn fresno. It
was a simple earth moving apparatus that consisted of a wide scoop with a steel
handle in back. Mid-front there was a big ring to hook a horse or team to pull
it with. The steel handle behind made it possible for a man to operate it himself. He would put the handle down, which would cause the bucket to run
parallel to the ground and scoop dirt into the bucket. When it was time to
dump the dirt, the tension on the handle would be released and the handle
would fly upward, dumping the dirt. Then the driver stopped the team and
pulled the handle back down with an attached rope. The trick was to not hit
a rock, stopping forward motion and throwing the driver over the team.
Charley borrowed it from Tom and built some dirt dams to keep the creek in
its banks in case there was another flood like that of the spring before. His
uncle Hy, who lived with Tom sometimes, came over to help. The rest of the
time Evelyn helped, and they plowed ditches, and cleared an area east of the
new garden. They plowed it deep, harrowed it smooth, and pulled ditches
through it. They planted alfalfa seed. Last of all they built an eight-foot-tall
fence of chicken wire surrounding the new garden and the newly prepared
plot. They made a gate wide enough to get the hay rack through. Then an exciting day arrived!

Charley rode in leading a pack horse with the slender, spindly limbs of
dormant fruit trees sticking out the backs of the panniers. Their order from
the Luther Burbank catalog had arrived. There were fifty fruit trees, including
many varieties of apples, plums, pears, peaches, apricots, cherries, and one
mulberry tree. The whole family carefully unpacked the trees, straightened the
roots of each one and lowered them into a pit they had dug. They covered the

Petroglyphs on the north face of Castle Rock near the orchard.

roots with straw and dirt, watered them until the pit was full, and left them to soak while they prepared the holes to plant them in. Evelyn was the undisputed expert, so supervised the project. The newly prepared area was to be a fruit orchard, with an alfalfa cover to keep down weeds as well as to provide a hay crop. They dug the holes three times as wide and three times as deep as the size of the roots, then filled the bottom one-third of the hole with aged cow manure mixed with rich soil. Each tree was gently planted and watered with many buckets of water. The irrigation ditches were trenched to each tree, allowing only a gentle trickle to reach the tree. The new trees were watered often, and soon began to sprout leaves and grow.

High water and floods came, but did not cause the damage they had on other occasions. Nonetheless, Evelyn wanted her new house built and her family moved out of that canyon. So far she hadn't even gotten her new stove. Ed and Guy came riding in one day right at dinner time. They sat down to a meal of fried venison steaks, corn on the cob, mashed potatoes, and some kind of green stuff Evelyn called spinach that was better than it looked. Full to the brim, they went out front to smoke. Evelyn wandered out and casually said, "I hope you can stay for supper. I've got some rhubarb pies ready to bake. If you have time you could haul the logs for the house." Needing no further coaxing, they hitched up the wagon, coaxed Charley to go with them to show them the little jag of logs, and took off. Making road all the way through the canyon left in havoc by the spring floods, they finally arrived at the biggest damned stack of logs they had ever seen. They were long and thick, too, and heavy as hell. They loaded as many as the horses could pull on the wagon, chained them on and hauled them to the site of the new house. Feeling used and pouty, they stopped by the house for a drink at the creek. Evelyn popped out of the house with a big smile and offered them some hot bread right out of the oven and a fresh pan of creamy egg custard to keep up their strength. It took supper, two rhubarb pies, plus breakfast, and dinner, finished off with two chocolate meringue pies the next day, but she got all her logs delivered and stacked neatly.

October, 1937, arrived and Miss McFadden was settled into her teacherage. The children were excited about school, but it would prove to be a difficult year. Miss McFadden didn't adjust well to this primitive life. Besides, she thought kids should be in school when school was in session, not out gathering cattle.

When shipping time came, Charley, Potch and Pat trailed the big, wild two year old steers to Lily Park to join the cattle drive there of the local ranchers. The cattle would be all trailed together from Lily Park to Craig to the rail head. Charley had taken a few cows along as the wild steers would stick with them, and be more manageable.

Henry Shank, plowing his field in Deer Lodge, heard the lowing of cattle arriving on the other side of the river. Riding over to investigate, he was greeted by the sight of two small boys with a cow roped and her head tied to a tree. Her hind legs were tied to another tree, and she was helplessly suffering the indignity of being milked. The bigger of the two boys would brave her thrashing feet to milk a cup full, then hand it to the younger boy who would empty it into a bucket. The process continued until she had no more milk. Henry watched in amusement as they turned her loose, coiled up their ropes, and returned to their camp fire where they cooked their supper. They even made coffee, and when he finally made himself known they invited him in and offered him coffee. He was surprised that they were proper little gentlemen. He learned they were Charley Mantle's boys and Charley had left them to hold the herd of cattle while he went to Craig to get a buyer to come out the next day to make a bid on the cattle.

When the boys returned, having missed four school days, the teacher was furious and berated them until they cried in anguish. Charley was baffled as to why she didn't realize they had to go drive the cattle to market. After all, what was more important than getting money to live on? The nine and ten-year-old boys understood it, you would think a grown woman could get it, but Miss McFadden could not accept that as a legitimate reason for missing school.

Guy rode into the ranch one day. He wondered if he might be able to spend the winter with the Mantle family and help them out with the work. Evelyn loved to have Guy around. He was a gentle man, and talked and visited with her almost as a woman would. He jumped in and helped with all her work, and the kids adored him. Charley was equally glad to have him. He was good company, could spin great yarns, knew how to cure hides, cut and braid the rawhide, and was good at twisting hair ropes. He always had a new or fancy way to make and decorate things. He was an expert with leather, and could repair saddles or even boots. He moved into the bunk house with the kids. They soon learned to try to beat him to sleep at night, as his snoring rocked the world. He accidentally told Evelyn that his birthday was next week and for years thereafter, every time he would show up, whatever time of year, his birthday was "next week" and she would make him a cake and the family would have a big ceremony of blowing out the candles. His big body would shake with laughter as the kids spanked him "with one to grow on." He was so old that they would lose count and have to start over.

Guy was missing half his thumb on his right hand. The truth was that he had gotten it dallied in his rope and a wild horse had pulled it off many years ago. Each night as they prepared for bed, the boys and Queeda would beg him to tell them how he lost his thumb and he would weave a gory tale of how a steamship had cut it off, a wild Indian had hacked it off with a spear point, a whale bit it off, a killer bronco had tromped it off, it froze off in a blizzard, he traded it for a squaw, a tornado dropped a house on it and endless other unique tales of the missing thumb. The kids would tingle with excitement as they drifted off to sleep.

Christmas was coming soon and Miss McFadden insisted she had to go out to visit her family. The drifts were deep and it wasn't a wise decision, but Charley finally agreed to try to get her out. They got as far as the first bench, and poor Mrs. McFadden was crying frozen tears and begging to return to the ranch. She was not an even a fair horse woman at very best, and Charley was relieved to not have to try to keep her alive for the trip over the dangerous mountain.

With four children anticipating Santa Clause' arrival with gifts at Christmas, property taxes due, and grazing permits to sign, Charley had no choice but to go out to town. Before dawn one day in late December Charley and Guy took three horses apiece and set out for Youghall. They would ride one horse to break a trail through the drifts and when he was tired, change to another. All six horses were jingling with icicles formed from their sweat and their heads hung low from exhaustion when they finally arrived at the Power's place just before dark. Charley and Guy were equally exhausted, but unsaddled the horses, rubbed them down, and put them in the shed out of the wind with hay and a bite of grain before they ever went into the house themselves. They had brought the Powers a quarter of beef, which was gladly accepted. Auntie Powers sat them down in front of the heater with hot coffee while she finished preparing the supper she had started when she saw them coming. How good it was, because all they had during the day was a couple of cold pancakes and some jerky.

The next day they caught a ride with the mail carrier into Elk Springs and picked up their mail. There was a big box from Eva, also one from Evelyn's folks. They were bound to be full of Christmas goodies. After he delivered all his mail the carrier took them on to Craig where Charley conducted his business. Afterward, they bought some supplies, and Christmas-shopped for the children and Evelyn. This finished, they caught another ride back to the Powers place.

Anxious about leaving the family alone, they saddled up, and packed two horses with supplies the next morning and started for home. The trail they had made coming in was blown over considerably, but still visible and a whole lot easier going than when they came. When they hit the benches at the foot of the mountain the trail was still broke and easy traveling. The horses were tired, but even with two of them packed were able to make the trip. It was bitter cold and as the afternoon wore on the snow that had melted for a while in their stirrups froze. The men covered their faces to keep them from freezing and rode doggedly on. When they rode into the ranch they could not dismount because their feet were frozen into the stirrups. Evelyn got a hammer and pounded their feet loose. The men were nearly frozen, unable to do more than stagger into the warm house. Evelyn and the two boys unpacked and tended to the horses. Charley warned her which horse the Christmas presents were on and she led that one away to the bunk house to unpack. She tied the panniers high on the rafter of the bunk house and cautioned the kids to not open the panniers, as there were some things inside that would explode if light touched them. The boys just smirked and gave each other knowing winks. From then until Christmas eve they circled beneath the panniers like small tigers antici-pating a kill.

A couple of days before Christmas the whole family went out and searched the benches and ledges close to home for the perfect Christmas tree. Finally they agreed on a six foot, perfectly shaped little Pinyon tree, already decorated with dried cones that had sprung open to drop their nuts. Charley cut the tree to the delighted yelps of the three older children. Queeda didn't know exactly what was going on, but joined in the joy of the occasion because Pat told her she was prob-ably going to get some candy. Lonnie toddled around squealing in glee at the activity. Charley made a stand for the tree and they put it up in the little cabin, which was now so crowded that Guy had to turn his ample body sideways to squeeze to the table.

Next day they popped popcorn and strung it. Guy went with the kids and gathered bright red rose hips to string with it. Miss McFadden had helped the students make Christmas decorations with colored paper. They had also made small clay gifts for their parents, which they wrapped to keep them secret and set them under the tree, cautioning their parents to not peek or the packages would explode.

On Christmas morning the kids woke up to find that the panniers had disappeared. They quickly dressed, woke up Guy to go with them, and raced to the house. The Christmas tree was laden with many wonders. Whole sacks of hard candy and nuts lay underneath. There were trucks and a pair of boots for each of the boys. For Queeda there was a stick horse and a new dress. For Nav (Lonnie's nickname) there was a quacking duck to pull behind him and some brand new overalls. Mrs. Powers had sent down a turkey, and it was already stuffed and baking in the oven. There were hot rolls rising to be baked and pies already baked. There was an SOB in a sack for Charley and a big chocolate cake for Guy. Dinner was complete with candied yams, mashed potatoes with giblet gravy, and canned green beans. Ed Lewis, Hy Mantle and Tom Blevins rode in about midmorning to join in the festivities. Everyone ate and ate again. Guy forbade Evelyn to wash any dishes, so she was able to sit down with the rest and enjoy the day.

The winter seemed longer than usual to Evelyn. Miss McFadden wasn't the pleasant companion that Ruth or Mrs. Snyder had been. Evelyn was bitterly disappointed that the Dinosaur National Monument had been expanded to include nearly all of their grazing range, thereby putting their ranch under innumerable new rules and regulations, and yet no effort had been made to build the road that had been promised. Her new house had not gotten started, nor had her new stove arrived. She had made a deal for their piano with some dry farmers who were leaving Blue Mountain. It was sitting in a deserted old shack, it looked like there would never be a road to bring it in on nor a house to put it in. She didn't want her children to be raised in a dugout and never get any of the music and culture and human contact they were entitled to.

One day a bunch of men arrived on the heavily iced-over river pulling sleds laden with lumber, cement, nails, and roofing shingles for the new house. Their friend at the lumber yard in Craig had decided to just make a delivery of the materials Mantles had ordered. The men were exhausted and it took two full days to tell all the tales of their trip. Evelyn was so joyful she felt she would burst. Her new house was actually going to happen!

Around the end of March, 1938, Evelyn came to the awful realization that she was pregnant again and cried bitter tears for days. Her fate now was sealed. She seemed destined to be a lonely drudge for the rest of her life. Charley would be taking the boys away as soon as school was out, to tend the cattle. More and more he stayed away with them on Blue Mountain and left her and the two younger children at home alone to tend the garden and can and preserve in preparation for the winter. He seemed to come home only to put up the hay and hated doing that. Longings to escape came unbidden to her mind. She had not had a new store-bought dress since she was married. Her riding habit, boots and hat were worn out long ago. Even the saddle she had come to the marriage with had been confiscated by Charley for the boys, and was worn out. Her legs were riddled with varicose veins from all the lifting and heavy work she did. On top of that, Charley had had a falling out with her parents and forbade them to come visiting, so they didn't, she was deprived of seeing them, except on those rare occasions when circumstances allowed her to visit them. She couldn't buy clothes for the children, she had to make them all from somebody else's cast off clothes. She just couldn't keep up with all that sewing, and felt that the clothes she did make looked shabby. Her spirits were at an all time low. What would Charley say about her being pregnant again?

Author Queeda Walker with her daughter, Freda Walker Bishop sitting on the east rim of Castle Park looking west. Left center is the "new" house then hay fields, then the orchard and the mouth of Hells Canyon where it empties into the Yampa River, with the Crows Nest cliff rising on the right side of the river. The red hills of Red Rock Ranch are beyond, with Blue Mountain looming along the left side of the photo.

Morning sun tips the cliffs on the north side of Castle Park.

Hells Canyon Gorge as it begins the plunge off Blue Mountain. The Mormon Cricket drive began here. Beyond are the deep canyons of the Yampa River where the Mantle Family lived.

Upper Hells Canyon bursts from Blue Mountain into more tranquil terrain before it enters the canyon walls. Author and grandson Jonathan Lisco on horses.

Bench Road west from Hells Canyon. Center, dome-shaped rock is the mouth of Red Rock Canyon. White cliffs of Pool Creek at Chew Ranch may be seen in the distance.

From Laddie Park, southwest with the "smile" of Marigold Cave at center right.

144

Pat's Cave, where Pat Lynch lived at times. One of his charcoal sketches of a sailing ship is on one wall. It is the tear-shaped cave mouth in the cliffs high on the north side of the river in Castle Park.

From Pat's Cave on the north side of the river. Ranch house, Castle Rock, south rim of Hells Canyon, and finally Martha's Peak and Roundtop Mountain.

The Yampa River flows through the "Narrows" and bursts into Castle Park. The first horizontal white cliff is Castle Rock. Beyond is the rim of Hells Canyon. Round Top Mountain rears up behind.

Author's son, Cody Walker and wife Kathy below the towering cliffs of Outlaw Park. On left the Yampa river flows below the renowned Tiger Rock.

From Outlaw Park east. Laddie Park on the left, Red Rock Canyon on the right. Martha's Peak far left, Round Top far right. Hells Canyon runs between them.

The "New House" about 1948 with the original red roof. The hay field and Yampa River and orchard are beyond.

Harding's Hole with the Yampa's deep loops, where the bulls were pastured in the winter, and where the Mantles camped during the drought.

24

Tim, 1938-39

CHARLEY NOTICED THE GAUNT, TROUBLED LOOK on Evelyn's face and saw the tears she tried to hide. He also noticed that she tired easily and was listless and quiet. He invited her to ride over to Mrs. Chew's one day, thinking maybe she was needing some woman companionship. Besides, the eagle eyed lady could tell him what ailed his wife if there was a serious problem.

They were of course invited to stay for dinner and spent a great day visiting and exchanging news. Lonnie got a lot of attention from the Chew family who passed him around like a new toy. Potch and Pat went fishing with some of the Chew kids, rode the milk cow calves while out of sight of the house, and followed the dogs on a noisy rabbit hunt through the foothills. In the afternoon Charley followed Mrs. Chew into the kitchen, out of earshot of Evelyn and asked her if she thought there was anything wrong with Evelyn? She spun around to face him with a look of total shock on her face. "Charley Mantle, you beat all I ever saw. You keep that poor girl pregnant all the time, and still can't tell?" Charley was dumbfounded.

Before they parted Mrs. Chew gave the now contrite Charley a long lecture she thought he needed. She told him that his wife was worn out from caring for four kids and a husband in the primitive way they lived. She told him that Evelyn needed a washing machine with a gas engine, a house to live in and a car to get to and from town in, which of course would require a road. She also needed someone besides Guy MacNearlin to talk to oftener than once a year, and she needed a whole lot of help doing all the work. Mrs. Chew said dry farmers had better houses and a whole lot better stoves. The most shocking thing she told him was that he was pampering his selfish self, staying away so much while she was home raising food and preserving things so they wouldn't starve in the winter. He protested "Them cattle need tendin' and them boys need to learn to work and be men." "Horse Feathers," she replied.

Charley thought hard on all these revelations on the way home. He thought she was probably right in everything except that Guy MacNearlin was not good enough company. He felt he was providing the best there, because Guy acted so much like an old woman sometimes, but he vowed to do better because he truly loved his wife and wanted her to be happy.

149

The next morning when the children left for school Charley came up behind Evelyn and folded her into a great gentle bear hug. Gently patting her stomach he said, "We been too long without a baby around here. What do you say we have another girl right away?" Sobbing and laughing together, they mended their tired marriage. The new baby would be wonderful, and they grew anxious for its arrival.

May arrived and school election time was upon them. Charley and Evelyn rode out to Three Springs where the election was held. The last check for Mrs. McFadden was signed and sent home with them and Evelyn turned in her carefully kept books for the school. They decided to go on to Craig to personally see the school superintendent about getting a teacher for their school in the fall. She gave them the names of several teachers that would be available.

Florence Shank, the oldest daughter of Henry Shank, was only twenty-three, but had taught the previous year in Lily Park, and was reported to be an excellent teacher. The Shanks were a nice, clean living, cultured family. They were ranchers and poor and understood about ranch life and getting by with very few luxuries. The superintendent said she would be seeing Florence that week, and would ask her if she wanted the job. As it turned out, Florence wanted the job, and the Shanks were very pleased to let their daughter go. They knew the Mantles were a nice family. People always commented on how the little Mantle boys were always neat and mannerly.

Charley and Evelyn stayed at the home of an old friend, Lou Seabaum while they were in Craig. He ran a garage, repairing wagons, cars and farm machinery. Charley asked him to start looking for a pickup truck for them. He figured that with the help of the gold prospectors who were camped at Hardings Hole they would have a road into the ranch finished by Christmas. Lou was pretty skeptical of that. He and his friend, Dick Toole, who ran the gas station, had been down there many times to fish and visit, and always had to walk the last ten miles. It wasn't even easy terrain to walk over because of all the deep gullies and rock outcroppings. Lou promised to get them the first good deal on a pickup that came along. Evelyn could hardly contain her excitement at the prospect.

Charley mentioned to Lou that he was also looking for a Maytag washing machine that ran on a gas motor. Lou said he had been in the hardware store yesterday and a new one had just come in. He drove them over to look at it and Charley bought it on the spot. Lou said he would bring it down to Johnson just as soon as the mud dried up. He smiled behind his hand and winked at Charley as Evelyn cautioned him to be very careful with it and brace it good so it wouldn't get scarred up.

When they got back to the ranch Miss McFadden was packed and announced that school was out and she wanted out of that canyon. Even though it was a little early the boys were ready to get out because spring had come. Green grass, baby calves, and baby chicks were everywhere. The best sign of spring was that Guy had taken off all but one shirt and one pair of pants of the many layers he had worn during the winter. He still needed the spring bath and hair cut, and Evelyn was going to see that he got them as soon as possible. It hadn't rained for a week, so the road shouldn't be muddy and Charley sent Guy to Hardings Hole to see a gold miner named Swede, who was bossing a mining crew there. Swede had his car parked at Johnson and Guy made a deal with him to take Miss McFadden to town the next day.

The signal had been given that summer vacation had started. The kids all took off their shoes and started toughening up their feet. The boys always went shirtless, too. Soon they could run like deer over the rocks and through the brush in their bare feet. The only time the boys could not go bare-footed was when they wore their boots to work cattle or horses. Queeda rode bareback and went bare-footed to gather the milk cows, go fishing, chase rabbits, and just wander endless hours on her beloved Mousy. He was a small white horse that Ed Lewis had caught from the wild horse herd in Utah. He was gentle and trustworthy in every way except that when he could escape he would return to Utah, join the wild herd and have to be chased down and roped. So he became the only horse that got to stay at the ranch year around and he and Queeda were inseparable.

One day, Ed Lewis showed up and he, Charley and Guy, along with the kids made short work of putting in the garden, relieving Evelyn of weeks of hard work. Then they planted the corn and hay crops. They hauled wood, chopped it into pieces that would fit in the stove and stacked it near the house. They even raked and cleaned around the cabins and tore out the dead sage brush and grubbed out rabbit brush. They repaired and cleaned the corrals and spread the manure on the garden and orchard, built pens for the milk calves, and cleaned the chicken house. They even worked hard at catching fish for the dinner table. Charley was shocked at how much of this "woman's work" there was to do and that a man was worn out after a day doing it. Old Lady Chew might have been right about Evelyn working too hard! Evelyn was grateful for the help and that Charley and the boys didn't leave her alone so much.

When the spring work was done Charley made a deal with the prospectors. In exchange for a beef in the fall and vegetables this summer, they would help him work on the road from the head of Hells Canyon to Johnson. He and Evelyn flagged the location for the road. They placed it around the heads of draws, along the narrow tops of steep-sided ridges, trying to maintain a grade that a vehicle could climb even with the handicap of the inevitable mud from quick rains and melting snow. With picks and shovels and the horse-drawn Fresno (a kind of scoop used to move earth) the men whipped the road through the rocks and trees. Sometimes they had to blast off a ledge. Often they had to fill washes with enough rocks to build a crossing, yet were careful to leave room for the water to pass and not leave washouts along the sides. It was by no means perfect, but it soon started taking on the shape of a road. They had set their goal for the road to be passable by December so Evelyn could ride out in the car when the baby was due. That would make her travel time one day instead of the three days the wagon would take. The prospectors worked their gold claim and Charley cared for his cattle, while they all relentlessly worked on the road every spare minute, sometimes far into the moon and star lit nights.

By July, Evelyn had gotten big and clumsy. She wasn't able to can as much as she usually did, and worried about the winter food supply. She got Charley to bring home a lot of venison to make into jerky and canned and preserved what she could. Guy, always her good friend, stayed around the ranch and helped her with the garden, the milk cows, the kids, and even sat patiently with skeins of yarn stretched over his hands as Evelyn wound it into balls. He kept her water buckets full and filled the boiler with water and heated it for washing clothes. He loved to chew and spit as he stood out in the shade of the box elder tree running the wet clothes through the wringer on the new washing machine, then hanging the clothes to dry. He would often say reverently, "Pretty soon we'll have lots of dydies to wash for a brand new little baby." The four children loved him dearly, and he organized an efficient work gang from them. The gang and their foreman required lots of cookies for fuel. The only time he left Evelyn was when he had to make a quick trip to town for tobacco. He was always welcomed by a cheering crowd when he returned because he had his pockets full of hard candy.

Dugan, the big white work horse that was Henry's mate got colic one night and died. He was a beloved member of the family and everyone cried. Henry hung his head dejectedly and whinnied hopefully for days. Guy tired quickly of all the sadness so next trip out for tobacco he returned leading a big horse just the size and shape of Henry, but jet black. He wasn't broke to work, but in just a few days with Henry as his tutor he became a gentle, dependable work companion for Henry, and the road work went on. They named him Nig and he was soon nickering when he heard his name.

Evelyn wrote Florence telling her that she was expecting a baby in December and wasn't feeling like traveling, so Charley would be coming to pick her up on October first. When Charley came for Florences' belongings he was greeted by the devastating news that she had been in a terrible car wreck. He tied up his horses and rushed breathlessly into the house. Florence told him not to worry, she was going to be fine, and that she was definitely going to be able to teach his children. However, she had a back injury from the wreck and was in a cast. The doctor ordered her not to do anything for two weeks, and above all not to go near a horse. So she and Charley made arrangements that he would come back for her in two weeks.

When he returned he came in Swede's car, thinking it would be easier on Florence than going on horseback. However, the car broke down on Swede in Bear Valley, so Charley got the postman, Kelly, to take him to pick up Florence. He brought Queeda with him, so Florence, Charley, Queeda, Guy and Swede stayed with the Kellys that night. The next morning Swede set out to get his car fixed. Guy and Florence, meanwhile, headed out horseback, leaving the Kellys at 3:00 a.m. Guy hunted down and checked his herd of horses pastured on the benches at Dry Woman, and he roped fresh horses to replace their worn out ones. It was after dark when they got to the ranch. Evelyn was worried sick because they were a day late. She fed them supper. Florence was so exhausted she could hardly stay awake to eat, and fell gratefully into bed. Charley and Queeda returned with Swede when the car was fixed.

Florence rearranged the school house and got ready to start school. She fell in love with the children and declared them to be the four sweetest little kids she had ever seen. She described them to her sister.

Navvy, the little fellow, is an adorable little fellow with a tousely white head and big brown eyes. Queedy or Queed is light headed and has big brown eyes. I greatly fear that she will be a regular little tomboy unless the next edition is a girl too, for she plays with the boys all the time and is a bigger rowdy than any of them. My little fourth graders are regular pals. They stick together through thick and thin and are always together. They are about the same size but do not look at all alike. Potch, the older looks more like his Dad while Pat looks like his mother. Pats eyes are a light hazel brown and his face is slimmer than Potch. Potch's eyes are beautiful but they have never decided whether to be blue or brown and sometimes look one and sometimes the other.

The whole family worshiped Florence from the beginning. She and Evelyn became immediate friends. She was terribly lonely for her family and felt isolated from the world, but the loving Mantle family took her as one of them and smothered her with love and company. Lonnie and Queeda begged to sleep with her and often she let them. She played endless games with the boys, and they played endless tricks on her. However, they became serious students once they passed through the schoolhouse door. They loved school and were quick to learn. Potch loved to read, and read everything he could get his hands on, even adult level books. Potch finished everything in record time, but skipped parts and left some things unfinished. Pat was slower but got everything right. He was much better than Potch at motor skills, but didn't care a hoot about reading.

Queeda was only five, but walked on her stilts back and forth in front of the school house, peering mournfully in the window until Florence and Evelyn finally decided it would be best to start her in the first grade.

Three year old Lonnie would appear daily at her door and pull himself up to full height and say, "I'm almost big enough to go to school aren't I?" Florence finally had to start having kindergarten for him for about a half hour after school let out. They went to school on Saturdays, too, to make up for lost time.

Evelyn was getting unusually heavy it seemed. She didn't feel like going out for supplies herself, so she sent Charley, which proved to be a mistake. Rather than taking the wagon like he usually did, he got Swede to take him in the car. Without the wagon he couldn't bring everything on the list and as a result got less of everything. This would prove disastrous, because it turned out to be a snowy winter, and they were often out of flour. Worse yet, both Guy and Charley were often out of tobacco and really got crabby when that happened. They borrowed Florence's flour and when it was gone borrowed from the prospectors. Charley covered himself by saying it would be all right because they were going out in December anyway when the baby was born and would stock up then.

The Mantles had no outhouse, they just went out in the bushes when nature called. Florence was amazed to see tiny Lonnie heading for the bushes even on a snowy morning with a couple of sheets of paper, with his 'barn door' hanging open.

Moffat County finally decided that they should put a road down into the canyons so tourists could visit the monument. However, Charley and Evelyn had decided to do it themselves rather then waiting on the county to do it. There would always be plenty more to do after the road was established. They hoped the county

Queeda on homemade stilts, longing to be old enough to attend school.

would do most of that. The good news arrived about the middle of November that a man named Brimhall was finally finished with the job he had been working on and could come down with his bulldozer and finish the road out the east side of Hells Canyon. When school was out on Sundays, Charley took the kids, and Florence, too and went up to watch the bulldozer work. It was a marvelous machine and they were in open-mouthed awe. It turned over huge cedar trees as easily as you would flick a fly off your nose. It could dislodge the biggest rocks and cast them aside, then scoop up dirt to fill holes. It began to look as though Swede would be able to drive to the very door to get Evelyn when she went out in about two weeks. Dr. Bailey had told her to come in about the first of December, which would give her one week before the baby arrived.

The bulldozer first got the road fairly passable from Johnson to the top of Hells Canyon, then Brimhall was ready to tackle the most difficult part of all, namely getting an acceptable grade down the steep incline to the floor of Hells

Canyon through the frequent outcroppings of ledges. Charley, Evelyn, and Brimhall scouted the route, dynamited the obvious outcroppings, after which Brimhall mounted his big machine to bust out the road. Brimhall and his audience knew that if he hit a rock-solid concealed ledge his bulldozer bucket would catch and if he was a split second too slow in reducing power it would roll the bulldozer down the steep slope and fall to the canyon floor far below. Carefully he worked his way down the dangerous incline, raising his blade to pass over ledges that wouldn't give. They would have to be blasted off later. A man with steel nerves, he teetered on the edge several times, saving himself and his precious machine by inches. Suddenly, with a terrible scream of ripping metal the bulldozer lurched off the edge of the road, and teetered at the edge. Only a solid cedar tree kept it from rolling over. A spring had broken, and it would require a tow truck to pull the bulldozer out then a trip to town for parts to repair it. It was slow and precarious work to get the bulldozer back on the road. Several times it began slipping and the men thought they had lost it over the edge. They feared that when it went it would take the tow truck and driver with it. Finally one last tug from the tow truck got it back on the newly dozed road. The parts had been brought in and finally the huge machine was ready to go to work again, but it was Thanksgiving Day before work could be resumed.

Charley had invited the road crew for Thanksgiving dinner, so they planned to eat in the evening. Evelyn had Guy kill the big white rooster, which they baked with a dishpan full of dressing. They made an SOB-in-a-Sack and Florence made two apple-coconut pies and two elderberry pies. They had hot rolls, mashed potatoes, gravy, pickles, plenty of whipped cream and sauce on pies and pudding. Florence searched until she found a cabbage root sticking out of the frozen ground where Guy had carefully buried the cabbage last fall. She made a big slaw. Everybody ate until they could eat no more, and although it was after dark the men went back to their camp.

About 5:30 A.M. on November 25, Charley came up to Florence's house and asked her to come down because the baby was coming, much sooner than expected. There was no time to boil anything, so Florence ironed everything for about two hours with very hot irons to sterilize it. Florence later declared, "Evelyn was sure one wonderful little woman, she told us everything to get ready and what to do when the time came and drilled Charley and me as to what each of us could do." She cautioned Florence not to get scared or she would be no help.

Guy, meanwhile, was getting breakfast and entertaining Potch, Pat, Queeda and Navvy up at the school house. He took them all down to check the traps that had been set for coyotes down at the fruit trees.

About 10 o'clock a little baby boy was born. He made such a a racket that Lonnie heard him from down at the corral and asked Guy, "What dat noise?" Evelyn had to cut the cord and tie it herself because her two nurses were shaking too much. The baby had a lot of hair for such a little fellow and a little fuzz for eye lashes. For Florence it was instant love, and throughout her life she told

The completed Mantle family, 1939: Charley, Tim, Evelyn, Potch, Pat, Queeda, Lonnie.

the story of delivering Tim Mantle, the most beautiful and best baby in the world. Tim Mantle was born on November 25, 1938, in Castle Park, Colorado. Evelyn was thirty-one and Charley forty-five when their last child was born.

Monday morning it was back to school as usual. The two boys were learning to type on Florence's typewriter and doing fine in all their school work. Queeda could count to fifty and read half way through her primer. Charley and Florence had their hands full taking care of Evelyn and the baby plus all the chores.

One evening after school the boys wanted to take Florence up to the cliff houses. Intrigued, she went with them. In the back of a nearby canyon, under a huge overhanging cliff in the shape of an upside down bowl was a deep, wide-mouthed, dry cave. Inside were old compartments made of rock plastered together with mud and fitted with chipped stone lids. You could even still see the fingerprints in the clay. Some old pieces of basketry and pottery had been found, but Evelyn had most of them at the house now, where she proudly and reverently showed them to all visitors, but guarded them fiercely from being taken away. People were always wanting to take them to be studied and dated.

Brimhall and his bulldozer finished busting the road into Hells Canyon on November 30. He didn't have time to smooth it out very well and the last fifty feet to the canyon floor was too steep for a car to get up. A horse or team of horses had to help pull any vehicle up this first fifty feet, but at least the road was passable by a wagon now, all the way into the canyon, and with some hand work cleaning up the flood damage at the creek crossings, you could drive all the way to the house.

Charley took Florence home for Christmas on horseback. Henry told him not to worry about coming back for Florence, that he would bring her himself right after Christmas. Charley was able to catch a ride into Craig and quickly buy a pack horse full of groceries and Christmas gifts. He was too concerned about his family at home alone to take the time to get the mail at Elk Springs. They had a sparse but happy Christmas together. On New Years eve Florence returned, ready to begin school again the next day. The Mantles were excited and happy to have her safely back. Florence was badly disappointed they hadn't gotten the mail, as she was expecting some.

Potch, Pat, and Queeda build an igloo.

Finally on January 5, Guy rode out to get the mail. A week passed and he hadn't returned. When he finally rode in with the mail sack Evelyn and Florence met him with a mixture of anger and relief. Cabin fever was setting in as the snow piled up and supplies ran low. Every possible event was celebrated at the canyon home, which kept spirits up. The next event was Evelyn's birthday on February 18. The hens had almost entirely quit laying eggs and the cow was giving very little milk; there was no butter, so the diet was monotonous. Florence made her a cake, and helped the children make gifts. They surprised Evelyn and had a wonderful time.

Florence wrote to her sister.

My birthday has come and gone. About daybreak on March 3, I woke to the tune of a terrorized squawk from the region of the hen house, and upon looking out beheld my three angels escorting a rooster to the Mantle residence in a most uncomfortable position. His head was well throttled beneath an arm. A hand or two was very effectively choking off another squawk. "Oh! Oh!" I figured

I would have rooster for my birthday supper. When my cherubs came to school that morning they were seething with suppressed mystery. At recess I put my dinner on to cook as usual but when I put my nose out the door three younguns besieged me and I had to rush back inside the school house. They vowed they would whip me (birthday custom of spanking, with one spank for each year of age) at noon so when I ambled forth at 12:30 I was not surprised when my darling angels suddenly turned inky black, tied me hand and foot with two of Charley's hand-made binder twine ropes and declared they had each given me 25 licks, which I suppose makes me somewhere near 100 years old. The extra 25 is for Navvy who couldn't decide whether to whip me or champion me and spent his time between the two extremes . . . first demanding they turn me loose and then taking to me with a stick. They untied me on the dot of 1:00 o'clock and we resumed our studies. I was invited down to supper and as I had guessed, we had stewed rooster, dumplings and all the trimmings. Under the bed was a great pile of hand made, wrapped gifts."

On March 10 Guy left to get the mail and some much needed tobacco. After waiting for him a month they found that he had gone to work for some Greek sheepmen. In the meantime, Hells Canyon was raging with floods. Evelyn had begun work in the garden, and Tim stayed with Florence at school a few hours every day. The cow freshened, making milk and cream plentiful. Eggs were also plentiful, as was fresh fish. On April 11 Pierre Morgan rode in for a visit and took out the mail. Potch rode out to Elk Springs to get the mail soon after. Although he was only twelve years old his parents were confident he would safely make the eighty mile round trip ride.

Florence wrote to the school superintendent, explaining that she would be unable to teach the Mantle school during the coming year. As a replacement, she suggested her sister Katherine, who would be receiving her teaching certificate from Greeley and would be available. Grateful, the superintendent gladly accepted the suggestion and on March 4 Florence wrote to her sister, Katharine, to tell her that the school board was willing to give her, Katharine, the Mantle school for the coming year.

On March 18, 1939, Florence's brother John brought in a car and took her home. The Mantle children were devastated. Florence missed all the Mantles, but missed Timmy something awful. It had been a good year for everybody, and would always be remembered as a year of joy.

Perry Mansfield, 1939-40

OOD NEWS HAD FINALLY COME IN THE MAIL. After lengthy negotiations, The Perry Mansfield school for young ladies in Steamboat Springs had signed up for a horseback adventure trip with the Mantles in August. All of these young ladies were accomplished riders and their director was an interesting, rather hard boiled lady who took great pride in seeking out a truly challenging adventure for the girls each year. She fearlessly drove her car in to the ranch to discuss the details with Charley and Evelyn. When it was time for her to leave she drove out to the head of Hells Canyon. From there she shouted encouragement from behind the wheel of her car to Henry horse as Charley hitched him to her car and pulled her the first fifty feet out of Hells Canyon.

One day a pickup drove slowly down Hells Canyon and pulled right up to the cabin. It said University of Colorado on it and a very attractive, personable young man stepped out. He stuck out his hand and introduced himself as Charles Scoggin and explained that he was the archaeologist the university had chosen to do an archaeological survey of Dinosaur National Monument. If the survey revealed evidence of permanent residence by prehistoric peoples in the area then the university would be asking permission to do some excavating. Evelyn had been corresponding with the university about this, and had agreed to give them permission to explore the Mantle property. She was very excited, because she had a consuming interest in the petroglyphs and artifacts she was always seeking.

Scoggin, as he was immediately named, instantly became very popular with the whole family. He was friendly and funny and could do absolutely anything the kids set him up to do and even played tricks back on them. Potch and Pat proudly showed him several caves and petroglyph sites. They tried to move him right into the bunk house with them, but he said he had to go make all the arrangements and come back as soon as he could. The whole family gathered to watch Henry pull Scoggins's pickup out the first incredibly steep fifty feet of Hells Canyon.

The garden was planted, extra big this year because of all the anticipated visitors. The fruit trees were producing now, so fruit canning went on all summer. Potch was twelve and a half, Pat was ten, Queeda was six, Nav was four, and Tim one and a half.

Evelyn working in the young but productive orchard and huge garden. The eight-foot fence keeps the deer out. House is in the background. Wood was pushed off the cliff behind the house. Burro Park overlook is on the far left.

While Charley was in Craig on business he went to visit with an old friend, who told him there was a guy in jail named Malcolm Campbell who was a carpenter. He had been put in jail for stealing money from his own friend. They made a deal, and Charley paid Malcom's bail and took him down to the ranch to work on the new house. Charley paid Malcolm's wages to his friend to repay the theft, and when the debt was paid off it was agreed that he would pay Malcolm directly.

Work on the house started and progressed rapidly. The frames were built for the foundation. Sand was mined from the river and hauled to the house site. A big wooden frame was built for mixing cement in. Tons of cement were mixed and poured by hand. Everybody worked. Even the kids mixed cement and carried lumber and nails to the carpenters. Evelyn was there for every nail that was pounded, many of them pounded by her. Malcolm grew moody and wearied of the hard work. Also, there were no wages. One day he was gone, and his big tracks showed in the dirt road all the way to Bear Valley. Work stopped on the new house. The basement was in, and a drain had been laid under the cement floor. The sunken windows were in as was the stairway and the outside door. The sub-floor of the house above was also put in, making the big basement dry and warm for winter.

Evelyn wrote to the Perry Mansfield school telling them the road was just too bad to go out and pick them up in a vehicle and it would be best if they just met at the Mantle summer camp on Blue Mountain and they agreed. Charley and the boys had been working hard at getting enough horses broke for the ladies to ride.

He felt that if he paired each girl up carefully with her horse there would be enough horses. The girls were bringing their own saddles and equipment.

The big afternoon arrived. Twelve young ladies landed at cow camp with screams and giggles enough to set the cattle running away wild eyed with their tails stuck high into the air. Charley had asked two young cowboys to help him. Boyd Walker and Cecil Connors were pleased to do it and never did ask for wages. They cooked huge stacks of buckskin and biscuits, along with water gravy for the girls for supper. Battered tin cups full of hot coffee hit the spot, too. Charley later told Evelyn, "They look like ladies, but they eat like a bunch of starved wolves." After supper Charley told them, "Find a sagebrush to roll out your sugans under, cause it's going to be a hard day tomorrow."

The girls were shocked. They had at least expected tents. The bathroom was anyplace they chose out in the darkness. They worried about rattlesnakes getting in bed with them and shrunk trembling under their covers at the howling of the coyotes. The cows bawled half the night looking for the calves they had lost in their flight to get away from the noisy girls. None of the girls slept much and at daylight the next morning they were called for breakfast, then told to roll up their stuff. Sleepily, they drank their coffee and choked down as much of the doughy pancake and buckskin as they could. Their morning hygiene facilities consisted of a bucket of cold water with a dipper and a wash basin beside it. A flour sack hung on a nail for drying off.

Then they heard the frantic jingling of a bell and saw a cloud of dust approaching from up the draw toward the corral. A large herd of running, romping horses materialized within the dust cloud, driven by a cowboy. The horses kicked, squealed and bit each other. The horse with the bell around his neck led the rest into the corral and the cowboy jumped off his horse and quickly shoved poles into place so they couldn't escape. They looked like horses from hell to the exhausted girls.

Charley told the girls to make a pile of things they wouldn't be needing today and prepare the stuff they wanted to carry with them today. They reminded him that no lunches had been packed. He replied there weren't any lunches, that only sissies carried lunches. There was a water hole or two they would stop to drink out of today, but they snuck down to the well, anyway and pulled up buckets of water to fill their canteens.

They heard a ruckus at the corral and saw that a cowboy had roped a big hairy legged horse that was having a fit on the end of the rope. His mouth was open, his tongue out, and his breath a hoarse rasp as the rope tightened around his neck as he sat back on it. Finally he leaped forward, the act of which loosened the rope around his neck so that he could get a breath of air. The cowboy then put a halter on him, maneuvered him out of the corral, and tied him up. Meanwhile, the other cowboy had roped and saddled his saddle horse, and got on him outside the corral. The horse bellered, jumped straight up in the air, then slammed his front feet into the ground and gave a great show of vicious horseflesh and heroic cowboy for the girls.

Boyd untied the big hairy-legged horse and handed the rope to Connors, who dallied the rope around his saddle horn and dragged the violently resisting horse up to the cabin and tied him to the hitch rack. They did this four more times until they got all the pack horses tied to the rail. Then Charley and the boys stuffed the girls' things into panniers, setting two of them behind each snorting horse. They scotched up a hind leg on each horse, making it impossible for the horse to refuse the panniers and loaded them up. The panniers were then lashed down so that they were almost like a part of the horse. Looking satisfied, the boys freed the horses' legs, left them tied to the hitch rack, and told the girls to go to the corral with their saddles, blankets and bridles. The girls looked pleadingly at their director, but she just smiled sweetly and reminded them that this was their adventure.

Charley took his saddle horse inside the corral and mounted up and asked which of the girls was a good rider? Four hands went up and he told them to step aside into a group. Then he asked, who was a beginning rider? Blushing furiously, two girls showed their hands. Charley then said, "Now you have all told me what kind of horse you are getting, so you have to live with it." Two more crossed over to the beginners group. The four girls that remained undeclared, fervently hoped for horses they could ride.

Expertly Charley roped four gentle horses, which Boyd and Connors then led to their riders, explaining that they should brush their horses' backs and bellies with a stick of dry, barkless sagebrush before they saddled them to get off all the burrs and caked dirt. They told each girl her horse's name.

Charley roped other horses, some of which he told the boys to take to the four undeclared riders. They helped each girl bridle her horse before leaving them to saddle up on their own. The other horses, Charley told the boys to tie outside the corral for now. When he finally finished there were six horses tied out there.

Charley and the boys tied up their own horses and went to help the four good riders saddle their mounts. Charley took the bridle from one of the girls, then walked up to the first horse on the right side and grabbed his ear. The horse squealed and threw a fit, but Charley twisted his ear until finally the horse stood spraddled out and rigid while Boyd bridled him. When Charley released his ear, the horse shook his head and walked off calmly behind Boyd. The girl bravely saddled her horse.

The next horse, a pretty sorrel, took the bridle easily, but when he led him up to his rider Connors hobbled his front feet before he directed the girl to saddle him. In a whisper he told her to go to the bathroom and get a big drink of water before mounting, because this was not an easy horse to get on and off of and it was gonna be a long day.

The next horse Charley approached lunged at him with his mouth wide open, teeth snapping. Charley passed him by. The next horse laid back on the rope around his neck until it seemed his head must pop off his neck. Charley kicked him in the belly and he lunged forward and stood trembling but quiet. Boyd and Charley had a low-voiced conference about him, and finally decided to use him because he was good at swimming. When Boyd delivered the horse to his rider he told her, "Never, ever tie this horse hard and fast. Just drop the reins when you get off."

The next horse calmly waited to be untied, turned around, then jerked his lead rope loose and took off at top speed toward the back of the pasture. The girls learned some brand new cuss words that they filed for future use around the school.

One more horse to get. Conference time. The bay has an eye out, but put him in the middle and he is good and steady on narrow trails. The black shies real bad, but is broke like a dream. That pretty little girl shouldn't be riding a one-eyed horse. She said she was a good rider. They brought the girl the horse that she named Black Beauty, although his real name was SOB. Charley told the girl about this horse's bad habit of jumping sideways quick and fast, or charging forward with no notice, over any strange sound. She assured him she could handle it.

Charley yelled to the girls to take one last trip to the bathroom, tie on their stuff, tighten their cinches, and mount up. While they were waiting the cowboys tied the head of each pack horse up short to the tail of another pack horse, making a caravan of the four, the front one to be led by one of the cowboys. The cowboys all mounted their horses first so they could take care of any problems the girls' horses might give. No problems. Charley was pleased at how well they had saddled and mounted. Connors took the hobbles off the sorrel and the horse walked calmly toward the others.

Charley told the girls to follow him, single file, being careful not to step on the heels of the horse ahead, and he started up the trail. The girls fell in behind, managing their horses well. Just as they got all lined out they heard a terrible racket behind them, and saw the four pack horses pitching and falling and bellowing with the girls' stuff while Boyd dragged the lead one along with the lead rope dallied to his saddle horn while Connors tried to encourage them from behind. The black horse leaped into a full run and the girl lost one rein. Charley yelled for the group to stop and took off hurtling through the sagebrush, shaking out his lariat rope as he raced at top speed. The black was fast, but Charley's horse was faster and he roped him and slowly eased him to a stop. The breathless, disheveled girl said, "Thank You. Let's tie my reins together so I won't lose one again." Charley admiringly said, "Girl, you can ride."

The girls rode along giggling and relaxed when all at once they came to the rim of Blue Mountain and looked off into the yawning depths of the canyons below. The trail had become rocky, steep, and narrow with protruding slab rocks and tree trunks grabbing at their legs. Refusing to show their fear by screaming they all settled firmly into their saddles and wondered if they could trust this bunch of mongrel horses to stay on their feet, let alone on the trail. Only the clicking of the horses hooves on the rocks could be heard. Rounding a sharp turn in the trail each girl was gripped by complete astonishment at the majesty that lay around them. Forgetting all fear and discomfort they rode the rest of the trail down the mountain and into Hells Canyon in a state of rapture. Charley stopped his horse in the bottom of Hells Canyon and asked them if they wanted to get off and lead their horses a bit to rest their legs. They all did, except the girl on the sorrel, who was determined not to be a bother by causing the cowboys to hobble her horse so she could get on and off.

After a short walk everybody mounted up again and to the girls' horror Charley took off at a body rattling trot down the canyon, motioning for them to follow. Chafed and stiff, it was pure torture, but at last they passed a cabin with a bunch of kids watching them go by, and soon after were unsaddling in a corral. Boyd and Connors herded the horses off somewhere, and Charley took the girls to the cabin and introduced them to his wife. What a lovely woman she seemed to be. She seemed perfectly content living here, deep in a remote canyon in a cabin with a dirt floor. Wonderful smells were coming from the cabin and a feeling of deep content blanketed the little home and everyone in it.

Evelyn directed the girls to the wash basin and towel, then told them to be seated. A long plank table with plank seats was set up under a tarp stretched over a framework of poles constructed as a shelter on the east side of the cabin in the shade of a cottonwood tree. Charley brought cups and a big pot of coffee, which they enjoyed while Evelyn and two young boys brought out plate after plate of wonderful food. There were roasting ears, green beans, squash, mashed potatoes, fresh hot rolls, milk gravy, and huge steaks. Softened yellow butter and big dishes of preserves were also on the table. A bucket of water with a dipper in it sat close by if they wanted a drink. They dug in and ate until they could eat no more. Then out came fat apple pies and more coffee.

The girls noticed that Evelyn had five children, including a toddler and a baby about a year old, and although still smiling graciously looked exhausted. Insisting that she sit down, they jumped up and cleared the table. Soon the dishes were clean, the dish towels hung to dry and the leftovers tucked up into the refrigerator, which was a small, cool cave overhanging the spring.

As the shadows started climbing up the cliffs, the girls found good level places to roll out their bed rolls in anticipation of crawling into them. The two boys and the girl of about six introduced themselves and asked if they would like to help milk the cows and do chores. They said sure and followed right along. Pat told one of them "I'm gonna let her calf suck until Brindle gives down her milk. When the calf starts slobbering, you know she has let down her milk and you pull the calf off and tie him up. I'll save him one teat." At the cue, the girl pulled back with all her mite, but couldn't budge the calf. Pat said, "Pull him off quick, or he is going to get all the milk." Two other girls jumped in to help and together they tugged until they popped the calf off the cow, dragged him to a post and tied him up. This was repeated for all four of the cows, as each of the children milked. When they finished milking, their buckets had great domes of foam-covered milk. They carried the milk to the house then returned to the corral. Potch stepped forward and commanded "Turn em loose!" The girls were delighted by the enthusiastic bunting and slobbering and obvious enjoyment as the calves got their supper.

Lonnie keeping his pet deer company, while she shares food with the chickens.

Feeling a light tapping on her arm, one of the girls looked down at Queeda who asked her if she wanted to gather the eggs? They all trooped to the chicken house. Stooping to go in, they found the hens already sitting on the roosts for the night. Queeda directed them to gather the eggs from the nests. A hen was sitting on one nest. Queeda said, "She'll peck you, but you gotta get the eggs." Having never been bitten by a chicken, the girls were reluctant, but not to be outdone by a six-year-old, they braved the grouchy hen's pecks and got the warm eggs from under her. Having very little daylight left, but determined to do her job, Queeda showed them well hidden nests in various bushes and under rock overhangs. She instructed them to gather all the eggs but one in each nest. That one egg they were to leave as a nest egg so the hens wouldn't abandon that nest and go hide out a new nest.

Navvy, the four-year-old, was in charge of gathering chips to start the morning fire. He was delighted to have the help and even directed them to bring in a couple of armloads of wood for the cook stove. He showed them some bark that had been removed from cedar trees and laid aside. He showed them how to ruffle up the bark until it was fine and fluffy. In the morning, a small bunch of that would be tucked under the kindling and lit.

Night had fallen and the moon was not up yet, but the millions of stars shining into the total darkness gave quite a lot of light. Finally, the exhausted girls were able to go to bed. That night they heard nothing and slept the sleep of sweet exhaustion.

In the morning they woke to the sound of running horses. Evelyn had a huge breakfast prepared of hot coffee, bacon, eggs, pancakes, and cool sweet milk. Everybody noticed right away that her pancakes were a lot lighter than

Girls from the Perry Mansfield school in Steamboat Springs ride the awesome canyons with Charley Mantle.

Charley's. However, for the rest of their week's adventure they would find him an excellent cook as he prepared pancakes, dutch oven biscuits, jerky gravy and fried steaks. They all learned right away to sneak a pancake and a piece of meat into their pocket for lunch, because otherwise lunch just didn't exist.

They saddled up and took to the trail down the Yampa River. All at once the trail was blocked by the river swirling in fast against the rocky cliff. Charley told them that they had to swim their horses to get into the next park, called Outlaw. He gave them a few instructions, mainly to hang on, took them up the river a little way then he and Boyd and Connors whooped and hollered behind the horses until they all jumped in, hitting deep water immediately. The horses were submerged all but their noses and paddled furiously to swim across the river. The girls clung desperately to them, especially when the drenched horses lunged up the bank on the opposite side of the river. The girls had their boots full of water and several of them got covered with sand as their horses rolled gleefully in great mounds of dry white sand.

They did some fishing every day and usually they caught quite a few, which Charley fried up for breakfast. One day Charley told them that today they had to fish for their supper. They did so poorly, however, that they had to eat canned sardines wrapped in a cold pancake. Each day was packed with fun for the city girls. They jumped up fawns still with their baby spots, chased half grown Canadian geese into the river and snuck off from the cowboys to swim nude. They rode their horses bareback, quit personal grooming, got sun-peeled faces and generally had the time of their lives. The dark canyon walls reared ever taller as they rode down the river on a usually nonexistent trail to Warm Springs. There they marveled at the roaring rapids of the river and drank and played in the fresh water of the warm springs surging down from Douglas Mountain. Finally they reached Steamboat Rock where the Yampa River joined the Green River. They visited briefly with the Chew family at Pool Creek, then rode home on what seemed a super easy trail, after the one they had been on along the river bottom.

On the last night they rode into the corrals at the ranch and regretfully unsaddled their horses. They told Evelyn all their wonderful adventures while they drank gallons of milk, ate corn on the cob, and slathered butter and preserves on slices of freshly baked bread. Friendships were formed that lasted a lifetime for these girls and for Charley and Evelyn. The next day the girls mounted their now-contrite horses and rode to summer camp where their director met them to take them out of this magical world they had been privileged to visit.

26

The Archaeologists, 1939-40

EVELYN WONDERED HOW SHE WOULD GET EVERYTHING DONE. There was still canning to do. She must get winter shoes for the children. They all needed winter clothes, too, and she would probably have to sew them. Winter supplies had to be purchased and brought in. Charley and Potch and Pat would be gathering the beef cattle and holding them someplace to get as fat as possible before trailing them to market, so they wouldn't be around to help. Winter wood needed to be brought in, but it could be cut later. Besides all this, Ed and Guy, Boyd Walker and Elbert his brother, and Cecil Connors were wanting Charley to go chase wild horses.

The teacher would be coming soon and the kids were like wild things. They needed to slow down and get prepared to change their life style for school. Luckily, it was Florence's sister, Katharine that was coming. If she was anything like Florence she could handle the school. Evelyn did have to go clean and dust the school house, though and air out the bedding Florence had used. The shelves and dishes had to be cleaned as well and she would need some fire wood stacked by the school house door, too.

To her surprise one day Boyd showed up and started working like a wild man to get all the work caught up. It was not at all like him, but she sure wasn't going to look a gift horse in the mouth. He took special interest in getting the school house ready "for them little kids."

One day Lou Sebaum showed up driving a second-hand Chevrolet pickup. He got out, and said, "Evelyn, here is your new pickup. I been looking for one for you, and this one is a dandy. Charley can just pay me next time he is in town." Evelyn was speechless with delight. Lou lifted the hood and told her what everything did, and how to fix it. He had even brought her a spare tire, along with a jack and pump and a package of patches thrown in. He spent the night, and the next morning Boyd took Henry to the head of the canyon and pulled them out. Evelyn had decided to go ahead and buy winter supplies since she had to take Lou to Craig anyway. He coached her as they went, but found her to be a good driver. She went to the court house next day, got her driver's license and registered the pickup. The five kids were having the time of their life, eating ice cream and riding in the pickup.

Evelyn was lucky enough to find shoes for the whole family in Craig. She bought material to make clothes from. She bought a winter coat for Potch, as he was the only one who didn't get hand-me-downs. Then she went to Mount Harris and bought the winter supplies. She stopped at Dick Toole's gas station to gas up and show him her new pickup. He was so excited he gave her a big hug, and had his wife, Maude come right down to see, too. The two of them had spent many days with Charley and Evelyn fishing and visiting. He threw in two five gallon gas cans, several cans of oil, and some brake fluid. He also promised her that next year he was going to bring in a county bulldozer and make a new road out of Hells Canyon around a gentler grade so she wouldn't have to have Henry pull her out every time she came to town. Worried about her driving home alone with five little kids, they insisted she spend the night. The next day was Saturday, so Dick closed the station and drove his pickup in behind her as far as the head of Hells Canyon. He watched her until she reached the bottom of the canyon, shook his head in wonder, and waved goodbye.

Katharine knew the Mantles only through her sister, Florence, and stories her dad told. Evelyn and the children met her at the door with huge smiles on their faces. The children helped carry her things to her new home in the school house. Evelyn had a big supper ready, and Katharine immediately felt at home. The two older boys liked her in spite of the fact that she was a teacher and was going to keep them inside a lot.

Boyd rode down often from Red Rock ranch where he was living. It was soon obvious to Evelyn and Charley that he was sweet on Katharine. He was too shy and gruff to ever let her know, though, so the romance never blossomed.

On one of his frequent trips, Boyd got trapped by Evelyn into helping build an outhouse. They located it a good distance away and down wind from the house. Boyd dug a deep pit, only just big enough at the top for the job it had to do. The earth mustn't be disturbed too much so the structure would have a solid foundation. It was only a one-seater, made of scrap logs from a driftwood pile. Boyd artfully fitted two bowed logs into place to leave an eye level peep hole in the direction of the path. The door opened away from the path so you could sit and enjoy the view with the door open if you chose. He searched out a flat rock for a step outside the door, reasoning that the boys and Queeda needed a step. All finished, he went to the cabin and asked Evelyn for an old catalog, put it in the new outhouse, and proudly stepped back to survey his work. About that time Katharine came along and exclaimed grandly over his work. It just didn't get any better than that!

On New Years day 1939 Charles Scoggin and his assistant, Ed Lohr, drove in. The Mantles were shocked to see anybody this time of year. Scoggin told them that he had finally gotten funding from the University of Colorado for the archaeological project and they had come to start work. He asked if they could camp somewhere near water with some shelter, like maybe an overhanging cliff. They did better than that, offering them the basement of the new house. It had a roof over it and a stove so they would be comfortable during the cold winter. They gratefully accepted and moved in. The Mantle kids were elated. It was the first time they had ever had neighbors, and Evelyn had to keep a watchful eye that they were not up bothering the men all the time.

Scoggin walked the length and breadth of Castle park, photographing, mapping, sketching petroglyphs, examining caves and overhangs and noting anything of archaeological interest. When they were not in school, Potch and Pat, showed him caves and petroglyphs he never dreamed were there and showed him how to get into them. He walked the canyons and the benches next, making a complete archaeologic survey. Scoggin and Ed ate many meals with the Mantles. They also gave the men all the meat, milk, and eggs they could eat. Evelyn was the best cook they had ever known, and they craved the company, so they spent almost all their spare time with the Mantles. In return they cut wood, helped butcher, and did anything else that needed doing. They loved to sit and listen to Charley spin yarns. Ed Lewis and Guy spent some time with them, too; both told of ancient Indian habitations they had seen in other canyons in Utah and Wyoming, and embellished what they had seen enough to make the two archaeologists' mouths water.

Evelyn was so fascinated with the archaeology of the area that she had to be very careful to not appear too interested in the men. Charley was a little jealous of the attention she gave them, and the two guys obviously enjoyed talking to her and showing her things they found. She devoured any literature they gave her. They also never tired of the many artifacts that she had found and preserved in a box and that she let them look at and touch and analyze to their heart's content. There were spear and arrow heads, an arrow, a cedar bark bag, reed mat, a goat horn with a hole in it for pealing arrows, and many other things. She had a collection of big dished out grinding rocks and the round stones for grinding the grain in them. The archaeologists went out every month for the mail. When they did Scoggin would bring something back for the family, usually calling for a celebration.

School election time arrived in February. Not much snow had fallen, so the road could be travelled. It had been ever more difficult for the Mantles to get their school funded with books and other necessary items because the officers of the school board all lived in the Three Springs district. Although there were no students in the district now, they kept control by outnumbering the two Mantle votes. This year Evelyn loaded her pickup with qualified voters, got Boyd with Henry the horse to pull her out of the canyon and set off for the elections, picking up Shorty Chambers along the way. Katherine, Scoggin, Ed, Shorty, Evelyn and Charley outnumbered the four from Blue Mountain and Evelyn was voted in as the new secretary of the school board. She needed to be bonded, so she and Katharine set out for Craig, where Katherine's Uncle Waller Barnes posted her bond. Now she knew how much money there was available for their school and where the money was spent because she kept the books and had a strong say in how money and materials were distributed.

Before spring even broke Johnny Milheim came in to hew and shape the big logs and construct the walls, rafters, and roof of the new house, which was going to be finished this year! On weekends and after hours Scoggin and Ed helped. Ed Lewis and Guy were called away on "urgent" business elsewhere when all this work began. Boyd still hung around and helped until Katharine finished school and went home.

Early in the spring Hugo Rodeck hiked in. He was Scoggin's boss and curator of the Archaeology Museum at the University of Colorado. The good news was that he had received funding to excavate a cave in the area. He studied the work Scoggin had done and did an extensive comparison of Marigold and Mantle Caves to decide which one to excavate. The better of the two they decided was Mantle Cave because it was easier to access. He wanted them to start immediately. Elated, Scoggin set out for Boulder to obtain supplies, promising to be right back. Charley assured them they could continue to live in the basement for the summer.

One bright spring day Evelyn asked Boyd to fill the wash boiler with water and build a fire under it. He also filled the barrel beside it with creek water. It was time to do the spring wash. She was very grateful for Boyd, because usually she had to carry the water and build the fire herself. She had done only small amounts of wash all winter, and now winter clothes and blankets needed to be washed and put away. She also got Boyd and Charley to take the washing machine out to the water barrel. She emptied a half can of Lye into the water in the boiler to "break" it, which meant that a scum rose to the top as the water heated. The scum consisted of all the water hardening minerals in the creek water. She would skim off that scum, leaving softened water that would get the clothes clean and white. Evelyn loved her washing machine, and trusted nobody to service it but herself. She practically took it apart and put it back together, cleaning and oiling each part. Then she filled it with gas and oil, removed the cloth between the rubber ringers, and carefully washed them.

Dinner time! Evelyn fed everyone the delicious stew she had been cooking on the back of the stove since the day before, with huge slices of homemade bread with butter and jam. Katharine said she would wash dishes and take the kids back to school, including Tim, so Evelyn could wash. Huge stacks of dirty clothes were separated by color and degree of dirtiness. Evelyn filled the washing machine with hot water, shaved some homemade soap into it, and started the engine. When she pulled the lever to engage the agitator the soap and hot water made a beautiful cap of snowy white foam. She dropped in dish towels, hand towels and Charley's white shirts. She had soaped the collars and cuffs first with the bar of handmade soap. While they were washing she placed two tubs on flat tree stumps on either side of the wringer. One she filled with a little hot water, and enough cold water to make it luke warm. The other she filled with cold water.

When the load of clothes was clean she stopped the agitator, turned on the wringer. The clothes were then run through the wringer and into the warm tub. About that time Charley came to help. He dunked and stirred the clothes to get the soap out of them. Then he ran them through the ringer into the cold tub, rinsing them again, then he ran them through the ringer into a basket. Meantime, Evelyn had loaded the next batch into the washer. It was shirts,

Laundry day in the early spring.

underwear, night clothes, and her dresses. Charley draped all the wet clothes over brush in the bright sunshine to dry. Next came sox and overalls. There were several loads of each selection. As the wash water became dirty and dark, and the rinse water sudsy, Evelyn changed the water This huge washing had taken all afternoon and it was growing dark. The clothes were left out overnight to dry. From the clear blue sky there was no danger of rain.

Katharine took Boyd aside and told him she thought Evelyn needed a clothes line and could he perhaps make one? Bright and early the next morning he came riding in dragging two sturdy pealed poles. He planted the poles deep, tamped them solid and even watered them in. Then he stretched a forty foot wet rawhide string between them. As the rawhide dried it tightened to a really fine clothesline. Katharine exclaimed grandly over it. Boyd grinned, hung his head and spurred some rocks, basking in the praise.

It had been a hard year for Katharine to teach because of all the interesting distractions to the children. She was pleased and relieved when all the children passed the final exams easily. Potch and Pat passed to sixth grade, while Queeda passed to third. Lonnie was told he passed, too, and his little chest swelled with pride. As Henry pulled Uncle Waller's Pickup out of the canyon carrying Katharine away, all the little Mantle faces were sad. Especially Queeda, because Katharine was as near a sister as she would ever have. They had spent time together picking flowers, hunting pretty rocks, and talking.

The Perry Mansfield plans to make another trip that summer fell through. Charley and Evelyn had been counting on the money and wondered if they could finish the house without it. The impending war was changing many people's plans.

As the summer of 1939 approached, a letter arrived from Eva saying they could not come out that year, but would surely come the summer of 1943. Evelyn sent a letter back immediately, insisting that they promise in writing that they would come in the summer of 1943. Eva promised, but with the reservation that "Who knows but what we will be at war on our own soil by then."

The summer brought a bumper crop of fruit from the new orchard. Evelyn canned everything as it ripened. The ever-nearer war was causing plans to be made to ration food, clothes and gas. Sugar would be hard to get soon, so she canned while it was plentiful. She stocked up on tin canning cans, and jar caps.

Henry horse pulling Katherine's pickup out of Hells Canyon.

She also bought all the half gallon jars she could get.

Scoggin returned from the university, and he and Ed set to work excavating the cave, which was a mile walk every day. Charley offered them horses, but they preferred to walk, although they did accept the use of a pack horse to carry in their supplies. It was tedious work, gently brushing and sifting tons of dirt to reveal anything that might lie under the surface. They found many things, among them a set of white flint ceremonial knives, a flicker feather head dress, mats, sinew for sewing, fiber ropes, bone needles and fish hooks. They found squash rinds and seeds and kernels of corn in covered storage pits fashioned of slab rock. Each day it seemed brought a new and exciting discovery.

There was a continuous flow of university people and Dinosaur Monument personnel all summer. All were very excited about what the excavation would reveal. The men worked industriously, but the one thing they couldn't resist was when Potch and Pat would show up and invite them to go swimming with them. The cool river water washed away the sweat and dirt and loneliness. They spent delicious minutes lying on the sand bar in the sun while the two boys buried them in sand or played checkers in the sand with them. There was the ever-present trot line to check, too, sometimes yielding a fish

Charles Scoggin, archaeologist from the University of Colorado on the right, with his assistant Ed Lohr.

supper. Scoggin spent hours in the evening playing with the children and visiting with Charley and Evelyn.

The radio blared the presidential election year campaign talks. Clowning around as they excavated the cave, Scoggin would take the part of Franklin Roosevelt and Ed would be Wendell Wilke. Working at opposite ends of the cavern, the cliffs would magnify their mock impassioned campaign speeches as they hurled political threats, promises and accusations at each other. The radio also carried ominous news of the accelerating war in Europe. It sounded like the United States would be in it soon. Both these young men were draft age and knew they would be among the first to go.

The new house progressed rapidly. Evelyn supervised every nail, log and shingle, and roll of roofing, much to Johnny's amusement. They were great friends and enjoyed working together. Charley helped when he could, but was very busy with the hay crops and the livestock. Under Johnny's supervision, Evelyn built the frames for the windows and doors. Once again she became thin and gaunt from over work. Most of all, she was frantic at the thought of having any more babies. She had hoped to move into the new house this year, but it just wasn't going to be ready. Maybe they would move in anyway and do the finishing work while they lived in the house.

Regretfully, Scoggin and Ed wrapped up their work and returned to the University of Colorado for the fall semester. All the Mantles had heavy hearts at losing their friends. There was nothing sure that they would ever see Scoggin again. They loved him so much.

27

A New House, 1941

WO ARTICLES BY JACK HOWELL had appeared in the December 1940 and January 1941 issues of *Western Sportsman* with pictures and stories of the canyon lands of Dinosaur Monument. It described awesome canyons inhabited by ferocious, stalking mountain lions, and it told of the family who lived there in the unconquered wilderness. People from all over the United States, including a few local people "discovered" the Mantle family at that point. It was the beginning of a trying time for the Mantles, as tourists began to arrive, intruding on their privacy and work time.

Charley had been suffering with a bad case of hemorrhoids for quite some time. It had become a critical problem and he now badly needed surgery. However, he said they couldn't afford it because they needed too many other things. He was thin and haggard and in much pain.

Their dear friend Johnny Milheim had a terrible car accident. He was driving and had run into a bridge. Two people were killed, another might not live, and Johnny himself was in critical condition with a crushed pelvis, broken arm, and a broken leg. He would be unable to work on the house for some time.

Although unfinished, Charley and Evelyn made the decision to move into the new house anyway. They had hardly any furniture, but could make do. Evelyn wanted to leave the livestock where they were. There would be somebody there every day since school would be in session, and the outbuildings and corrals at the new house were not yet finished. The new place was relatively close; about half a mile, it would be easy to take care of everything where they were.

The move was a very traumatic time for the children. They loved their home and couldn't imagine moving into that big lonely house set out in the flats, with not even a cliff behind it! All their friends, the chickens, cows, horses, and pet rabbits were being left behind. It was some comfort that the cat got to go and Evelyn said they could even let the dogs in the house on occasion.

Trip after trip with the pickup finally got all the essential things moved. They were set up so they could be comfortable. The house seemed hollow and lonely, though, because it was so big but things changed when the cook stove got moved and put together. Evelyn cooked a big meal and they all sat togeth-

The new house. Note the big basement where the archaeologists lived.

er at the table and enjoyed the moment. Charley told stories and they all laughed. Each one of the kids got to talk, too, just as long as they didn't interrupt somebody else, or talk with their mouth full. When they could talk about it they didn't feel so lonely leaving their old home.

A big worry had beset Queeda quite some time ago and now it was about to happen. The move to the new house had begun. Her mother was very excited for her because Queeda now had her own room. To this little girl who had always lived and slept among so many people, this was a terrifying thought. She thought she would have to sleep, eat, and keep house in that room all alone and wouldn't be a part of the family any more. She became quiet and withdrawn and saddened as she considered what a lonely outcast she would be. Being the only girl, you got left out of most things anyway, but now it would be more so and she couldn't bear it. She crept away by herself, hiding away in the bushes and small caves to cry. Reluctantly, she helped with the move. She got Navvy to say he wouldn't sleep any place but with her and moved into the room with her. Tim got to join them frequently, too. Her door was always open and she got to eat with the rest of the family; maybe it was all going to work out! It sure wasn't as great as their old house, though.

The two older boys had their own room in the basement. Their bed in the bunkhouse had been a wooden frame nailed to the wall and couldn't be moved. They gladly rolled out their bedrolls on the cement floor like real cowboys. They managed to sneak the two dogs, Roughy and Kelly, in to sleep with them at night.

Evelyn had gone to the county superintendent early in the year to ask for a teacher. Opal I. Bennet had been assigned to them. When the time came to pick up the teacher Evelyn drove out to meet her. Opal Bennett complained the whole trip in about the road and the dust. When she met the smiling children, she coldly announced that they were to always call her Miss Bennet. It was not going to be a pleasant school year, but this teacher had come highly praised for her teaching ability. Evelyn hoped it would work out. She was afraid Miss Bennett would not thrive, living alone at the school house, so she moved her into the basement of the new house.

Evelyn cleaned and put away things at the old homestead as she always had. The kids were more content at school with Miss Bennet, knowing their mother was nearby. She cleaned the chicken house, carefully piling the manure for next spring, Then holding her breath and dashing outside when she needed to breathe, she applied a very thin stream of nicotinic acid the length of each roost and in each nest. She did this periodically to kill all the mites and fleas and lice chickens always had. She also went down into the spider web infested potato pit and raked the floor and swept the walls and ceiling. She put fresh straw in the bottom to get ready for the potatoes that would soon be harvested.

Next she cleaned out the food cellar. There were always a few cans and jars, the contents of which were spoiled that had to be taken out and the contents buried. She thought of the time Charley took a can of spoiled corn out to bury it, and fed it to the chickens instead. There had been dead chickens everywhere. Since that she always buried the spoiled canned food herself.

Last spring Charley had made some chokecherry wine. Apparently something went wrong with his recipe because right after sealing the wine and storing the bottles in the cellar they were awakened by what sounded like gun shots in the night. Jumping up to investigate, sneaking quietly through the darkness, following the sound, they were led nearer and nearer to the cellar. Finally Charley stood in front of the cellar door and said he expected his wine was exploding and they couldn't go look until it stopped or they would get full of glass. Finally the next day the activity in the cellar stopped and Charley went to look over the damage. Bottles had exploded and scattered glass all over the shelves and food. Many broken bottle necks had been embedded in the ridge logs overhead and just hung there. Charley picked up some of the glass, but Evelyn picked up the rest, prying the bottle necks out of the ceiling, then moved the canned goods and washed the sticky shelves.

In the cellar there were the never-ending spider webs to sweep down. Once she had seen a garter snake in the rafters of this windowless place, so she hated cleaning it. She lined the squash and apple bins with fresh straw. She brought in fresh dry sand for the boxes that the carrots and turnips and beets would be stored in. When they were not in school the children all helped with these jobs, laughing and teasing all the while. It was their job to get this work done, and it was very important, but that didn't mean they couldn't have fun while they did it.

Before he was injured in the automobile accident, Evelyn had asked Johnny to partition off a back room in the basement of the new house. Here, she built sturdy shelves and would at last have a nice, clean, dry place to store supplies. It took all summer to complete the move to the new house.

As fall approached, there was much to be done. Evelyn and the kids harvested the root crops and winter squash and put them in the cellar. Charley came home from gathering the beef steers and helped them plow out the potatoes, gather them up and put them in the potato pit. Apples and pears were picked and stored away. Evelyn buried the cabbage upside down in a protected place. They cut the corn stocks and shocked them for winter feed for the milk cows and chickens. Later they would have to move it where the deer couldn't get to it.

As soon as Evelyn got time, she worked on her "secret" project, which involved building a huge wooden box, thirty inches wide by forty inches long by thirty inches deep, with a hinged lid. When she had finished she and Charley put it inside a closet in a basement bedroom. She piled quilts and a feather tick on it, concealing it so well that even the children didn't know it was there.

The Mantles often stopped at the Cross Mountain store to buy a few things and also to spend the night. They would order winter supplies in Mount Harris and have them shipped as far as Cross Mountain, then haul them the rest of the way home in the wagon. The people there had a separate room they used as a store room, which made it a good place to stop on the way home. Things were going badly for the people who ran the store, however, and they finally made plans to leave. The Cross Mountain Dam had not materialized, and business at their store was not enough to keep them going. She had an upright piano that Evelyn enjoyed playing when she was there. The lady wouldn't be able to move the piano when they relocated, and asked Evelyn if she would be interested in buying it. Evelyn could barely contain her eagerness and they made a deal on the spot.

Charley was less than excited about the piano. It was just irritating noise to him. However, after much grumbling he finally paid for it since Evelyn had made a commitment. At the same time the people sold them their beautiful big oak dining room table and eight chairs. The table had so many leaves that it would easily expand enough to seat the whole family and then some. Evelyn's dream of having furniture she could polish was nearly realized. Now all she had to do was get it home.

The groceries and supplies they had ordered finally arrived and the team and wagon were waiting to take them on the forty mile trip home. There was enough room on the load for the piano, but not the dining room set. Charley got the delivery driver and his friend, plus the man from the store to help him, and they laid the piano down on its back in the wagon. Evelyn sobbed, "The piano will be ruined. Set it upright." They did, but there was just nothing to set it against to steady it for the ride. Finally Charley talked the two delivery men into going with him to steady the piano. He would bring them right back out when he came to pick up the dining room set and salt and cottonseed cake. They had always heard about the wild, beautiful canyon home of these people and so readily agreed.

They found a strong plank and after much discussion found a way to lash it to the sides of the rack on the wagon so that it formed a secure back brace for the piano. They then lashed the piano to it under Evelyn's watchful eye, so it was firm but not scratched. Off they went with the two men sitting primly on the piano bench with their hands firmly on either side of the piano to prevent it from tipping or bouncing. Evelyn sat on the wagon too, watching closely to see that her piano wasn't scratched. Charley had never driven so carefully, nor had it ever seemed so far. He rough locked the wheels of the wagon until the horses could only move it at a creep down the switch backs. It was an enormous test of the strength and endurance of the men to hold the piano upright on the wagon. The trip down into Hells Canyon was the greatest test, but the men were true heroes and all went perfectly well except for one deep lariat rope scar in the piano finish. The tired men were rewarded with a huge supper and soft beds. Evelyn sat down to her piano and played a few of the songs she remembered from her childhood in New York. The next day the men were shown the best fishing holes, and their fish got served in a big cele-bration feast that night. They felt that the grueling trip had been well worth it.

True to his word, Charley took the men back to Cross Mountain to their truck. He caught a ride with them to Craig where he bought rock salt, cottonseed cake and a little grain. The delivery truck delivered him and his purchases to Cross Mountain and the driver helped him load everything on his freight wagon, along with the dining room table and eight chairs. Driving along home, chewing and spitting, he got to thinking how much easier life had been without that big old house. He sure did have a happy wife, though, and that was worth a lot. Life could be a whole lot easier if the road ever got finished.

28

The Road is Finally Finished, 1941

NE SATURDAY AROUND THE LAST OF SEPTEMBER the roar of heavy equipment rumbled through Hells Canyon. Charley saddled up and went to see what was going on. There was Dick Toole on a huge Moffat County bulldozer ready to knock a new road out of the east side of Hells Canyon onto the bench above. All he needed was to have a route mapped out for him to follow. Evelyn soon drove up with all the kids and together they searched out a route for the road. To get an acceptable grade, it would have to be bulldozed dangerously close to the edge of the cliff overhanging Hells Canyon. Solid, protruding ledge rock would have to be dynamited in several places. Dick had the dynamite, so he and Charley set the charges off one by one. When it looked like it might make a passable road, but far from a smooth one, Dick mounted his dozer and started work. Teetering on the edge of huge loosened rocks, lunging into holes left by uprooted cedar trees and judging the edges within inches when dumping buckets of debris, Dick maneuvered the huge, wonderful machine. By Sunday afternoon it was roughly finished. The grade was easy and the road wide enough so that there was little danger one would spin out and fall off the edge onto the canyon floor far below. Now it would be just crowbar and shovel work, which Charley assured Dick he would get some help to finish off the road before it snowed. The Mantles were very grateful to this wonderful friend, and also to Moffat County for probably not noticing the bulldozer was in use that weekend.

When Evelyn drove out for the first time it seemed to her that Henry horse had a big smile on his face. No longer did he have to pull her and the pickup up that hill. She drove right out of the canyon without his help. Charley rode over from summer camp and joined her in Bear Valley, then the whole family went to Craig. Charley bought quite a load of cottonseed cake and oats. He also bought a sack of wheat for the chickens. It looked like they were going to have to make two trips anyway, so he bought a bunch of rock salt to finish out the second load. They spent the night in Craig with old friends Roy and Thelma Grounds. Roy said he had wanted to come down all summer but hadn't been able to make it, so why didn't he just haul in that extra load as an excuse to go. He had heard about the new road from Dick, and was anxious to try it out. The Mantles were glad for him to come and loaded his pickup. Potch and Pat and Roy's son Don piled in with Roy and they went on down ahead of the Mantles. They spent a couple of days fishing, eating fruit out of the orchard, and enjoying the beautiful quiet place.

Charley and Evelyn shopped for their winter supplies. Evelyn had ordered winter coats, shoes, long underwear, sox and flannel sheets from Montgomery Ward and they had already arrived in the mail. She had also ordered flannels and cotton and wool materials to sew into clothes for her family. She shopped for thread and darning cotton. Charley got two pair of new Levis. Cowboy fashion dictated that they had to be four inches too long to allow a four inch cuff to be turned up on the outside. He also bought each of the older boys a pair of Levis.

Charley carefully selected a piece of thick, partially tanned cow hide to make shoe and boot soles of. They had a set of shoe lasts at home and as the family shoes wore out Charley would resole them at least once. He also bought heel caps.

After all this shopping was finished they went to Mount Harris, an old coal mining town a few miles east of Craig, and loaded up with a large supply of groceries. They only shopped for groceries once a year, so the pickup was stacked high. How nice it was to have the new storage room. They decided to spend the night with Walt Hammond, a friend who was the post master in Craig, and get an early start the next day. Walt asked Charley why he didn't learn to drive now that he had a pickup. Charley replied that "The SOB don't look where it's goin' and it don't neck rein."

When Evelyn got home with the year's supplies that fall she stacked the sugar in her big wooden box. Rationing was in effect on some items to help with the war effort. It was against the law to have an extra supply of rationed items on hand. It was hoarding and punishable as a federal offense. There was no other way for her to have what she needed on hand other than to buy it all at once with her allotted stamps for the year. Nevertheless, she didn't want some government agent stopping by and seeing all that sugar and getting wrong ideas. Evelyn was such an honest person that she felt like a criminal doing this, and knew her face would show it if there was any question ever raised.

A couple of years before, the Dinosaur National Monument had been closed to hunting and guards placed around the rim to enforce the law. Everyone was aware, so the fall meat had to be gotten more carefully than usual. It was too early to butcher a beef and Charley would be damned if he was going to feed those bucks all summer and then not eat some of them when he needed them. The meat was brought in and half was canned. They had made jerky during the summer. The beef steers were trailed out and sold. Around Christmas, Charley weaned the calves and placed the cattle where they all had water and feed. They were as ready as they could get for the winter.

The usual wild horse chase took place. The men planned and built wild horse traps, toughened up their saddle horses and all had that special sparkle of anticipation in their eyes that only the hunt for wild horses put there. The big day came, and was a great success. They cut the little studs and bobbed their tails to show that they had been done. The few colts that had flaws were sold and most of the fully developed young horses were kept out to break, leaving only a few fillies to maintain the herd size. It was Charley's year to get Pearl's colt. She was a classy little three-year-old bay filly that he named Rambler. He planned to break her that winter. Rambler would prove to be the seed for possibly the greatest bucking horses ever produced.

Winter at the ranch was long and you needed a good supply of people food, as well as grain and cottonseed cake for horses, chickens and milk cows. Thanksgiving was the time to butcher a beef because it would stay frozen until mid-February. Charley usually gave a quarter to the Morgans or Gadds, or whoever the Mantles stayed with when they went to town. They often traded fruit during the summer for a hog to butcher when winter started. The pork would also stay frozen, but needed to be eaten before mid-February.

Miss Bennet did a good job teaching the children, but they didn't enjoy the learning as much as they had in the past. Navvy started with great enthusiasm, but soon lost interest in Miss Bennet's teaching. He was only five, however, and was allowed to quit. Tim was very pleased to have him back, and the two of them played school.

Back in February 1941 Scoggin wrote that he had been hired by Dinosaur National Monument as a park ranger for the summer. In that capacity he was to ground survey the rest of the monument for archaeological sites and artifacts. He had a horse that he would be riding and promised to come see them first thing. Sure enough, just as spring broke on the mountain, he rode his horse down the now nearly impassable trail off the side of Roundtop Mountain. He rested for awhile at Red Rock, then rode on to the Mantle Ranch, arriving at almost dark. It was a grand reunion and the children got him up before daylight the next day.

For a whole day Scoggin and his horse rested. Then Charley asked him if he would like to see Schoonover. He said yes. They saw Schoonover, all right, but Charley hadn't told him they would be roping, throwing, and dehorning a bunch of wild yearling steers. Scoggin was beat up and tired but could still grin and say, that rangers ought to get paid double for that kind of work. Always conscientious and disciplined about his commitments, Scoggin began work immediately on his job.

When school was out in the spring the two older boys begged to ride with Scoggin and accompanied him all over the monument, climbing into every cave and hidden park. Queeda wanted to go, too, and cried secretly, because you weren't supposed to let anybody see you cry. Every day she would ride Mousey to the limits she was allowed to go, hoping to catch a glimpse of them. She had all the chores to do and never got to do the fun things boys got to do!

Every morning and every night it was Queeda's job to round up the milk cows, bring them home and milk them. Her companion in doing this job was her beloved small white horse, Mousey, who had started out a flea-bitten gray with lovely steel gray legs, but time had turned him white all over. She always rode him bareback and nearly always at a dead run.

It was spring, the Yampa River was running high and when the river was high a whole lot of debris floated down it. This debris was deposited along the bank at every curve the river took, and was referred to as drift wood piles. It was great fun to see what sort of treasures the river had carried into these drift wood piles. There could be cans, buckets, dolls, balls, animal parts, chairs, furniture parts, boots, boards, etc. Mousey and Queeda would make a pass by a couple of drift wood piles each morning on the way to get the cows.

One morning Queeda saw a mass of something brown and sodden lying in a crevice in the top of the pile. Curious, she dismounted

Charley with his pistol strapped on and Queeda mounted on her beloved Mousey.

and climbed over the wet bunch of debris to see what it was. It was a huge brown bird, apparently dead. His head was not visible, nor his feet. She lifted him so she could see what sort of bird it was. He moved ever so slightly, so she knew he was alive. She could see his huge beak and knew it was an eagle! She folded his wings and held up his drooping head, and clutched his feet in her hand, cradling him in her arms. She climbed back to the dry sandy bank. The big bird weighed almost nothing, and was obviously near death. She had to help him!

The cows had to be brought in before any nursing could begin, so Mousey and Queeda raced on down the river and brought the cows home a whole lot faster than Evelyn would have liked. The cows hurried on home, and Queeda jumped off Mousey to get the eagle. A quick check of the eagle proved him still alive, so she tenderly tucked him under her arm and led Mousey to a big rock from which to mount. Mousey realized she intended to carry that big eagle on him, so just as Queeda got in position to mount he took off for home full speed without her.

Queeda carried the pitiful eagle home and into the kitchen. Evelyn didn't even scold her about running the cows or letting her horse come home empty and scaring her to death. She took one look at the eagle's water soaked feathers, drooping head and defeated eyes. She got a big towel and wrapped the eagle in it and laid him tenderly by the stove.

Later, after chores were done and breakfast eaten Evelyn and Queeda took on the task of saving that eagle's life. His feathers were nearly dry. He could hold up his head, almost, and his eyes had a wary look. Queeda held him on her lap while Evelyn spooned a little warm broth down his throat. His once powerful beak was easy to open. His huge talons were powerless. Every half hour they repeated the feeding. Finally he stood up shakily. Then he began to hiss at them when they came near. He didn't want the fingers-on-the beak feeding any more and struggled against it. He began to look stately and proud and his feathers took on the golden sheen of a golden eagle.

Lonnie came in with a small fish he had caught for Eagle, as his name now was. He cut it into small pieces and Eagle greedily gulped it down. The endless job of getting enough to eat for Eagle had begun. Tim, Lonnie and Queeda caught mice, fished, snared birds, and even caught lizards for Eagle. He lived in a shelter made of sticks and saddle blankets out by the apple cellar. He didn't seem to have any broken bones, just very severely sprained wings and legs. They speculated and concocted possibilities of how he could have fallen into the river, gotten mixed up in the driftwood and been carried far down the river. The kids had never seen a golden eagle before. He was such a noble, aloof fellow that they were fascinated by him.

He walked with a hop when he came out. Finally after about a week he began to straighten out and walk better and flap his wings to exercise them. He was ravenous all the time, and ate anything that was brought to him in the line of meat. Evelyn began to fear for the chickens as he roamed farther and farther from his cave. He got heavier. There came a time when they couldn't heft him any more to see how heavy he had become because he would back up on his tail and stick his talons out front and make rude noises warning them to respect his space. Eagle never harmed any of them. He enjoyed their company and graciously accepted their food. He would eat it in the company of the children, rather than carrying it off to eat alone. Queeda felt honored to be his friend and to be allowed to sit by his side while he enjoyed his meals. His wings were becoming strong, and he didn't limp any more. He was beautiful and gleaming gold. His dark eyes were lively. One morning Queeda went to see Eagle, and discovered he was gone. Not a trace of him did they ever see again. They believed he flew back up the river and joined his eagle family, wherever they were.

Evelyn had always wanted bees. Now she had a good excuse because sugar rationing was in effect. She went to Jensen one day and went to visit Ross Snow, Hilda Morgan's brother, who directed her to where she could buy some bees and bought four hives of bees that same day. She had been studying for quite some time how to care for bees, but none of the instructions told what a problem it would be to get the bees home in a bumpy pickup. Johnny had gone with her and the two of them were enjoying their ride home when all at once Evelyn saw a cloud of bees through the rear window. She slammed on the brakes and both of them jumped out of the pickup wringing their hands in anguish. All that preparation and they had lost the bees. A steady stream of bees flew into a hive that had lost the plug in its entry way. Evelyn poured a thin stream of corn syrup that was their supplemental food in front of the opening and the rest of the bees returned to the hive. Evidently they had just escaped when she saw them and hadn't wanted to leave their queen.

Firmly plugging the hole, they drove on. Johnny was watching and all at once yelled for her to stop. The bees had escaped again. This time they were not friendly and Evelyn and Johnny had several stings apiece by the time they got them back in their hive. This time they pushed and stacked building supplies they had purchased tight up around each hive. Then they wedged the hives tight among all that padding and lashed them together so they couldn't move. Johnny rode in the back all the way home watching for escaping bees, but this time there were none.

When they got home Evelyn and Johnny unloaded the bee hives in a protected place in the new orchard. Evelyn decided to check and see how they stood the trip. For his part, though, Johnny said, he'd had all the bees he wanted and suggested to Evelyn that she check them out while he, Charley and the kids got supper. Evelyn was excited as she put on her long sleeved shirt and loose pants tied at the shoe tops, and slipped down over her shoulders with the netting hanging from a wide brimmed hat. She put on her wide cuff canvas gloves. Next she filled a smoke pot with a long spout with oil and lighted it, making a great cloud of smoke. She could reduce the flow of smoke through the spout or increase it as needed to control the bees. She took off the lids of the hives and checked the insides, finding everything in order. The angry bees were soothed by the smoke. Last of all she put out dishes of the corn syrup near each hive doorway. She would have to keep feeding them until the natural flowers produced enough nectar for them. She loved her bees.

Johnny built an outhouse of logs to match the house. It had two holes side by side at the regular height. It had a small hole, built very low, in the corner, which was three year old Tim's. He was very proud of his very own seat, and went to sit on it several times a day. Unfortunately he could unfasten his own overalls but he couldn't fasten them back up, so he would just drag them around with him after each visit to the outhouse. He often wandered away to the orchard dragging his pants, and there he ate mulberries until his face and fat little belly were painted purple with the juice.

An orphaned baby fawn joined the family in May and was named Bucky. He and Tim were constant companions. Bucky loved prunes, and knew where they were on the third shelf in the storeroom in the basement. Whenever he saw the basement door open he would bound down the stairs, race through the first room, butt open the storeroom door, stand on his hind legs, and eat prunes from the third shelf. Tim liked to tease Bucky. He would open the basement door, which swung in, then when Bucky came top speed down the stairs he would slam the door and Bucky would crash into it, a tangle of legs and neck. Then Tim

would swing open the door and do a maniacal dance of glee at the fate of poor Bucky. But Bucky was a fast learner. Tim would close the door, Bucky would tiptoe to the bottom of the stair and wait quietly. There was no window in the door, so Tim, wondering what was going on would open the door to peek. When he did, Bucky would butt open the door, throwing Tim screaming onto his back as the door hit him and Bucky would run on in and eat prunes.

In June, Charley told Potch and Pat they had to come home from riding with Scoggin and help him

Bucky the deer and Tim run off from the house to the orchard for a shared feast.

brand and shove the cattle up onto Blue Mountain to summer pasture. Scoggin missed them. He spent as much time as he could with the family, but his work took him on river trips and far to the east and to the west of the ranch. When the boys could get off work they would join him "huntin' injuns" as they called his work.

Last of all Johnny put up the logs for the new chicken house. They couldn't yet afford the roof, so he just anchored the structure so it wouldn't fall over. The chickens would have to move later. Somebody had given the children several Bantam hens and a rooster. These wily girls hid their nests out in secret places and hatched big bunches of chicks. They sneaked around the cliff and into the garden and feasted on all the vegetables and fruit. Evelyn finally had to do something about them. They roosted high in trees by night and were too wild and fast to catch during the day. So, when it was time for a chicken dinner she would take her .22 rifle out and bag as many as needed. A lot of chicken dinners were served that summer.

29

Pat Gets Sleeping
Sickness, 1941

EVELYN HAD JUST GOTTEN THE SUPPLIES IN. On September 16, Esther
Campbell, a new teacher, arrived. She and her husband Deward moved
into the homestead cabin and prepared to open school just as soon as
the two older boys got home. They were still on the mountain finishing up
work with the cattle. Deward had to leave right away to get back to complete
fall work at their ranch on Douglas Mountain, but planned on spending the
winter with Esther.

Potch came riding in, his horse lathered and dripping with sweat. He told
his mother that Pat was sick. He couldn't move his arms or legs hardly at all
and was real sleepy. Esther told Evelyn to go, that she would take care of the
kids. Terrified, Evelyn drove as fast as she dared, to summer camp, where she
found Pat partially paralyzed. She and Charley rushed him to Steamboat to a
chiropractor, thinking something was wrong with his back.

After ten days in the hospital Pat was diagnosed as having a streptococcus
infection in his head, and a touch of sleeping sickness. He was semi-paralyzed all
over and was in the hospital for four weeks before he could even sit up and then
was in a wheel chair for a week after that. Evelyn never left the hospital. Many
friends came to visit and some insisted on taking a shift so she would take a short
nap. Charley had to tend to the cattle, but kept in touch as much as he possibly
could. They gave Pat sulphathizole, a new sulfa drug, which didn't seem to work,
and they were about to call in a specialist, when finally he began to respond. He
had no permanent nerve center damage, and recovered movement rapidly. He was
still too weak to sit up for very long, but the hospital staff could see that this family wasn't doing well with him in the hospital, so he was released. They brought
him home on the Sunday before Christmas in a spring suspended bed in the back
of the pickup.

Precious Esther just smiled and welcomed everyone back as if she had enjoyed
being the mother of four children to cook and clean and wash for, with a ton of
ranch work to keep up with three children all in different grades to teach each day,
while coping with a two-year-old blasting around the school room.

Pat and Queeda milking the cows.

Pat got his strength back very slowly. He made a mighty effort to catch up on his school work, but it was too much strain on him in his weakened condition. He was feeling depressed because he thought he was letting everybody down by not catching up. Esther reassured him he was doing just fine and refused to give him more material than he could manage easily. That summer, all over the ranch, rabbits had died from a disease that everyone called sleeping sickness because the animal just went into a sleepy stupor, wasted away and died. Everyone was accustomed to eating the plentiful rabbits. It was believed that you could catch the disease from contact with an infected rabbit. Although the doctors did a blood test on Pat for "Rabbit Disease" (tularemiaremia) and it came back negative, most of the hospital staff believed that was what he had.

◆ ◆ ◆ ◆ ◆ ◆

Evelyn loved her new house. First she made built-in wood boxes to store fire wood in the living room and the kitchen. Long winter days when she wasn't sewing she made built-in cabinets. She set up a work shop in the basement, but it was so dark there that she did a lot of the work out in the yard. She and the whole family also gathered and hauled in big flat sandstones and created an elevated porch outside the kitchen door. There she set up her washing machine. Since water had to be hauled in she brought in two fifty-gallon barrels with the tops cut out and set them under the drains to catch snow water off the roof.

Water was a problem at the new house. Drinking water had to be carried from the creek. Water for other household uses was hauled from the river, which was about 100 yards away. The way they did it was to balance a fifty-gallon barrel of water on a wide tree fork flattened on the upper side, which was pulled by a big gentle horse named Red. He would stop on command and they would bail out buckets of water for the newly planted trees around the house and fill tubs and containers at the house. On the wash stand in the kitchen there were always two buckets of water. One was drinking water with a dipper in it. The other was river water and had a different dipper. It was for washing hands and faces and dishes. Used water was carried out to water plants with. Garbage was saved in a "slop bucket" and carried out to the pigs and chickens.

The new cook stove that Evelyn bought from the old lady upriver had finally arrived and was set

Bath time in front of the cook stove.

up in the kitchen. It was beautiful, blue enamel with a big cooking surface, and a warming surface. The oven door was heavy and ornate. Ornate arms supported a warming oven above the cooking surface. The warming oven had two beautiful blue and chrome doors. The stove had a big reservoir on the side by the fire box so that there was nearly always hot water.

On weekly bath night a round galvanized tub was brought in and set in front of the warm kitchen stove. A nice comfortable mix of hot and cold water filled the tub about half full. The kids were scrubbed and dried one at a time, starting with the youngest. Evelyn thoroughly cleaned noses, ears, necks, elbows, knees and feet. There was a water change after the first three. The bathing order made Queeda last, right after Nav. He always told her he had done evil things in the water while he was bathing. Evelyn had a deal with Potch and Pat that she wouldn't "look" and would let them wash themselves if they got everything clean. Hair was washed separately, and rinsed in vinegar water to make it glossy and soft. Even Charley and Evelyn took their baths in the tub on that designated night. Everybody got clean sheets that night. The water that was cleanest got saved for scrubbing floors the next day. The rest got emptied on newly planted shade trees. Not a drop was wasted.

In the winter, everybody got up before daylight and started chores. Charley started the fire in the living room heater and the kitchen stove. The kids milked the cows. Charley fed the chickens. Evelyn got breakfast on the table and strained the milk. Queeda ran the milk through the separator, then carefully washed all its parts. Evelyn usually started a batch of bread. There were dishes to wash, dogs and cats to feed, and beds to be made. The house had to be tidied up and of course nobody could come to the breakfast table without washing their hands, brushing their teeth, and combing their hair.

School started promptly at eight o'clock. It was about a half mile walk to school for the children, and although they had been threatened with lots of inventive consequences for being late, Esther often had to come looking for them to start class. Usually they were taking just one more ride down the sledding hill, or chasing a rabbit the dogs had jumped up. Every morning the children stood stiffly at attention, with their hands over their hearts and recited the Pledge of Allegiance as the flag was raised. Afterward, they sang either the National Anthem or America the Beautiful. After school the flag was lowered and folded. Reading, studying, and recitations continued steadily in the one room until a fifteen minute recess at ten o'clock.

When Esther rang the recess bell the kids would jump up, grab their two sleds and run like deer to just below the dam on the iced over creek. Each older boy would put a smaller kid on the front of the sled, then run like fury behind the sled until he got up good speed, then jump on the back of the sled on his knees. He would lean over the child in front to reach the ears of the sled, and guide it down the creek, trying to miss the rocks sticking up through the ice. On a good day they could sail all the way to the river. Then they would run back to school as fast as Nav's short little legs could go back to school, usually arriving just as Esther rang the bell for class to begin. Evelyn often laughed as she watched, because she was pretty sure the bell rang on cue at the kids' return, not at the correct time.

Esther and her students found dinner on the table at noon. They would eat and go back to school. An afternoon recess was just about long enough to run around the rocks out front and back, but it woke everybody up. Tim would usually show up at the school house door just as school let out in the evening. Esther would ring the bell for him and he would smile hugely, very pleased that he had arrived just in time. Potch or Pat would give him a wild ride all the way home on a sled. If there was not enough snow he got a "bucking bronco" ride home on one of their backs.

School election day in February was snowy and bitter cold. Nonetheless, Charley and Evelyn rode off horseback before dawn to go vote. They were not about to let a little discomfort for themselves deprive their children of every opportunity they could give them for an education. Esther worried about them until they got back the next day because it was so bitter cold, and she knew Blue Mountain would be dangerously drifted.

The kitchen cabinets were finished and looked beautiful. Evelyn brought out the broken parts of fruit jars she had been saving and started scraping the rough oak floor. Everybody wanted to help at first, but it ended up just Evelyn and

Queeda sticking to the job. They scraped down through the rough surface of each narrow board, then smoothed out the high places. After finishing all the floors in the two bedrooms, the dining room and the living room, it was time to start back over it all with sandpaper, first medium then fine. It was beautiful and glossy. Evelyn couldn't wait to apply the finishing coat, which would bring all the beautiful grains of wood to glowing splendor. Spring came on before they could finish, however, and with it came the hustle to get the spring work and planting done. Nobody was allowed to take any food into the living room, or to walk in there with shoes on. The rule was that only Evelyn could fill or light or blow out the kerosine lamps. The floor was not to be dirtied up and stained until the finishing coat could be applied.

Esther Campbell with her students. In back, l-r, Pat, Potch, Esther. Front: Tim, Queeda, Lonnie. Note the flag pole on the left.

On the first trip out in the spring Walt and Juanita Hammond gave Evelyn a kitchen table and chairs to take home. She bought some second hand beds and a comfortable chair for Charley. She went to Siebots Hardware store and got what they said she needed to finish the hardwood floor and paint for her new cabinets as well. Her beloved cousin Eva, and daughter Barbara, from new York, were planning to come out that summer and she wanted the new house to be as nice as possible for them.

30

War, 1943-44

WE WERE IN ALL-OUT WAR NOW. A flu epidemic and severe coal shortage crippled the East Coast. The nation was braced and ready to endure anything to further the war effort.

In very early spring the weather turned cold. Fruit trees were budded-out, ready to bloom and Evelyn was sick with worry that their fruit crop would be frozen. The whole family dragged and piled huge heaps of limbs and brush in different places around the orchard. They cut green cedar branches and laid them on top of the pile. One night the mercury plunged and it seemed sure to freeze. Evelyn took her kerosine can and went out in the dark and after pouring a little kerosine on each one, set all the piles on fire. Black smoke billowed up and as luck would have it the atmosphere held the smoke within the canyon walls, making a thick blanket over the orchard. Evelyn fed the fires until about three in the morning, when she was so exhausted she finally had to quit. Breathlessly, she waited for a week and danced for joy when the trees broke out in full bloom. That summer the trees bore the heaviest crop ever.

It was a hard summer. Evelyn had to spend long hours irrigating and tending both the garden and orchard, then hauled the produce to the new house to can and preserve. All the single young men had been drafted, so laborers were few. Young women could make fantastic wages doing defense work, so most of them were also unavailable. Gas and tires were both scarce and rationed, so they very seldom drove the pickup. Batteries for the radio were hard to get, too, so they only listened to the news in the morning, an occasional boxing match, and "One Man's Family" in the evening.

Scoggin brought his girl friend, Charlene Knudsen, to meet the family. She was a very pretty, exotic looking girl from Goodland, Kansas. They met at the University of Colorado. It was obvious that they were in love. Queeda was jealous, but Charlene made over her until finally Queeda could resist the friendly girl no longer. The clincher was a small bottle of perfume so they both smelled alike. The family was very sad when they left because they knew that Scoggin was going to be drafted and go to war soon.

Charley, Potch and Pat hand dug a well behind the house. They hit good water at only fifteen feet. The rich soil of the pasture below the house was plowed and irrigated and became the new garden. Pat built an eight-foot fence

Charlene Knudsen, Scoggin's fiancé in the sand box with Lonnie and Tim.

around it to keep the deer out. The garden was irrigated with water pumped from the well. The water was good for drinking, but still had to be packed up the steep hill to the house. The well lasted a couple of years, then began to cave. Without a casing it was too dangerous to work the well any more. Charley had planned to case and finish it when he could get some help and do it right. They already had a pump and were waiting to buy a windmill in the fall if they had enough money. Meantime, they watered the little honey locust trees they had planted for shade, using Big Red the horse to pull barrels of water from the river to the trees on a skid.

They got the roof on the chicken house and the chickens moved in. They also partitioned off a third of the building and made a snug little granary. Egg production should be good all winter with the hens in this nice warm place.

It looked like they were not going to be able to get a teacher, causing some concern. Potch was entering the tenth grade and Pat the ninth. Lonnie (Nav) was in the fourth grade and Queeda in the sixth. Although Tim would only be five at Thanksgiving they had hoped he could start kindergarten, since he was so anxious. They would need a teacher with the credentials to teach high school as well as grade school. Finally one day in September the county superintendent sent word that there was a teacher available. She was an elderly lady, born in New Haven, Connecticut, but had lived in Colorado since 1905. She was presently teaching a summer school and would not finish that until November 12 and had another school starting in April, so the Mantle school could only have her for four months. The superintendent thought that they could finish the work required in that time, because Lucy McInturf was an excellent teacher, and the Mantle children had always done well on their tests. So a contract was signed, and Mantles agreed to pick up Mrs. McInturf in Craig on November 13.

When it was time to get in the winter supplies Evelyn took Queeda with her and they rode horseback the forty miles to Lily Park. She borrowed a car at the Shanks and went on to Craig to shop. With rationing in force, even when you had the necessary stamps, supplies were short. Evelyn shopped in Craig, Hayden, and Meeker for shoes. She could only find nine pair, which was not enough and hoped that she could get what she still needed by reordering from Montgomery Ward. Since the Mantles bought groceries only once a year they were given certificates worth all the points in the books which had already expired for the year. She got 100 point coupons, and traded on them. She used 283 points on meat, which was mostly bacon and ham. She used 216 points on the other groceries that required stamps. It was mostly for grapefruit juice, because there was no orange juice or raisins to be had. The size 116 film Evelyn's camera used was not available.

Evelyn got new congoleum rugs for the two bedrooms downstairs and for the kitchen and pantry upstairs. She bought all the suitable yard goods she could get because she had to make all the overalls and shirts for the three smaller kids and shirts for the two older boys and Charley. Her own clothes were worn out, but she never sewed for herself until everybody else had clothes. She hired a pickup to take the purchases to Thanksgiving Gorge, at the rim of Blue Mountain. There, Charley met the driver with a team and wagon and took the load the rest of the way home. Evelyn and Queeda made their tired way back to Lily Park and rode home.

Charley was extra busy hauling and chopping wood. He had to get in enough Pinyon wood for the living room heater, the basement heater, and the school house heater and had to cut seemingly endless amounts of cedar for the cook stove. He had to go out on the benches for a supply of both. His favorite place was on a high cliff top south of the house. With the help of his horse and lariat rope he would drag big dead trees to the edge, then roll them off the 700-foot cliff. When he picked up the pieces at the bottom they were fairly well chopped, ready to be hauled home in the wagon.

On November tenth Evelyn started out for Craig to pick up the teacher. Guy had showed up, so she left all the kids with him. She was to be very pleased with that decision. When she met Mrs. McInturf, Evelyn was hard put to keep her mouth from dropping open. The lady weighed 245 pounds and barely fit in the huge dress she wore. Never in the world would she fit in pants. She better not get sick during the winter because they would never be able to get her on a horse. They loaded up her things and covered them well with a tarp so they wouldn't get covered with dust. The trip in to the ranch was a tiring, terrifying experience for Mrs. McInturf. Even though she had been told in detail about where she was going and the condition of the road to get there, she was totally unprepared for the bouncing and jolting, let alone the unbelievable terrain. All at once they left Blue Mountain straight down such a steep road she felt like she was riding on the hood ornament. The little woman driving had to slide forward on the seat to effectively operate the brake and clutch. The turns were so sharp as they wound down the mountain that it seemed their front would meet their back.

Finally they reached the bottom, and the teacher announced she needed a rest stop. Evelyn stopped in a rabbit brush flat and helped her struggle out of the pickup. They drank from a canvas water bag and continued on. Not far along, a loud hissing suddenly announced a punctured tire. Evelyn unloaded her passenger, got out the jack from behind the seat and strained and stomped on the wrench until finally she got the tire off. Then, to Mrs. McInturf's horror Evelyn told her there was no spare and she would have to patch the tube. Evelyn pulled the tube out, spit on it here and there until she found the leak, scraped the rubber with a piece of steel, then cut a patch from a sheet of patching, and glued it in place. She laid a flat rock on top of the patch, and dug out sandwiches for them to eat while the patch dried. Stuffing the inner tube back into the tire, and adjusting it so the stem stuck out, she pried it back on the wheel, then proceeded to pump up the tire with a tire pump. She pumped until her arms ached, then rested and pumped again until the tire was fat and firm. She wrestled the tire back on the axle, tightened the bolts and they were ready to go.

Just before every steep hill Evelyn would rev up the motor, floorboard the gas pedal, and go hurtling up the hill. As they neared the top the pickup would go ever slower and barely be moving when they topped the hill. One time she gunned it and speeded up on a level spot, then plunged through the mud in the road caused by a small seep above. The windshield was plastered with mud, so Evelyn scrambled down the bank to some small puddles of clean water, found a coffee can left there for that purpose, filled it with clean water, and washed the windshield. At one point the teacher looked off her side into 200-foot-deep Bull Canyon. All she could do was hold her breath and close her eyes until they passed.

Finally, they made one last terrifying descent into Hells Canyon, drove to a friendly looking log house, and Evelyn announced they were home. When Evelyn had first seen the big lady she made the decision to house her in the basement so she could take care of her rather than letting her batch in the old cabin. The giggling, friendly kids and the big cowboy put her stuff in the room, which Mrs. McInturf was unaware that this was Potch and Pat's bedroom and they had just been moved out. Guy had a big pot of beans with a venison shank simmering on the back of the stove, and he made some sour dough biscuits. Hungry and tired, but grateful, the two women ate, and went to bed.

The next day Mrs. McInturf got the school materials and room set up like she wanted it. She told stories and read books to the children. Even Potch and Pat listened spellbound because she made the stories very real. They liked her and could hardly wait for school to start the next day. She wondered if maybe at her age she had bitten off more than she could chew with this energetic bunch of kids with such a wide grade span and in this isolated place where everything, even going to the bathroom, was hard. She became more and more dissatisfied and didn't teach up to her potential as the winter wore on. More and more, Evelyn had to do the teaching, and her patience with Mrs. McInturf wore very thin. Potch had turned sixteen in October and Pat fourteen in August. Next year they would have to go out to Craig and board with somebody while they went to school. Most of Evelyn's free time was spent teaching them so they could do well in school the next year. Navvy fell far behind, and she knew that next year he would have to repeat fourth grade, while also doing fifth grade work if he was to catch up. How Evelyn and Charley dreaded losing their boys! Queeda was now eleven, Navvy eight, and Tim five. Evelyn felt old and tired at the ripe old age of thirty-seven.

Eighteen inches of snow lay on the ground by the eighteenth of January. It was cold and the cattle had to be watched carefully. Potch and Pat had a good trapping business. They caught a bobcat about every week. The bobcats had moved in last summer and killed lots of turkeys. They also caught coyotes that came near the home place. They would skin the animals, salt the hides, and stretch them to dry on a green willow branch they bent and lashed into a circle. They had about $200 worth of furs to sell. Also, Rial Chew paid them five dollars per cat and coyote that they caught around his sheep. They also caught an occasional skunk and drove Mrs. McInturf wild with the way they smelled.

The winter passed without a single visitor, or chance to send or receive mail until March. Charley and the boys made hair ropes. Evelyn painted the floor in a basement room and finished making the cabinets. She crocheted rugs from old socks cut in strings and sewed together. She also cut quilt blocks from old denim pants, others from scraps of wool, and still others from cotton scraps. By March 9 the wild geese started arriving, two hens were setting, and Charley was setting out to dehorn cattle. All were welcome signs of spring.

Getting Mrs. McInturf out by March 30 was a real problem. There was too much snow to drive out and she was too fat to take out on a horse. Finally, Charley saddled up and rode to Rial's to see if he could help get her out. He could and showed up with two big stout saddle horses. They hitched up the team to the rubber tire wagon, tied two relief work horses to the back and left early one morning over the frozen ground. The wagon made it fine to the steep switch backs at Thanksgiving Gorge. Then Rial tied a heavy rope onto the end of the wagon tongue, and he and his saddle horse helped the team pull the wagon up the steep mountain side. On top of Blue Mountain they kept switching horses around, tromping through crusted drifts to break a trail, and finally arrived at Elk Springs, where they put Mrs. McInturf on a bus. They left the wagon in Elk Springs with Johnny Milheim, and after a two day rest for the horses they rode home, leading the teams.

A new family member joined the Mantles that spring. To paraphrase Evelyn: Early one morning in May, while the grass was still whitish with the heavy dew and the air had such a crispness that even the echoes sounded louder and longer in the canyon, Pat came in from the fields holding something, seemingly precious or tender, tucked under his chin. It was a baby wild goose.

So it was that Poose came to live with the Mantle family. He was a fluffy greenish-yellow puff of awkwardness, wholly dependent upon these humans for his welfare. After Poose got acquainted he wanted to be with someone all the time and to find that someone he would go peeping around at the top of his lungs just as he had the morning Pat found him tangled in the tall grass.

The big problem was what to do with this baby goose at night. They got a cardboard box and arranged an old wool sweater in it so he could snuggle among the folds and he seemed to be satisfied, that is until the early morning hours, before it was hardly daylight, then he put up an awful racket and managed to squeeze out of the box, to prance and peep all over the house. In desperation to keep him from waking up everybody, Evelyn grabbed him and pushed him down in a wool sock and took him to bed with her. He snuggled down with just the tip of his beak showing and never made another move until the household awakened. After that, every morning at the same time he would hunt up his wool sock and warm place in Evelyn's bed.

From then on Poose pranced along with the family everywhere they went. Along the way to the garden, about 200 yards from the house, was a pond, where he was always treated to a swim. He always wanted just one more dive or splash and it was always ended by one of the children wading in to get him out before they could go on.

At the garden Tim, aged six, and Navvy, aged eight, would put in all their time feeding Poose. He never seemed to have enough, but unless the boys fed him he would go along helping himself, walking up a garden row, either trampling on the tender plants with his unusually big feet, or mowing them down with his scissor edged bill. His diet was mostly green stuff, such as clover, cabbage, lettuce and dandelions.

As Poose got older he began going to the pond alone, peeping his way along through the tall grass as though telling everyone to come along, the swimming was going to be fine. His coloring soon blended with the surroundings, so he was very hard to see. Many times somebody would go looking for him, calling him and when his answering peep came he would be real close by but hard to see.

With everyone feeding him constantly, he grew and grew. The boys gave him minnows, while Queeda, age eleven, fed him a cup of new milk and bread every morning and evening at milking time. Soon he began to associate the tinkle of the cow bell with that feast. This presented another problem, because he was right out among the cows, unconcerned over the waving horns and menacing hoofs. Since we had always tried to protect him from all harm he had no fear of anything. Queeda began calling him to her while she milked to keep him out of danger. Then, like an impish child he got to pulling the cow's tail with his bill causing the cow to step around, and on one or more occasions, slop the milk. He was quick to see where that milk came from, so then he got on the other side of the cow and would try to sneak a bill full out of the bucket at every chance. All of this pleased the children a lot.

Since they had a cat that would sit up and lap milk while a stream was squirted at her, they wondered if Poose would too, so, the test began. At first he only shook his head, then he realized this was the stuff he liked so much, so he began working his bill and coming closer to the source until they were afraid he might even develop a technique for trying to milk for himself.

His down gradually gave way to tiny feathers and he began to take on the general appearance of his kind, the Canadian Honker. He was so proud of his new wing feathers and was always opening out his wings full spread, much like the small boy seeing how high he can reach. Even with his new sized wings (for so long his body had been so much bigger in comparison) he was unable to fly for a long time. It seemed like his body was too, too heavy for those new and tender feathers to hold up, but this did not stop his travelling.

If anyone left by horseback he would follow, just as far and as long as he could see or hear them at all. One day some relatives were visiting, and the children and their Daddy, all on horseback, were showing them around the canyons, through the different parks up and down the river. Poose was with them all day. When they were near the river, he went by water. When they got too far away for that he would squawk until someone would go back after him or, as once, he got in the trail in the middle of the procession, slowing up everyone so much and being in danger of getting stepped on all the time, that Charley got off his horse, picked up Poose and gave him a ride on his horse with him. He told the folks, apologetically, that Poose had to be excused for getting in the way so much, he just didn't know he was a goose.

As summer advanced, so did the swimming. The high water in the river was past, so every day the children had fun swimming, but not nearly so much fun as Poose. He took swim time as a personal favor to him, and his efforts to show his happiness were a sight to behold. From the time the first child made a splash in the water he did everything imaginable to attract attention and laughter. His antics included a tail spin in which he reared back on his tail, flapped his wings, spinning around on the water, or flipping over on his back to splash water over his breast with his wings while his feet stuck up in the air. As soon as anyone dived, he began to show how that was done, too. With a quick flip of his wings and tail he was out of sight with everyone wondering where he would come up. After what seemed too long a time he would appear right beside or behind someone—then in a flash was under again to tag someone else. The more noise and hilarity the better it pleased him.

On these swimming occasions he tried his wings by flapping along in the water until just his feet were touching. Each day he was able to fly a little better and a little farther. His first real flight was quite late in the summer. Charley was going to the mountain leading a pack horse one late afternoon and Poose followed along the trail until Charley would be nearly out of sight, then he would fly to catch up. About half way up the mountain side, with the canyons in a dusky outline below, Poose had lagged far behind again, but soon he came flying overhead making a circle, and headed out over the canyons for home. Evelyn and the children were outside when he came over, high above the house, emitting excited honks as he sailed for the river, a short distance below the house.

After that he really enjoyed this new excitement, but caused much anxiety at times. Anyone leaving on horseback needed to keep a good watch or Poose might come sailing right over the horse's ears as though he was going to mount up, too. The young horses the boys rode were always frightened and capered around.

Everyone felt sure Poose would leave when fall came and the other wild geese began going south. At times he was very restless, but stayed on, never mingling with any of the flocks which flew over from time to time. As it grew colder, he would fly to the house every morning from the river about the time we started the fires in the stoves. Many times his feathers were a pattern of ice. At those times Evelyn would let him in beside the fire for a spell and give him his favorite dish of bread and milk. Always, before she could stop him, he would flip the melted ice from his feathers all over the kitchen. Finally, they made a practice of putting him in the warm chicken house on these cold nights. He seemed to feel this was below his standards somewhat, but there was just too much goose to share the house with any more.

With the spring thaws and ice melted in the river Poose was all set for another summer of swimming until the appearance of the wild geese from the south. He seemed to be afraid of them and stayed close to home all the time. However, this attracted the wild ones so much there were from six to fourteen in the field by the house most of the time. Some even ventured to the corner of the yard to see what manner of goose that could be standing on the very steps of a human's house. We all hoped he (or she) would choose a mate and raise us a family, but this did not happen. Mating season passed and then came the most tragic period of his life.

Because of molting, Poose's wing and tail feathers came out so he was temporarily unable to fly. Also, now the river was at its highest flood stage and Poose seemed to be afraid to go around it very much. But seeing Pat start down the trail horseback one day Poose took to the river and followed along, unknown to Pat. Down river some stretch, Pat dismounted to shoot at a wood-chuck. While he was aiming and waiting for the chuck to get right for the shot, Poose slipped out of the river, sneaked up behind Pat and took a nip at his leg, causing Pat to nearly jump over his horse before he could turn to see what had taken hold of him, and there stood Poose looking wise and a bit tickled over this prank.

Another time Poose followed some of the family down the river when we were after a new milk heifer and her baby calf. He got stranded on an island. It was several days before anybody missed him. Evelyn remembered seeing a goose on the island, so they went to the bank and called. Sure enough, there he was, but the current was too swift for him to swim toward home, and he couldn't seem to reason that he would have to cross below the island and come back around the trail. He had just waited there for somebody to save him. They coaxed him over and he was one pleased goose, talking and craning his long neck at everybody. He never lagged a step on the way home until they got through the lane and could see the house. Then he opened his wings and flapped them for joy to be home again.

After those four days alone on an island even the chickens looked good, so much so that Poose adopted a mother hen and her brood of thirteen. Everywhere they went, he went, even at times trying to coax them to the river. At feeding time he always shared his food with the baby chicks. Anything else was sure to have a fight for even looking his way. Even the bum lamb had to steer clear or Poose would grab a lock of wool and beat poor Fibber, an orphaned lamb, all over the yard with his wings.

Poose got his new wing feathers and was again able to fly through the canyons and up and down the river to greet everyone with a friendly honk. "How Evelyn hoped he would continue to be as safe, happy and free always as he had been with his family."

Dick Toole was a terrible tease and prankster. He tried to teach Poose to attack Maude when she would go to the outhouse. He was a very good teacher, too. Poose would not bother Maude, but never let Dick go to the outhouse without attacking him after his education. Dick would sneak noiselessly out the yard gate, and walk silently toward the outhouse. Somewhere along the route the vigilant Poose would waylay him. He would run toward Dick with his neck stretched out and a mean look in his eye. He would grab Dick's pant leg in his beak and hold on to it while he beat Dick's leg with the joints in his wings. The entire family would shriek with laughter at the sight of the tall man shaking his leg wildly to dislodge the big goose clinging to it while beating it up with his wings. Dick always had great black and blue marks on his shins every time he left after a visit.

31

Eva Comes West, 1944

PRIL 30, 1944, FOUND CHARLEY AND EVELYN camped in a shallow cave beneath an overhang in Schoonover. They had left home at noon, leaving the children to take care of the ranch while they were gone for the school election. They had to get to Bear Valley to vote by noon the next day.

This small cave was headquarters for Charley's dehorning operation each year. He had counted on the cave as their camping place for the night. It had sleeted and rained on them ever since they left home and they were cold to the bone. They picketed their horses in the tall grass, then gathered pinyon wood and set two fires to dry out the wet bedroll. While Charley piled fluffy cedar boughs for a bough bed, Evelyn gathered up some dead cedar limbs and started a cooking fire. Charley produced his meager dehorning camp outfit that he had left hanging in a tree to keep the pack rats and porcupines out of it. He produced a blackened coffee can out of a crack in the ledge, filled it with water from a nearby pot hole, dumped coffee grounds in it, and set it on the fire. He dug out a dutch oven and added some tallow to it and put it on the coals. Then he got out a flour sack, some salt, and a little envelope of baking powder. He made a small depression in the flour and after adding salt, baking powder and hot grease, he added water, and mixed until he could handle it. He squeezed off little balls of dough into the dutch oven, set it on coals and covered the lid with more coals. Then he pulled a hunk of meat from a sack tied on his saddle, heated tallow in a skillet, sliced the meat thin and fried it. They had one fork and one knife between them and ate right out of the skillet. They wallowed the hot biscuits in the meat pan for flavor, and drank coffee out of two tin cans. Coyotes yipped around them that night. Evelyn's last thought as she drifted off to sleep was that Eva would get to hear some coyotes for the first time when she came west. The next day they were the only school district members that showed up for election of officers. There was nothing to do but elect Charley president, and Evelyn secretary.

A heavy snow storm suffocated many of Rial's sheep and lambs that spring. Others died of cold. He had already sheared them and then a big storm hit as the lambs were being born. He was in bad need of help. Potch went over to help Rial as soon as school was out. The Mantle's cattle were all right because there were bare ridges and lots of feed on the benches that they could get to. Potch brought two orphaned lambs to Queeda, who named them Lucky and Frisky. They followed her everywhere. One day Lucky disappeared. She looked everywhere, sniffling all the while because Charley and the boys teased her by speculating on what might have eaten Lucky. Finally she heard a pitiful bleat from the outhouse. Lucky had fallen through a hole. He smelled terrible, and Charley was the only one who helped her rescue him.

Charley had injured his back several years earlier, while they were building a dam in the rocky creek bed. He was pulling a heavy log by a rope dallied to his saddle horn when his cinch broke. He was thrown down across a big rock on his back. From time to time after this he had partial paralysis when lifting heavy objects. He had gotten X-rayed while Pat was in the hospital and it showed him missing a joint of backbone right at the coupling. Every spring he had trouble when the heavy work began. This spring he was really broken down. He was haggard and exhausted. Everything he did hurt, and there was so much to do he couldn't stop. Evelyn doubled her work load to save him as much as possible.

The Chew children were nearly of school age and it was looking as though they were going to have one central school to serve both families, making it necessary to have a road between the two ranches. There was an old wagon road that came from the Chew Ranch across the bench, past Red Rock and on to Hells Canyon. The last part from the bench into the canyon was too steep and rough for a car and even a wagon could not safely negotiate it. Once again, the Mantles were struggling to build a road. The Mantles were caught with a worn out old pickup when the war made it impossible to buy a new one. Besides, tires and gas were rationed, so they just got along with no car. Then their old friend Brimhall and his bulldozer became available. Having not used their car, the Mantles had lots of gas stamps, so Brimhall agreed to make a whirlwind trip in with his dozer.

Brimhall knocked a road across the benches from Pool Creek to Hells Canyon, sticking more to the high ridges than had the old wagon road. Much of the snow would be blown off the road that way, making it more passable in winter. It was a bear cat getting the road off the bench into Hells Canyon. Long gray limestone outcroppings ran parallel to the natural grade. Charley, Evelyn, and Rial planned out a grade that would work and the bulldozer made a passable road through, aided by a few charges of dynamite. Just as they reached the bottom of the hill and stopped for a drink of water and short rest, Jess Lombard, Superintendent of Dinosaur National Monument came roaring up in a cloud of dust. Jumping out of his pickup, he shouted for them to stop immediately, explaining that they were not allowed to do that on public land without a permit. But Jess was a good friend of the family and although he professed anger, the hint of a smile crossed his features as Charley offered him a drink and said they'd quit.

Since Eva was coming, Evelyn asked her to bring zippers, denim and twill gabardine if it was available back east. It was no longer available in the West because it was all being used by the military. She was accustomed to buying forty yards of denim at a time to make overalls for the kids, and was desperate. Nancy had sent a little denim from California, but it was light weight.

In counting up gentle horses for Eva and her family to ride, Evelyn named Nig, Big Red, Jigs, Dummy, Simp, Brigham and Mousey. She described each horse's looks and his personality. Eva felt like she knew these horses personally when at last she arrived.

Eva, Barbara, and her friend, Isa Coles, finally arrived in mid-August. The canyon was sweltering hot, and they were complete greenhorns, but game to tame the West. Charley and Evelyn took them on a couple of short horseback trips so they could learn how to ride. Then they took them on a week-long

Evelyn's New York cousin, Eva McCormick Reymore, daughter, Barbara, and Isa Coles. Eva made this book possible by saving a lifetime of letters exchanged between herself and Evelyn.

pack trip down the river into Outlaw Canyon, then on down the river to Warm Springs, moving camp each day. The first new experience was the deep water leading into Outlaw that their horses had to swim across. Terrified but remembering Charley's repeated caution that they must trust their horse at all times, they clung to their saddles. When the horses lunged out of the water onto the dry sandy beach Brigham gave a happy nicker and dropped to his knees in the sand. Barbara yelled at him to get up, then scrambled off and crawled away from him on hands and knees as he plopped over on his side and rolled and rolled in the sand. So much for trusting him!

When they made camp the first night Charley told them he was going to make a Brigham Young bed. Intrigued, they asked what a Brigham Young bed was. He explained he would lay down a wide bed of fluffy cedar boughs on a slight slope. All of them would crawl in the bed, and as the downhill woman rolled out she would rotate to the upper side. That was how Brigham Young got around to all his wives. The cliffs of Outlaw Canyon rang with laughter.

Poose the goose with Eva's daughter, Barbara. Lonnie, Roughy the dog, Kelly the dog, and the sheep Frisky and Lucky. Queeda and Tim hold a cat.

They stopped early the next night in a lush green park. Charley assured them it was the best fishing hole on the river and they would have a big mess of catfish for supper. He cut green willow fishing poles for everyone. They tied their line, hooks and sinkers on as instructed and rushed to the river bank. Each determined woman baited her own hook with a fat worm from a coffee can full of worms Evelyn had dug from her garden, and they set about catching supper. They caught a bucket full of big beautiful catfish.

Charley fried up skillet after skillet of fish well salted and rolled in flour. He served them on fat biscuits baked in a dutch oven. They washed supper down with hot black coffee boiled in an old coffee can with a bailing wire handle. They were impressed watching Charley cook and listening to the yarns he spun as he leaned on his pot hook. Barbara was impressed that she got to drink coffee with the grownups. They washed dishes with sand and river water and rolled out their sleeping bags in level places before it got dark.

They decided it would be fun to build a bonfire to light up the canyon walls and visit around. They dragged drift wood up on top of a huge boulder that jutted way out over the water. They fished awhile more, listened to Charley tell tales, caught Evelyn up on news of the family in New York and just relaxed around the big fire. Suddenly a gust of wind came rushing up the river and scattered live coals into the vegetation. Instantly flames started up. The jointed, hollow Goose Grass built up hot air inside, then exploded and arched into the sky. The noise was like gunfire, and the canyon cliffs were fairly leaping with the reflection of the flames and rocketing joints. It was bright enough to see the horses panicking and tugging at their picket ropes, and the flames were fast advancing toward their camp site. Everybody ran along the bank at the river's edge to the camp and grabbed everything up and dragged it to the safety of a fresh rock slide. Charley and Evelyn and the children ran to the terrified horses and managed to wheedle them into letting them lead them to safety. The fire finally burnt itself out in the small park. Morning dawned to a sorry sight of people, beds, pack outfit and clothes black with soot.

After they cleaned up their camp outfit, the ride continued, but first with a stop for a bath in the cold river. They used lye soap to scrub each sooty body. It left their hair pretty witchy looking but it sure smelled better. Isa complimented Charley on the wonderful entertainment he provided. Amazed by the enormous mule deer, the cliff swallows swooping low, the clear echoes from the canyon walls, and the sheer beauty and majesty of the canyon and river, the three New Yorkers and their escort of seven Mantles had the time of their life for one wonderful week.

When they returned to the ranch Isa asked if she could teach Queeda to play the piano. She was a piano teacher and was unable to remember ever having anybody that she couldn't teach to play. However, this girl had no ear whatsoever for melody or beat, and it was a failure. Evelyn was devastated, because she came from a very musical family and had dreamed of Queeda being able to enjoy music. She knew it was probably because they had never had any kind of music in the house, not even on the radio.

When Eva's vacation time was up, Evelyn and Queeda took them out of the canyon. They rode horses over Blue Mountain to the K Ranch, which sat right on the Utah Colorado border. Pierre Morgan, the owner of the K Ranch and his father, Tom Morgan, had been Charley's lifelong friends. Pierre and Charley had served in the army together. Pierre and Hilda graciously welcomed the Mantles any time they stopped by. Hilda was an excellent cook, and put a wondrous feed on the table for them that night, then bundled them off to clean beds. The next morning the Morgans were reluctant to let Eva leave, because they were so fascinated by these Eastern ladies' impressions of the West. They finally took them to the bus stop and sent them off home. Eva had tears rolling down her cheeks as she looked out the bus window and Evelyn was overcome by uncontrollable sobs as she watched them go. Hilda tenderly hugged her, letting the tears flow. Evelyn took home some sewing to do for Hilda and for her two kids. She felt that was the only way she could repay their generous hospitality all the time. Her friend, Hilda, was always there for her.

Evelyn and Queeda rode back to summer camp, but there was nobody there because Charley and the boys were driving the beef to Lily Park. How Evelyn wished she had a car. Her boys were starting high school in Craig this fall and she wouldn't even be there to settle them in and hug them goodbye. They were practically independent men now and she knew they would never be at home with her again. She hurried on home to Lonnie and Tim.

Their teacher would be coming October first, and there was so much to do. Katharine was teaching again. She had married George Rinker. He had been her neighbor and friend, and when he had shown up in his army uniform looking handsome and brave, she had been overcome. He was being shipped

L-R: Queeda, Pat, dog with the hat, Katherine Shank (teacher), Tim in the wagon, Florence Shank holding Lonnie.

out soon and as thousands of girls in the U.S. were doing, she married him and was left behind. She was bringing a thirteen-year-old girl with her to go to school. This girl's family had lots of problems and it was thought best for the girl that she get away. Who knew how this disturbed child would adjust in a home with strangers. She fervently hoped it would be a good thing for Queeda to have this friend.

Evelyn had to hurriedly can all the fruit she could pick. The box elder bugs were at plague proportions. They would attack a fruit tree in masses and suck all the juice out of the fruit. Fruit was best if tree ripened, but she had to pick it a little early to beat the bugs. Also, the turkeys could fly over the eight foot fence surrounding garden and orchard. They were eating the tomatoes. It was a pretty sure thing those turkeys were all going to be in cans this fall.

Charley rode home with the news. The two boys had to leave the herd and go on to Craig because school was starting. They bought their own clothes, with one hitch. They couldn't leave the store with the shoes they bought because they didn't have their ration books with them, and had to start school in their boots. Charley took the ration books back to Craig a couple of weeks later and got their shoes for them. Charley and Evelyn had made arrangements last spring that the boys would live with Walt Hammond, the post master and his seventy-six-year-old mother. Their room and board was costing fifty dollars a month and a beef.

Both boys had gotten jobs to help pay expenses. Pat was working at the stockyards, taking care of the livestock at the weekly sale. Potch got a job with a building contractor, who Charley was pleased to see was going to teach him a lot. He made eighty-cents an hour. It did seem to Charley, though, that Potch was working much too hard. Charley had a healthy respect for what hard work school was and considered school the number one job the boys had to do. However, if the boys wanted any spending money at all they had to get a job and earn it, because Charley just didn't hand out money easily.

Charley told Evelyn that he had made a "hell of a deal" on the cattle. A buyer had bought them right in Lily Park for a flat $4,200. He wouldn't have to take the weight loss or pay for the shipping on the train to Denver. The money would pay for a lot of education for the kids and a lot of necessities.

Without the boys to help, Charley had triple the work to do that fall. He felt lucky because even dry as it was the benches and river bottoms had good feed to winter the cattle on. It would take his constant care to get them through, however. He would have to camp out in cold caves and move the cattle to fresh feed all through the winter. The sheep men were in big trouble because there was no corn and cake to be had and what little hay was available cost the unthinkable price of twenty-five dollars a ton.

Evelyn got a chance to go to Craig and see her boys. They were so grown up and self sufficient that she felt less worried about them. However, her tears flowed in secret at the passing to manhood of her precious little boys. Queeda, on the other hand, who had come with her to Craig, had some adjustments to make to modern plumbing. They stayed with Walt Hammond and Evelyn sent Queeda to take a bath. There was no bath tub! Just a shower. She had never seen one before. Fully dressed, just trying to figure out how she could get clean in this thing, she turned a knob and water hit her on the head. She tried to turn it off with the other knob, but even more water came down on her. Panicked, she turned the knobs frantically one way then another, becoming soaked from head to toe with first hot water, then cold. Finally she got everything turned off. Her heart was hammering. Embarrassed, she crept out of the bathroom. Evelyn reprimanded her for getting her shoes wet, and sent her to change clothes, never realizing Queeda had barely escaped from the shower with her life.

32

Trauma, 1944-46

HE HEART BREAKING NEWS ARRIVED that Scoggin had been killed in action. The Mantle family didn't think they could bear it. Losing him left a huge lonely vacancy in their lives. When Charlene wrote she told them that she was pregnant, how they ached for her. Charley wrote to Charlene, "You poor little bastard."

One moonlit night Evelyn was wakened by the turkeys. The noise of their terrified chatter and flailing wings filled the canyon. The cows were wakened by the racket and ran bawling to the calves locked in the corral. She grabbed her shoes and shotgun and ran through the moonlight in her white nightie toward the tree all the noise was coming from. The great horned owl heard her coming, stopped his stalking, and flew to the top of the tree. The big gun boomed into the darkness and the owl flew away. She had missed! She heard the screech of the owl in a tree farther west. She ran toward the sound of the screech, but the moonlight gave her away and the owl flew on. He screeched again where he had landed. This time she moved stealthily through the shadows in the direction of the screech. Her progress was slow, but she finally saw him sitting in the top of a tree, illuminated against the sky. Carefully and silently she advanced through the trees until she was within range. Sighting the heavy gun by the glint of the moonlight on the sight, she finally braced herself and pulled the trigger. She heard a great cracking of branches as the big bird fell down through the tree. She listened and heard no movement. Fearing the tearing beak and ripping claws, she did not search for him in the darkness. In the morning she checked on the turkeys and found one with a wound on his back, but not a fatal wound as she had feared. She found the dead owl lodged in the tree and felt a surge of victory that she had overcome one more obstacle in her life.

◆　◆　◆　◆　◆　◆

Katharine arrived to begin teaching at the Mantle school house in September, 1944. The girl she brought with her was not happy for personal reasons and her unhappiness brought a cloud of gloom over the household. Charley was surly and lonely without the boys. He and Katherine had some serious conflicts. Evelyn and the children felt sad and uncomfortable. Finally, as she was leaving for Christmas vacation, Katharine told Evelyn she wasn't coming back. It had been a hard decision for her, but she saw no other way. In addition to the obvious problems, there were others she just didn't want to discuss.

Just before Christmas break, Charley led two horses the forty miles out to Elk Springs and left them there for Potch and Pat to ride home. The two boys jumped off the bus with their saddles, caught their horses and hurried home to their family for Christmas.

Since Katharine had quit in the middle of the school year, they were left without a teacher, so Evelyn took on the job. She studied the school books of the children late into the night and planned each day's program. She never let any part of their subjects go unlearned. The children missed Katharine because they loved her, but they were happy to have Evelyn as their teacher. She made lessons fun. Also, she was always game to organize an activity for them that they could all participate in. It was spring before she could apply for an emergency teaching certificate. There was a critical shortage of teachers during the war. The small country schools were allowed to employ teachers who passed a proficiency test given in the county superintendent's office. They were issued emergency teaching certificates. They had to teach in a building other than a home. Evelyn only had a high school education, but easily passed the proficiency test. The students of a teacher with an emergency teaching certificate had to be tested at the end of the school year in the superintendent's office. Evelyn was very proud that her class of three passed.

The superintendent was relieved when Evelyn asked for a teaching certificate for the following year. It was impossible to get enough teachers for all the schools and she knew Evelyn would do a better job than most teachers, even if she could find one that would go down into that canyon to teach.

Charley remained an unhappy, brooding man. The kids didn't know what the trouble was, but mostly tried to stay out of his way. Potch and Pat were hardly ever home that summer. They and Charley stayed at the cow camp on the mountain, except for a few days when they put up hay at the ranch. Charley let the boys rodeo every weekend. They would wash their rodeo shirt in a dish pan, and carefully hang it up to dry, after which they would iron it with a flat iron heated on the little cook stove at cow camp. Then they would wash their good Levis, crease them perfectly and lay them under their mattress to dry and get pressed. They would ride their horses off the mountain to a point where they could leave the animals and catch a ride to the rodeo. They were on the winners list regularly. Potch's style was to ride and spur wildly and either make a winning ride or be bucked off. He seldom got bucked off, but occasionally drew a lemon that even he couldn't look good on.

Pat loved to ride the bucking horses. He was almost impossible to buck off, but did not always put on a grand show as Potch did. On the other hand, he often won because he stayed on and Potch got bucked off. He began team roping with Earl Wilson and really enjoyed that. Earl often let him ride one of his calf-roping horses and he nearly always came out a winner. He also started bulldogging. Shorter and lighter than most of the bulldoggers, he still won consistently. He longed for a roping horse, but didn't seem to be able to make a good one out of any of the ranch horses. Finally he bought a roping horse for almost nothing because it had a terrible cut right in its hock. He faithfully and tenderly doctored it until he was able to rope off it once a week. How he wished he had a trailer or a pickup with racks to haul it in, but that just wasn't going to happen! They could do anything they wanted to do, but Charley never gave them any money to do it with. Pat rode down to the ranch often to help his mother, but Potch and Charley hardly ever came to the ranch that summer.

It was a long, hot, hard, lonely summer for Evelyn and Queeda. They shelled peas, snapped beans, canned and preserved. Lonnie and Tim watered and weeded and picked and cut wood for the cook stove. They all hauled water endlessly with Big Red. Not once did Evelyn go to town. Always fair and never overworking her children, Evelyn would let them go to the cool basement in the heat of the afternoon. They would play Monopoly and read and do jigsaw puzzles for about two hours. Then they would run for the river. They would swim and skip rocks and ride driftwood over the mini-rapids. Sometimes they would plaster slimy blue mud on a steep bank, then wet it and use it for a slide. That called for a bath with soap before they got out.

When fall came Evelyn got the school house ready to use. The supplies she had ordered arrived in the mail. Charley got in the fall supplies and got Pat and Potch enrolled in school in Craig after they finished the beef drive into town.

In October, 1945, Irma Chew drove in to the Mantle Ranch with her two children to start school. Evelyn showed Stanley and Eula where they would be sleeping. The next day school started. Five students in five different grades was a heavy load for Evelyn. She had to study the work of each child for the next day and make up the necessary materials for them. In school she found herself the adversary of the two Chew children. She quickly made them understand that she was not the enemy, and they were all there to learn all they could and it was supposed to be fun. They finally relaxed. The kids loved having each other to play with and thought it was great to be together the entire week. The two Chew children stayed with the Mantles during the week, and Irma or Rial would pick them up on Friday night and bring them back on Monday morning.

One Friday Evelyn hesitantly approached Irma, "Irma, you are just going to have to make Stanley quit cussing in school. I just can't have it." Irma looked shocked and said, "Of course you can't. I wonder where the hell the little bastard gets it?"

The Chew family went out to town every weekend, and brought back colds that quickly spread through all the children. Irma kept her children on sulfa drugs constantly, and that concerned Evelyn greatly. Stanley Chew was eight years old and Tim turned seven in November. Stanley was very good at forming his letters and coloring, almost to the point of being artistic. Tim was better in school work. He progressed quickly to third grade work and Evelyn just let him go as he needed more to keep him busy. Queeda was beside herself with anticipation of the new Smith Corona typewriter they had ordered for her. It had been back ordered two months, but was going to be worth it.

Charley's sister, Lena, had come for a short visit. Her husband had died in August and she was very lonely. She had no children. Charley hadn't seen her for twenty-three years. She had lived in California with all the modern conveniences and naturally found Charley and Evelyn's way of life very crude. Evelyn found no common ground between them, and was not sad to see her go.

On the other hand, Charley's other sister, Nancy, was planning a visit. She and Evelyn were soul mates, and Evelyn yearned for her arrival. Nancy's son, Tab, was in the navy. He had been on Okinawa when the big typhoon hit. They had no news of him since, so were worried. He was found to be safe later on.

It was a hard year, but Evelyn was pleased when her students all passed their tests, and were promoted to the next grade. The Chews were pleased, but had found it a very lonely year without their children at home. They were going to try their very darndest to get a teacher for the next year who would teach in a school half way between the two ranches and have each family deliver their kids daily. That would be a round trip of about five miles over rough, muddy roads both ways, mostly in the dark, but they figured it would be worth it. All they needed was a teacher.

Just before high school in Craig let out a horrible thing happened. Pat was boarding with Walt Hammond the post master. One morning Walt shot himself in the head in the bathroom. Pat heard the shot and broke down the door to get in. He found Walt there, mutilated, in a mass of blood and gore. Pat acted calmly, held Walt's mother so she couldn't see into the bathroom, and called the ambulance. He did everything right, but in truth he was terribly shaken. He was only sixteen years old. He had nightmares and would relive that terrible experience for the rest of his life.

Potch had come home from school in the spring surly, angry, and abusive to the younger kids. Early in the school year he had moved out of Walt Hammond's home and gone to live with some people who were as crazy about rodeo as he was. He fit right in, as he loved to ride bucking broncs and he got a lot of notoriety in the country as a rodeo bronc rider.

He came home to discipline, hard work, and absolutely no hero worship from his siblings. He harbored a raging resentment against his mother and referred to her as "That Old Woman" and grew increasingly more bitter. One day he, Pat and Charley were working cattle in Schoonover when it all boiled over. He said he was going to kill "That Old Woman," because she just never laid off of him and he was sick and tired of having his life run by her. Pat stepped up to him and told him, "If you ever set a hand on Mama or say anything like that to her, I'll kill you." They fought and finally Charley tore them apart. He could tell that one of them would kill the other sooner or later. He asked Potch what he wanted to do. Potch said, "I want to get out of this damned country and never come back. You can run this god-damned outfit any way you want to cause I'm leaving." Charley gave him what money he had

Charley and Pat, the cowboys out to get the job done.

in his pocket, and Potch rode off on Diamond, a horse Rial had given him, spurring, whipping and jerking the horse to vent his hatred and anger.

Charley left Pat to finish the work, and he rode home. He told Evelyn, "Today we lost a boy." He told her only that Potch had wanted to leave and wouldn't be back. Nobody ever told Evelyn of Potch's terrible words. Tears for her sons drenched Evelyn's cheeks as she sat alone in darkness that night and many nights thereafter.

It was the fall of 1946 and the dreaded time when her only daughter left home was upon Evelyn. Her beloved cousin, Eva, begged Evelyn to send Queeda east to stay with her and Barbara for her high school years, but Evelyn couldn't bear to give her up for a whole nine months and declined the offer. Evelyn faced the task of getting Queeda ready for her first year of high school. Evelyn longed to move to Craig, rent a house and stay there with her children while they went to school. All the other ranchers they knew did that, and it worked out well. Charley, still deep in his dark mood, said she could go if she wanted to but she sure as hell couldn't take the two little boys. Evelyn wrote to Eva of her pain, "If I can ever live through this it may all iron out. I have cried buckets of tears thinking of this fall."

Eva sent patterns and leaflets showing up to date fashions. Evelyn told her she had lots of hand-me-downs she could make nice dresses of for Queeda if she just knew the styles. She wanted her daughter to have nice clothes she would not be ashamed of.

Isa and Eva sent outdated clothing to Evelyn. They were fine woolens, cottons, and silks that people in the civilized world replaced from time to time as styles changed. They knew Evelyn's limited resources, her needs, and her skill in making over old clothes to look new. A young woman from the Perry

Mansfield school named Lillian von Quailin had become a dear friend of Evelyn. They corresponded regularly and Lillian understood the sorrow and need Evelyn was feeling. She, too, sent a large box of things a girl would need for school. Personal items of clothing, scarves, socks, lounge wear, personal hygiene items and a few nice school clothes. She also sent Evelyn a nice dress for herself. They all hoped Evelyn would not be embarrassed by these gifts, and were relieved to get letters from her expressing her thanks for their help when she needed it.

To her horror, Evelyn discovered a lump in her breast. She didn't tell Charley, and urged Eva not to tell Charley, whom she felt had enough worries this summer. She just had to get the older kids in school before she could go to a doctor.

The Chews were looking for a school teacher, but Evelyn had no hope they would find one. They had a sheep herder with three children and wanted them to go to the school, too. They planned on putting a school house out on the road at Red Rock. Evelyn thought maybe the Mantles would have to lay up a log cabin at Red Rock and she would have to live there this winter with the school children. They had nothing to drive back and forth the five miles to school. Pat and Charley were looking for a car to buy when they went to town, but even if they found one a car couldn't be depended on to get them back and forth during the winter. She wrote Eva, "Gosh will it ever work out so I don't feel so upset? *I hope soon.*"

Charley, Pat, and Nav left Schoonover pasture with the beef herd on August third heading for Craig, hoping a buyer would take them off their hands along the way. They were the biggest, wildest steers ever. Let a brush pop and they would take off, their hooves sounding like thunder. They were driving what they figured was about $9,000 worth of beef if they could just hold the herd together until it was sold. Pat was working doubly hard. He felt as though everybody considered him responsible for Potch leaving, when in fact he left because he wanted to go. They had a number of cows and calves with the steers because they were cutting way back on the herd this fall as it looked like a hard winter coming.

The only thing that saved the steers from scattering beyond hope of ever gathering again was the gentler cows. They had been driven before, weren't terrified of cowboys on horses, and the wild steers stayed close to them. They finally made it to Craig with the herd and a buyer bought the cattle. As part of the deal Charley had to agree to deliver the cattle on to the train station and see that they got loaded. He was glad to do that since he already had the money and he didn't have to worry about weight shrinkage on the cattle, so he could get them to the train station any way he had to.

After shipping the beef Charley surprised everybody by sending Pat to Denver to buy a Jeep he had made a deal on. It was bright yellow and brand new. Pat drove it proudly into Craig. Charley had left him a message with Roy Grounds to bring it on home. The only bad news was that Nav had begged his dad to let him stay and ride home in the new Jeep with Pat. Pat gathered up a girl friend and together with Don Grounds and his girl friend they were ready to to deliver the Jeep to the ranch. Nav was about as popular as a skunky dog, but he didn't care because he really wanted to ride in that brand new Jeep.

Evelyn took Pat, Queeda and their belongings right back out for school in the Jeep. Queeda was moved into the home of Henry Mobley, the county clerk. Helen and Hank had raised three fine girls of their own and Evelyn felt comfortable that they would take care of Queeda. The daughter of a Douglas Mountain rancher, Lillian Sheridan roomed with the Mobleys, too. Evelyn stayed a week finishing up Queeda's wardrobe and getting her settled in. Helen often did sewing for people and offered to make a suit for Queeda, so Evelyn provided material. Evelyn also got material for Helen to make a topcoat for herself, which pleased her very much. When she returned a couple of weeks later she found that the suit turned out grand. Evelyn also searched out a music teacher and signed Queeda up for piano lessons. She thought it worth one more effort. It wasn't.

After Evelyn left Queeda was very lonesome. This was such an unknown world to her that she was afraid to venture out for anything but school. Pat came by and took her to the movies, took her out to dinner, introduced her to his friends, took her to school activities and tried in every way to get her to relax. He played on the football team and worked almost full time in addition to going to school, so it was a great sacrifice he made to pay her all that attention.

Suddenly and unexpectedly, a comic strip started appearing in the Craig paper. The main character was Queeda Cantle. This girl lived in a canyon and had all sorts of adventures with a river and horses and deer and wild animals. A man from Craig wrote the comic strip. He had spent many happy times at the Mantle home and knew them well. Each day the librarian, Mrs. Coles, would cut out the comic strip for Queeda and give it to her in home room. At first Queeda was embarrassed at all the attention it brought on her, but finally got into the fun of it and made friends and started enjoying life again.

Evelyn went to a doctor in Hayden to see about the lump in her breast. He wanted to send her to Denver immediately for surgery. She and Charley quickly caught up on chores, after which she left. On her way to catch a bus into Denver, she went after the mail at the K Ranch. Pierre and Hilda begged her to go to Salt Lake to a specialist Hilda had gone to. She and Hilda got on the bus at ten a.m. Friday, the fourth of October and reached Salt Lake at four that afternoon. Evelyn suffered from motion sickness most of the way. The next morning at 9:30 they went to the doctor's office, only to find that he had just left for a two-month rest.

Evelyn had made a long trip and wanted some resolution to the problem, so they went to the Salt Lake Clinic, where a doctor worked her into his busy schedule that very morning. He examined her and said she had chronic mastitis and unless the kernel grew noticeably in three months she had nothing to worry about, adding, "I don't mean growing in your mind, either." He said it might last fifteen or twenty years. Evelyn knew that the nagging worry that it was cancer would never leave her in peace, but she would try as hard as she could to put it out of her mind for three months.

Charley's yellow Jeep that changed the lives of the Mantle family.

Evelyn and Hilda returned to Jensen to Hilda's brother's house at 2:30 a.m. Sunday. Later that morning they went on to the K Ranch. The weather was terrible and rained three days straight. Evelyn finally got in the Jeep and headed home because she just couldn't stay away any longer. It was time for Nav and Tim to be in school. She wondered who the teacher would be and what arrangement the Chews had made for a school house. It was a terrible trip home, with the Jeep all over the road in the mud. She reported the Jeep to be "a daisy in mud and on rough, impossible roads." After she got home it rained another three days, then snowed six inches. At least it didn't leave much time to worry about her lump.

Precious Old Red, the horse, came down sick. He had a bad stomach ache for days. He would stand as near the house as he could get, as if begging for help. Evelyn nursed him desperately. She gave him charcoal and even tobacco for worms and gave him warm water to drink afterward. In spite of all her efforts he died. She felt like one of the family had left them. She felt lonesome, and also helpless without him to help with all the chores.

Evelyn's class: Back: Queeda (not a student), Lonnie, Evelyn, George D. Chew. Front: Stanley Chew, Tim, Eula Chew, Carol Chew.

33

Bench School, 1946-47

WHILE EVELYN WAS IN HAYDEN TO SEE THE DOCTOR about the lump in her breast, she learned that Potch was competing at a local rodeo. She looked him up and explained the situation; how his dad was in a jam and needed help. Since it was the end of the rodeo season anyway so Potch came back home. His feelings toward his mother had not really changed, but he was at least civil toward her. He and Pat patched up their differences and agreed to work together through this family crisis. Potch had been in California, Nevada, and Utah, and after considerable urging would tell Pat about his travels. He almost never talked to anyone else. He wouldn't go back to school, but his mother would always be guilt-ridden, believing he sacrificed school because he was needed so much at home.

Evelyn received another blow when she got home from Salt Lake City. The Chews had been unable to find a teacher. Rial begged her with tears in his eyes to teach the kids one more year. She tried to dissuade him from having the school out on the bench because of the bad roads and floods and the pure difficulty of doing it. Evelyn said they would be glad to keep the kids at their house and she would teach in the school house where everything was set up, but Irma would not hear of it and said, "I by damn want my kids home every night!" Rial was so dear to her and Evelyn could see how much pressure he was under, so she agreed to do it.

They moved what they needed from the school house to the small trailer Rial had parked out on the Bench. It was certainly not going to be as convenient as the little cozy schoolhouse, but what must be done must be done. Evelyn set up a little emergency kitchen at the school. They hauled wood from along the road each day and Rial usually helped cut it up into stove lengths. They hauled water in five-gallon army cans from the spring at home.

Both families drove back and forth every day. It was a five-mile drive for the Mantles and seven for Chews. Nav, Tim, Stanley, Eula, and sometimes Carroll, who was really too young for school, were the students. Rial's sheep herder whose three children were going to attend school got fired, so Evelyn would not have those children. Nav was eleven, in sixth grade, Stanley was nine, in third grade, Eula was eight, in second grade, and Tim was eight, in third grade. George D, the youngest Chew was two years old and wanted to go to school too. Every day he threw a major fit when he got hauled away after the other kids got delivered to school. Sometimes Evelyn gave him "classes" when they arrived early to pick up the kids after school. The mixture of ages and grades made Evelyn's teaching job very difficult. She always managed to give each child his full due in education and spent long hours into the night studying by the light of a kerosene lamp for the next day.

Chews had an old International truck and an old beer distributing van that advertised Blatz beer. Everybody called this "The Beer Wagon." They drove their kids to school in it. The two Mantle boys learned to be expert Jeep drivers by trial and error. Tim needed several pillows and blankets behind him so he could reach the foot pedals. Usually he just sat on a cinder block with a rock behind him. When he had to use the brake his head would disappear from sight while he got his foot low enough to touch the brake. He fastened a block of wood on the gas pedal so he could reach it.

How glad Evelyn was that Potch was there to help his dad. Charley & Potch shoved the cattle off the mountain, dug potatoes, hauled wood, and cleaned chimneys. The cattle were going into the winter poor because it had been such a dry summer. They butchered a lot that fall. It cost thirty dollars a month and half a beef for Pat's room and board with the Grounds family, and twenty-five dollars a month and half a beef for Queeda.

Evelyn managed one trip into Craig after school started to see that Pat and Queeda were settled in. She delivered the beef to Craig when she went and she also took a mutton.

Pat was a starting player on the football team and she got to see him play just that once. How proud she was. Queeda seemed all right at Mobleys, and Evelyn was relieved that she didn't seem too lonely.

Evelyn had found after her teaching year began that she needed reading glasses. She got tested and measured for glasses and chose the frame she wanted while she was in Craig. The glasses had to be mailed to her. When they arrived they fit fairly well and it was a great relief not to suffer headaches from eye strain anymore.

The winter started off snowing, and soon became dangerous to the livestock. Charley and Potch spent most of the winter camped out far from the ranch, keeping the cattle alive by continually moving them to shelter and feed.

School was from 8:00 am to 5:00 pm. The winter sun went down at 4:30, so there were no daylight hours at home. Saturday and Sunday Evelyn washed, cleaned, mended, made more clothes, and baked and cooked. She tried to console herself that the long hours were good because she couldn't worry so much about Queeda and Pat.

One day at school Stanley broke his arm at the wrist. During afternoon recess, the kids were jumping over cardboard boxes. He didn't quite make it, fell back, threw out his hand to catch himself and broke both bones. Evelyn loaded all the kids in the Jeep and took him home, then helped Irma get ready to take him to town. Luckily it was his left arm and he was a very tough kid, so he was back in school very soon. Evelyn had trouble getting the Chew kids to not cuss. It was just part of their everyday conversation, but she finally got them to cut down on the most offensive words. She compromised by letting them get by with the "By Damn's."

That winter and the next were also the times of enormous herds of deer inhabiting the Red Rock and Blue Mountain area. The Mantles saw coyotes surround and kill weak deer on the bench as they went back and forth to school. The deer were forced off the mountain by deep snow and ate everything including the sage brush. In fact they killed much of the brush on the bench from Hells Canyon to Red Rock. That, at least, was a blessing because the sage brush often grew too thick for grass to grow under it, ruining the grazing.

Tim and Nav ran a trap line and would often walk home from school via the Ladder Canyon or Cliff Dweller Cave, or often down the trail off the bench in front of the homestead cabin. They got a good price for the pelts. On a weekend they would walk the full rim from the head of Hells Canyon clear to the school house and on north to the rim above the mouth of Red Rock. If they caught a coyote or bobcat they usually skinned it on location so they didn't have to carry the heavy carcass all the way home. On a weekend Evelyn would wash clothes. Before they left, the boys would make sure she had plenty of water and wood to heat water. They would reset and work over their whole trap line on a week end. They could hear the old Maytag washer popping and echoing off the canyon walls around the full three or four mile trap line route. If the washer stopped over fifteen or twenty minutes that usually meant Mother was having trouble so they would hurry home.

One day after school, they were passing above the Mantle Cave in the Jeep. Evelyn would stop and let them check a trap if it wasn't too far from the road. This day, sure enough, the trap and drag (a log the trap was tied to) were gone. They trailed the drag out, but eventually lost the trail. Finally Kelly, their little Terrier dog got to barking up a tree and they found the bobcat had climbed the tree and was sitting in the crotch about six to eight feet up, watching them. He was caught by a hind foot. They didn't have a gun, so Tim and Nav knocked him out with rocks. He fell out from the tree and was swinging about two feet off the ground by one hind foot when Kelly attacked him. Well the hair was really flying and there was a lot of growling, so to save her dog Evelyn picked up a cedar club to hit the bobcat with, missed and knocked Kelly out by mistake. They finally got the cat killed and skinned. Rial would get five dollars bounty per coyote or bobcat for them in Utah and they could also sell the hide for about five dollars. They took the skins home, stretched and salted them, and stored them high in a small cave above the granary out of the reach of scavengers.

They used dead rabbits for bait, tied in a tree above a trap. If you hung it too high you got a hind foot because the cat had to stand on his hind feet to get the bait. It seemed they very seldom shot the rabbits—they usually "smoked them out." There is a fine art to smoking out a rabbit, as Lonnie delighted in telling his sister, to her disgust.

"When you see him run in a pile of rocks or a hole you plug it off with rocks so he can't get out. Then for about a quarter mile around you strip cedar bark off of trees till you have about a bushel of it. You ravel it up good and stuff it in the hole or holes where the rabbit went in or might escape. You set it on fire and let it get to burning pretty good before you ravel some more and stuff it in on top of the first burning bunch. After the fires get to going good smoke will start to come out of the cracks or other entrances so you need to plug those with cedar bark, dirt, or if it's warm enough, your coat. It takes about thirty minutes to choke the rabbit to death. If you listen you can hear him coming and trying to get out scratching and coughing. Pull the bark and fire out of the hole he went in and he'll be dead and scorched right behind the first cedar bark you put in. It's a lot simpler if you remember to take the gun when you need bait."

Sometimes in the winter the Jeep would get so cold it wouldn't start , so Nav dug a trench, which they filled each day at dark with hot coals. They then dove the Jeep forward to straddle the trench, and threw a blanket over the hood of the Jeep. At daylight the engine would still be warm and it would usually start. They would have trouble with water in the gas and occasionally have to drain the water out of the settling bulb to keep the engine running.

The winter of 1947-1948 was a nightmare for Evelyn. It was a wet winter, but the ground didn't freeze enough to keep the road solid. The Jeep wallowed to and from school in mud up to its axles. Usually the Chews chose to let their kids go home with Evelyn on school nights rather than fight the mud to come after them. She and the kids threw rocks and brush in the ruts they made, trying to make it passable for the next day. Only once were they hopelessly stuck. On that occasion, the wheels of the Jeep were completely out of sight. She had fought the mud for so long since leaving the school house that it was already completely dark. It was just at the head of Hells Canyon, so she decided to walk home down the canyon the two plus miles. With four children in tow she descended into the inky blackness of Hells Canyon. A coyote or something about that size jumped out of a bush in front of them and came hurtling past them. Startled and frightened, they all found a stick to carry for protection, and they hurried on down the seemingly endless canyon to the warm home.

The next day they went after the Jeep. It took them until two in the afternoon to get it unstuck and home. The ruts across the bench made it impossible to drive the road. Evelyn and the kids took a pack horse and brought the necessary school supplies home. Finally Rial had to ride in on horseback to pick up the children. He and Evelyn decided it would be much better to have the children stay at the Mantles and have school until the weather dried up, so for nearly a month school was held at Evelyn's house.

Evelyn had not heard from Queeda and Pat since January 6 when she had delivered them back to school after Christmas vacation. The snow had been too deep to get out. Finally on March 27 the canyon started flooding, indicating that at last the snow had started to melt and they could soon get out to see how the two high school students were getting along. Evelyn was thankful for Mrs. Mobley and Mrs. Grounds, and how she hoped and prayed they were looking after her children.

Finally in a fit of enraged motherhood, Irma Chew demanded that her children be able to stay at home and travel to school daily. The school on the bench was once more put into session. With the spring thaw came yet another problem. The flooding creek made it impossible to drive to the school. The alternative route was a tough one, but Evelyn's determination to educate the children was unwavering. Every day Evelyn and her children crossed the flooding creek on a plank spanning the creek at the dam. They had to walk the plank over the raging waters, then shinny around a ledge of rock, drop onto the other side of the creek, and walk down the river a mile and a half to Ladder Canyon. There was the remnant of an old

Potch, Pat, and Tommy Peterson hand dug a new well.

ladder there. They repaired the ladder a bit so they could climb out onto the bench, and walk on a half mile to the school. Evelyn was pretty skinned-up after the first climb out, so Rial completely rebuilt the ladder. He put new rungs on, tied his brand new lariat into knots, and tied it to a cedar tree for the final ascent over slick rocks after the ladder climb ended. Nav was always amazed that Rial left that brand new rope there forever. They left before dawn and returned after dark. Chores and meals were all done in the dark.

One night in the spring of 1947 a terrible crunching and crashing filled the canyons. The next morning revealed that the river had risen four feet during the night, carrying ice from lord only knew where upstream, shoving it over and under the ice from nearby with so much force that it ultimately made a huge dam of ice in the river. The water backed up quickly, threatening the orchard. Finally a channel opened up that released the backed up water. They heard on the radio that an ice jam had been threatening to flood Craig, so they had dynamited it. The water released there had come down the river all at once, causing the ice jam and the river continued to rise from spring run-off.

The milk cows had crossed the river, and Evelyn couldn't cross to get them, but Charley came down from camp four days later and went over and

A wagon load of produce on its way from the orchard and garden to the house.

got them. Engorged with milk, caked and miserable, the cows had started the process of drying up. Evelyn and the boys worked diligently with the cows until finally, to Evelyn's intense relief, they started making milk again. Evelyn couldn't even imagine how she could feed her family without the milk, cream and cheese from the cows.

The end of school found Evelyn almost ill from exhaustion and the spring work of the ranch was upon them. While Charley and Potch were away working with the cattle, Nav and Tim worked their hearts out helping her all they could. They cleaned ditches, plowed the garden, spread fertilizer, planted and built fence. They were like two small tanks.

On Memorial Day the whole family except for Potch went out to Craig for Pat's graduation from high school. It was a grand affair and they were so very proud of him. Evelyn cried for joy as she hugged him hard.

As the ground dried out something had to be done with the mess the winter had made of the road over Red Rock Bench. The ruts were so deep that the road was nearly impassable. Nav and Tim fashioned an old car bumper as a drag to pull behind the Jeep to fill some of the ruts. They weighted it with rocks to make it dig in and move the dirt. Dick Toole came along one day and saw them working with this contraption. Not long afterward he brought in an old horse-drawn road grader. He brought it in from the east, pulled by an old Allis Chalmers tractor. The Mantles were elated. They pulled it behind the Jeep to grade the road and it kept the ruts leveled and the roads passable until Moffat County took on the job of keeping the road graded.

Charley and Potch came home to dig another well. Pat, Potch, and a friend dug it. This one was near the house, and they hit a good supply of water at fifty feet. It caved on them, and once again the dream of a well failed. The well below the house had long since caved so badly that it was not usable at all, and the garden had to be moved back down to the orchard. Evelyn despaired of ever having a lawn with flowers and trees as she had dreamed of. Also, the back breaking job of getting water for use at the house was endless. They dipped water from the river into barrels mounted on a skid and pulled it behind a work horse or the Jeep to the house. Drinking water was hauled from the spring. The bathroom which Evelyn had built in the house remained an empty room.

The summer brought scientists to evaluate the archaeology of the area. The chief archaeologist for the US Department of Interior looked over the caves and the materials left behind by prehistoric man. It was concluded that the area might contain important historical evidence of prehistoric man. Using tree rings, it was determined that the Basket Makers lived here 1300-1500 years ago. It was the farthest north this culture had been traced thus far. A man named Bob Burgh was sent in and worked in the canyons, finishing up Scoggin's work. Evelyn and Charley were especially pleased that Burgh was going to publish Scoggin's work, under both their names, with full credit to Scoggin for his work.

The orchard produced a bumper crop. Evelyn canned all they could use, then traded the surplus for turkeys, chickens, grains and honey. Charley's sister Nancy had come from California for a visit, and had helped Evelyn. The two women had a very special friendship and Evelyn was refreshed by her visit. She was the only person in all the world who knew everything about Evelyn, her past, her loves, her pains, and her joys. She was in turn Nancy's support in her own very difficult life.

It seemed that the Ranch had been discovered as a place to spend vacations. Tourists and friends poured in. Evelyn entertained, guided, answered questions and cooked for people all summer. Many friends came to visit. Once Tommy Morgan and Doris Karen came to visit. The whole family took the rubber raft to Hardings Hole and made a day of it floating to the ranch. They had a great time swimming and fishing. They cooked the fish they caught on a small camp fire and that was lunch. They caught more fish and that was supper.

Potch and Pat competed in every rodeo in the area that summer. They usually split the first prizes, one winning one day the other the next. Potch had won a beautiful flower-stamped, all-around saddle early in the season, which he had given to his dad. Both boys competed in both saddle and bareback broncs events. Potch won a saddle in Vernal, to be built to order. He ordered a regulation bronc-riding saddle and he and Pat competed on it for years.

34

Surgery, 1947-48

HEIR SHY, GRUFF YOUNG COWBOY FRIEND, Boyd Walker surprised everybody by getting married. He met a girl from a ranch in Wyoming named Wanda Ramsey. She could ride and rope and live as tough as Boyd thought he wanted to. She was very pretty, intelligent, and soft spoken. It didn't take her very long to polish off the rough spots on the tough cowboy and make a first class husband of him. Boyd was so proud of her that he took her all over the country showing her off. He moved them into a nice house in Browns Park. They fixed it all up, and he even started mumbling about having a baby. He even milked the cow. Everybody was amazed and thrilled at how happy he was, and what a happy couple they were.

Through Wanda, Evelyn heard of a boarding school named Wasatch Academy. It was operated by Presbyterian missionaries in the little predominantly Mormon town of Mt. Pleasant, Utah. She had gone to high school there, and loved it. She said that there were many kids there who came from isolated places, especially Western ranches, where there were no schools. It was highly accredited, and she had no problem going right into college from there.

Evelyn was worried about sending Queeda back to Craig without Pat being there. She applied for admission to Wasatch Academy for Queeda starting in the fall of 1947. The waiting list was very long. The only chance Queeda had of being accepted was on the grounds of the family's extreme isolation. Wasatch Academy gave preference to kids from isolated ranches and other areas from where access to good schools was difficult.

Finally the letter arrived! Evelyn opened it with trembling hands. It was late, and the dorms were full, but they could take Queeda if she would room with another girl across the street from campus at a private home. She would take meals on campus. Evelyn joyfully said yes, and Queeda was enrolled for fall as a tenth grader. It would be a 250-mile trip from the K Ranch to Wasatch, but somehow they would do it when the time came.

On June 27 Evelyn labored as the temperature reached 108 degrees. She picked from the garden and the orchard as soon as it was light enough to see in the morning. Then she prepared and canned the produce in the sweltering kitchen. Vehicle loads of curious people arrived daily. She would drop her work and graciously entertain them with chilled fruit juice and a visit, answering prying questions about her life and family. She had a box of Indian artifacts she had collected over the years that she would show them and explain what they were. A mountain goat horn with a hole in it for peeling arrows; a cedar bark pouch she called the squaw's shopping basket, a reed mat, an arrow with sinew to secure the point and feathers, her extensive arrowhead collection, pieces of pottery, corn, squash, etc. Her graciousness was unfaltering (This box was later stolen from the house). Her work was still there to be done after all the questions were answered and the rude snooping around the house and yard had ended.

Boyd Walker and his bride, the former Wanda Ramsey.

On Labor Day weekend Charley and Evelyn drove to Wasatch Academy to enroll Queeda in school. Nav and Tim went also, because if this school worked out for Queeda, they too would soon be there. The trip was a great adventure to the three country kids. They drove up beautiful canyons, over a mountain pass and past many interesting cattle ranches, and most interesting of all, towns. The school was very good at orienting frightened parents.

A senior girl took the family on a tour of the campus and some class rooms. They visited the Principal, Mr. Gunn, and the Vice Principal, Mr. Hansen. Everyone was cordial and friendly, but the emphasis was on the education they could give. Both Evelyn and Charley were pleased by this. They checked out the infirmary and both the girl's and boy's dorms. They also met the obviously vigilant dorm mothers. All the campus rules of etiquette, dress, and deportment were explained in detail. Attendance at weekly worship was required. Every student was assigned jobs that were rotated each quarter. They ate in the school cafeteria and found the food to be very good and everybody happy. Queeda had never had the chance to experience this type of relationship, and it sure looked good to Charley and Evelyn.

The schoolhouse trailer on the bench at Red Rock.

Very quickly Queeda was moved into a nice room in the home of a moth-erly lady and her husband. A bank account was set up at the school. A set amount was deposited, from which she could draw her weekly allowance. An additional account was set up with emergency funds that could be withdrawn by getting permission from the principal. The school preferred that no extra money be sent to the students. Queeda's classes were assigned and books bought at the campus bookstore. The dining area was a big room below the gymnasium. Tables were covered with white table cloths and white cloth nap-kins. Meals were family style, all you could eat. Satisfied, Charley paid the tuition for a whole year rather than just half, because he would be unable to return with Queeda following the Christmas break.

Pierre and Hilda also talked with Wanda about Wasatch, and they enrolled Tommy there, too. He and Queeda were great friends. His constant good humor and big smile always brightened her day. He came home for a weekend visit with the report that she had been voted sophomore attendant to the homecoming queen. Queeda was fitting in, and her letters told how much she liked being in school there. Her first report card showed her to be doing very well in school. She had gotten a job at the school managing the pantry, which helped out on her expenses. Evelyn felt very comfortable with their deci-sion to send their daughter to school at Wasatch.

When she got home Evelyn found that Rial had moved the trailer house school even farther away. It was on a hill just east of Red Rock draw, overlook-ing the slab rocks and cliffs at the head of Red Rock Canyon. She set it up for school. There were three Chew children and two Mantle children. This was an even farther drive for Evelyn, but it was shorter for Chews. Evelyn started school on October 6.

Pat had been working for Pierre Morgan at the K Ranch all fall, so nobody was around to help with all the fall work. Nancy stayed until October 24, which was lots of help and comforting company for Evelyn. Pat had decided to wait a year before starting college. He got time off from his job, and he and Charley were on the mountain for hunting season. Charley had finally agreed to having an operation to relieve him from the terrible pain he was having from hemorrhoids. No date had been set for the surgery, however.

Potch was working for Rial. Everyone referred to him as "Charley" now, and he preferred not to be called Potch any more. He was spending a lot of time at Doug Chew's ranch. Doug's son, Dean and Potch were good friends, but the main attraction was Dean's pretty red-headed sister, Melba Ellen. Charley gave her an engagement ring, but was very reluctant to share the news with his family because he knew he would get teased. Evelyn was very happy for him. Charley had no comment.

Evelyn had not seen her parents for a long time and was longing for a visit with them. She could not even approach Charley about it, as he didn't want her to ever see them again. She would just have to sneak away for a weekend and have Nancy teach in her place for a day.

The Chews had just bought a new Chevrolet sedan. The road in from the west end was good enough that they ran in and out of their ranch to town all the time. Evelyn warned Eva, however, not to try to drive their trailer in when they came. The road could become totally impassable with the slightest rain.

Always great friends, the children shouted and clowned for each other when they gathered for the first day of school. They quickly settled in to the routine of classes. Carroll was old enough for first grade this year and very proud to be in school with the big kids. Nav was in seventh grade, Stanley in sixth, Tim in fourth, and Eula in third.

One day Eula was out playing at recess. Something went terribly wrong and she broke her elbow. Tears of pain streamed down her face, but there was no yelling and screaming as Evelyn quickly loaded all the kids in the Jeep and took them to Pool Creek, where the Chews took her the forty-mile trip over rough roads to town to get her arm set. Unfortunately, the doctor did a terrible job of setting the elbow and it was crooked for the rest of her life. Her sweet little face was clouded with pain for many days after she returned to school.

Recess usually consisted of running around through the rocky canyon full tilt, playing some kind of chase game. One day Nav fell on a sharp rock right on his knee. It was cut really deep just below the kneecap. Blood poured out of it and the tendons were bared. Stanley half carried Nav back to the school. Evelyn told Stanley to get the horses ready while she stopped the flow of blood. She got the Chew kids on their horses and started home, then she and Tim loaded Nav in the Jeep and headed home.

Charley was cutting wood on the hill overlooking the homestead and came running down to the road when Evelyn started honking the horn. They got home and they laid him out on a bed in the living room, cleaned the cut out and of course it had to be sewed up. Nav got kind of hysterical after the first stitch and Charley told him if he couldn't take it he would have to knock him out and then sew it up. It was easier to stand after that statement. Evelyn left a drain in it, kept him quiet that night and over the week end. She changed bandages regularly and checked for infection. The wound healed slowly and was stiff most of the winter, but healed completely although it left a bad scar. Nav never missed a day of school.

The Chew kids rode in one morning on their horses, which they often did. Eula was crying and couldn't get off her horse. Evelyn thought she was just cold, and rushed to help her off. She discovered that the horse had fallen and crushed the stirrup on her foot, so that she was unable to remove it. All the Chews were excellent riders from birth, and she had managed to stay with the horse when it got up. Evelyn undid the cinch and took saddle and Eula off the horse as a unit. She had to get the tire tool and pry the stirrup off Eula's foot. To this bunch of tough little kids that was just another incident of the day and school went on as usual with never a what if.

Rial left three year old George D at school one day during the critical time when the lambs were being born and he had to be with the sheep day and night. Carol was supposed to be watching him but he had the scissors and was working some of her stuff over when she caught him. She said, "Oh honey don't cut it all to hell."

Evelyn was worried about Queeda and very lonesome for her. She kept an ominous secret all to herself. Everyone was just too busy to be burdened with her problem just now. Pat and Potch were both working and not at home. Charley was down in the back, his piles were giving him misery, and he was terribly depressed and grumpy. She felt like the two younger boys were way overworked going to school and helping her do all the ranch chores besides. A diphtheria epidemic broke out in Utah, so all school children were inoculated, including Queeda. How she hoped the boys at home and the Chew kids would not get the disease, since there was no chance they were going to be inoculated.

In March Evelyn could keep her secret no longer. She had to see the doctor about a lump in her other breast. Besides, she just had to see Queeda. She went out horseback over the snowbound west end of Blue Mountain. Potch went with her and they bucked snow to the horses' bellies all the way. Evelyn's legs got so tired she had to keep getting off and walking to get the circulation going again.

The Morgans took Evelyn out to a cancer specialist in Salt Lake. She had been having a constant ache under her arms. Another woman graciously gave up her own appointment to Evelyn or she would not have been able to get in. The nurse didn't want to take her in the other woman's place, but finally after finding she had ridden thirty miles horseback through drifted snow to get there, she let her see the doctor. The doctor examined her and told her to come back June first for surgery. He explained that he was almost positive it wasn't cancerous because cancer doesn't ache, but he said the lumps should be removed anyway. The doctor instructed the nurse to make an appointment with the hospital for the first of June. The nurse said she couldn't make an appointment for that long in advance and he told her she would just have to, explaining that this lady lives too far away not to have some consideration. Pierre, Hilda, and Evelyn then drove to Wasatch to visit Tommy and Queeda. It was a tearful reunion and a healing visit.

Evelyn rode back home alone over the bleak, unforgiving mountain. She drove over to Pool Creek and told the Chews school was in session again. The little Jeep plowed faithfully through snow and mud. About mid-April the floods started in Hells Canyon so they couldn't get out to school. As before, she took all the children and taught them at her house until the flooding was passed. How tired she was when school let out. She just didn't know if she would be able to do it another year.

The day after school was out, Evelyn and Charley drove out for her operation. It was a stressful drive to Salt Lake to the hospital. Evelyn's operation went well. The tumors were very large, but benign. They both cried tears of relief. She stayed in the hospital only until the stitches came out. Faithful Nancy had come all the way from California and stayed with the boys during the two weeks that Charley and Evelyn were away. After Evelyn got out of the hospital they took time to go pick up Queeda from school, and enjoy a very welcome vacation. Evelyn had to do the driving because Charley didn't have a driver's license. It was painful, but she bore it gladly. The post-surgery pain was nothing to Evelyn compared to the dread and anguish she had suffered over fear of cancer.

35

Grasshoppers and Snow, 1948-49

UNE 1948 STARTED OUT with a full fledged grasshopper invasion. Evelyn made up a poison bran recipe mix given to her by the county agent. They scattered it about, but the grasshoppers wouldn't eat it as long as there was anything green left. They sprayed with a strong insecticide dust, but it was too dry for it to cling to foliage long enough to help. The grasshoppers stripped the garden completely. Then they ate the fruit off the fruit trees. Next they ate all the leaves off the fruit trees. Evelyn was sure the fruit trees would all die that winter.

Hilda Morgan had been Evelyn's good friend for many years. The blow was almost more than she could bear when she heard that Pierre and Hilda Morgan had sold their home, the K Ranch. They had been offered $100,000 clear for it and that was just too much money to turn down. Cattle and equipment all went with the ranch. They planned to leave right away to travel all over Mexico and the Southwest for six months to a year.

It looked like Pierre had done the right thing to sell the ranch. By July 13 it had not rained since the end of April. Charley was talking of selling every head of cattle they had except for a few milk cows. Prices were high right now, too. Rial, too, had sold nearly all his sheep with the plan of buying a herd in the spring.

An added misery was that the talk had become serious of building a dam in Echo Park just below where the Green and the Yampa rivers joined. The dam would back the Yampa river up and fill the canyons with water. The Mantle Ranch would be under 200 feet of water. All the Colorado River Basin states wanted the water and were fighting hard for it. Folks in Vernal wanted the dam because they would profit mightily from such a huge recreation area. Mantle's ranch would be condemned for a very low value, and all those years of work would be for nothing. Their security, both financial and personal would be gone.

The University of Colorado had an archaeological group headed by Bob Lister camped at the ranch doing research. They were doing intense work on Hells Midden, a site that promised to identify the different civilizations of ancient men that had lived in the area. If they found enough rare and rich evidence of ancient civilizations predating the basket makers, that could just possibly stop the dam from being built. The CU excavation team was camped by Hells Midden for two summers, and the Mantles enjoyed these congenial neighbors.

Hugo Rodeck, also of the University of Colorado, was in charge of the team that was collecting local specimens of plants, birds and animals. They shot the lizards and birds with buckshot in a .22 caliber shell. They then preserved them in formaldehyde bottles. Tim and Nav thought they were helping by shooting every lizard, bird, and toad that they saw with a single shot bb gun and bringing the mangled bodies to Hugo. They also ran down elusive roadrunner lizards for the delighted onlookers and brought many cans with specimens in them to Hugo.

Adair Feldman was a student worker collecting specimens that summer. He took a liking to Tim and Lonnie and they were eager to please and impress him. The boys would perform for him by shooting the head of a match off at about twenty feet. Apparently they impressed Adair because he sent them a pump-up pellet gun in the mail. It was powerful enough to kill a rabbit not too far away. In the summer the two boys were always shirt-less so Hugo gave them two old shirts of his because he didn't believe they had shirts of their own.

For the fourth of July Adair got a big stick of dynamite (BIG, like a foot long and three inches wide). After much ceremony he set it off on the ledge above the old orchard by the campground. It made an impressive boom that bounced around the canyon walls for quite awhile and about two hours later the fire lookout from Round Top showed up and asked for an explanation. Was there a war going on, he wondered, or just what was all that shooting about?

Charley took Queeda to the summer camp presumably to help with the cattle. She and Doris Karen became good friends and were able to spend quite a bit of time together. Lonnie also spent most of his time up there. Evelyn was lonelier than she had ever been. Tim felt left out, but worked faithfully through the hard summer. She and Tim held the home place together as best they could. They climbed deep into the well and cleaned the sand out well enough around the pipe to get some precious water. Evelyn had a pump in the well to bring the water to the yard. By moving the pipes and hoses around they got grass to grow into a nice green lawn. Evelyn planted a small garden by the house so they would at least have some vegetables that survived the grasshoppers.

Queeda had been asked to be a bridesmaid at the wedding of Pierre and Hilda Morgan's daughter, Rebecca. It was to be a grand affair, and Evelyn didn't see how she could make the bridesmaid's dress fine enough. She was in a constant state of worry, anyway, trying to dress Queeda so that she would not be ashamed of her clothes. She made fine cowboy shirts for the boys, which were the envy of all their friends at the rodeos. She never got all the clothes mended and shirts and pants made for the young boys that they needed. Sometimes she felt chained to the sewing machine. The dress she made for Queeda was beautiful, and Queeda felt like a princess in it.

Nancy left on the bus on July 13, so now Evelyn was completely alone and had all these burdens to handle by herself. Also, she was not very strong yet after her surgery, but had to keep up the work. She became more worn and haggard looking every day.

The Chews bought a house in town, and moved out for the winter. Evelyn was shocked that they could pay $12,500 for a house in Vernal. Rial would undoubtedly stay at the ranch and care for the sheep. Evelyn was greatly relieved that her days of teaching at some lonely place between the two ranches was over. She would have school at home this year for Nav and Tim. She wouldn't get paid for it, because school must be conducted in a school house removed from the residence in order for the teacher to be paid. Her teacher's salary was the only money she had ever had in her life that was hers. She hated to give it up, but she was very relieved not to have to make the miserable drive every day.

Charley brought in a floor sander and Evelyn finished the wood floors. She also made drapes for the living room, re-dobbed the house and put rock-wool insulation in the ceiling. She had lots of house plants and was proud of how her home looked.

Charley and Pat gathered beef early in October and trucked them to a pasture outside Craig to hold them until the market was more favorable. Wild and terrified by any sight or sound of civilization, the steers got spooked and tore down the fences and scattered into the thick oak brush. Pat rode for six weeks trying to gather them. Some he had to hire an airplane to help locate. Finally they shipped what they had just before Thanksgiving. There were still eleven missing when winter set in and it started snowing on November third.

The Jeep was out with Charley and Pat. Evelyn, Nav and Tim were alone. They hadn't had a chance to get supplies in for the winter yet, and Evelyn was worried. It snowed nearly every day from then on. They had no supplies, nor even kerosene for the lamps, and snow was piling up on the mountain to a frightening depth. Charley got a truck to bring in supplies to the top of the mountain, where they could bring it on in Jeep loads, and they finally got set up for a hard winter.

All at once it began to thaw. It thawed for ten days straight and bared the ground. Even the mountain didn't have much left on it, so they decided they could drive out and get Queeda for her Christmas vacation. Charley and Evelyn went out the east way on Friday, December 17, leaving Nav and Tim at home to do chores. They made it to Pop's Place along Highway 40. Queeda's bus was held up by a snow storm in Salt Lake, so they waited beside the road for her until 12:15 that night. They had been made welcome at Earl Gadd's home at Pop's Place just outside the little village of Blue Mountain, and spent the night there. Saturday they shopped in Vernal and Sunday they started home. They decided to go the east way because probably the road on the mountain had had some traffic over it to break up the snow drifts. They had to shovel through drifts twice, and it took them all day to get home, which looked mighty good when they arrived.

Pat wasn't able to make it home for Christmas. Mr. Calder, the new owner of the K Ranch had kept him on. They paid him a fabulous $175 a month, room and board and he could have his own cows to feed and look after. He also charged Calder for the use of his saddle horses since Calder had none. He was free to help his dad whenever he was needed. His parents were very proud of their nineteen-year-old son. Later, Pat worked for other absentee ranchers on Blue Mountain, who also paid for the use of his horses. He took advantage of every opportunity to make some money.

Over Christmas vacation Queeda gave Evelyn a Toni Permanent. Everybody feasted, opened presents, and had a wonderful time, although it was very lonely without Potch and Pat. It seemed very strange to have only five places at the table for Christmas dinner.

Every year since Evelyn married this wild cowboy, Eva had sent a Christmas box. When Eva was the wife of an ailing man with her own hands full she still sent the box. When she was a struggling widow with a child to support she sent the box. Now she had married a man who was generous and loving to her extended family. He insisted that she send an even bigger Christmas box each year. Eva knew that Evelyn yearned for the nice things she remembered from her childhood, as well as knowing that she needed a multitude of practical things. In the box was always included some delicate crochet work, pot holders, aprons, perfume, toys, nuts, candy, fine fabrics, used and new, patterns, fashion flyers, magazine subscriptions, muslin, soap, sheets, towels, flower seeds, lace, buttons, socks, mittens, gloves, tobacco, and on and on. She was a wonderful angel in the joy she brought to Evelyn. Evelyn never had much money to spend on gifts and she was so grateful to Eva for supplying this glorious experience for her children.

Evelyn wrote to Eva. She told her of her fear and discouragement around Thanksgiving time with no supplies in and winter upon them. The beef they so needed to sell to pay expenses were scattered. Her family was scattered. She was alone! She wrote, "I marvel at our peace and contentment now." Once again they had survived cruel trials and lived to find peace in their home in "Hells Hole," as the place was called.

The stallion, Shafter, that ran with the brood mares had to be replaced because his own offspring would be breeding age in the spring. Charley bought a huge chestnut stallion from Pierre Morgan. The powerful horse was not broke to ride, and the battle began. Charley couldn't afford to get hurt, so he let the horse tire himself out at every opportunity. He packed him with heavy loads of rock salt to distribute to the range cattle. He rode him unshod so he would have to think about watching where he stepped rather than bucking. He scotched him up and got on him and let him throw his fits on just three legs until he was too tired to care, then untied his leg and mounted up. Finally, he settled into a fairly dependable state. Charley was excited about the big horse. He had huge shoulders, long powerful legs, and the quickness of a cat. He was fearless of ropes and mud and ice, but very smart about staying out of jams with his rider. He got to test the big horse much sooner than he had expected.

It snowed for sixty hours straight right after Christmas, but didn't leave much lying except on the mountain. It was obvious that Charley would have to take Queeda back out to school on horseback. They started out before daylight on January first for the ride to Jensen. Charley was riding his Morgan stud who he predicted would be well broke and much gentler after breaking through snow drifts all day. Queeda was on a big, stout horse and everything they were taking was tied on their saddles. As they rode off Evelyn uttered a tearful silent prayer for their safe journey and Charley's safe return alone. It was a bitter cold day and even though they trotted along at a good pace their hands and feet were so close to freezing that they had to stop in the Barn Cave in Red Rock Canyon to warm up. Charley built a hot little fire close to the cliff to reflect as much heat as possible. When the feeling was back in their toes and fingers they continued on, pushing the horses at a fast clip while the snow was only knee deep. They had to get all the way across the mountain before dark. Charley knew there would be huge drifts to break through on the mountain, if they could make it at all.

As they started up the side of the mountain from Iron Springs the drifts and crusted snow started getting progressively deeper. The higher they got, the deeper the snow. It was a battle to get through the last big drift hanging at the rim before they broke out on top. The horses had to stop and catch their breath often, but the big stud really showed his stuff. Their lives depended on him, and he seemed to know it. After topping out on the mountain it was a little easier because the snow was blown off the tops of the ridges. Getting through the drifts between the ridges was slow, hard work. Charley would put Queeda in front to break trail at intervals to give his horse a rest. A couple of times his big horse got into drifts he couldn't break through, and then Charley would have to get off and break trail afoot for awhile. Both horses were trembling from exhaustion, and Charley was so tired he feared he couldn't get them to safety. At last they reached the rim and dropped off the mountain toward Jensen The snow gradually became softer and not so deep. How glad they were when they finally reached Jensen just as darkness came. The Haslems warm house, hot food, and a sheltered place with hay and grain for the horses was just too wonderful. Charley called Pat at the K Ranch to come get Queeda, who was then put on the bus the next day to return to school at Wasatch.

Charley stayed the night in Jensen and left as soon as he could see a little daylight the next morning in order to get home before the trail drifted shut, but as he feared, this had already happened. It became a fight for life as he crossed the mountain. Several times the horse Queeda had ridden got down then struggled until he was stuck in the snow drifts. Charley tromped the snow around him until he could get back up. As the day progressed and the horses got increasingly tired and darkness started settling in, Charley thought seriously about the wisdom of leaving the tired saddle horse and going on without him, but he couldn't bear to leave the faithful horse to die in a snow drift. By alternately stomping him out of the drifts, pulling him out with the stud, and letting him rest, he finally got him off the mountain.

His horses' heads drooping and barely able to go on, Charley finally arrived at the ranch at midnight. It had been sixteen hours since he had left Jensen. The dogs barked to announce his arrival and then Evelyn heard Charley's call, "Come help me off!" Already out the door, she ran to him in the darkness, fearing greatly of what had befallen him. She had spent hours worrying about him, and knew there had been a big problem because he was so late. She found him crouched helpless on his horse, his feet frozen into the stirrups so he couldn't dismount. He had gunny sacks cut up and tied around his legs with string to keep the snow out of his overshoes and boots. The melting snow had formed great cakes of ice around his feet and the stirrups. Evelyn had to break the ice with a hammer to get him loose. She and the boys got him into the house and sat him in a chair far from the heater, as he would need to warm up very slowly if he was going to survive.

The boys went out and unsaddled the horses and fed them and put them away. Evelyn got a hot toddy down Charley to warm him from the inside. She buried his feet and hands in a pan full of snow and massaged them until her shoulders ached. Finally a heavenly pink glow began to replace the dead white of his skin. He also began to howl and cuss as sharp pains shot through his feet and hands as the feeling returned. Evelyn continued the gentle massage and exchanged the snow for cold water. Gradually, through the night and morning hours she added tiny amounts of warm water. Finally his skin took on a healthy pink color and it appeared he was out of danger of losing his toes and fingers to frost bite. He was in extreme pain for several days, but it was nothing compared to what could have been his fate.

It began to snow and continued until the land was covered. It was bitter cold and nothing melted. It was a terrible winter that tested the pioneers of the Mantle ranch. Tim and Lonnie were on their own at school, with Evelyn out from daylight until it was too dark to see helping to try and save the cattle. She would test the boys about once a week on their school work and they actually did pretty well by themselves. They understood the gravity of the situation. They would do their school work, do all the chores around home, cook the meals and also fought for the lives of the cattle right alongside their parents.

News of dead cattle, stalled trains, and a frozen world came over the radio every day. They had a limited supply of cottonseed cake, which would only last until about mid-February. Lonnie would forever remember trailing those old cows out of Red Rock Canyon to the cabin. Every day they cut down more trees and the cows would eat them down to the size of a half dollar stub. Most of the old Bar Diamond cows Charley had built his herd from died in Red Rock Canyon. Charley cremated them in the Barn Cave next spring. It burned quite a while and created "Huffman's burnt rock shelter." After they had cut down all the willows and trees around the cabin they started cutting those down the river from the orchard and up across the river from the house. Lonnie explained it to his sister, "Our butts dragged our tracks out in the snow as we followed the cows around." About half the cattle at home lived and amazingly about half of the range cows survived east of Hells Canyon.

Everyone was worried about the Mantle family and the newspapers carried stories of them being snowbound and starving. Even though he knew they always had a good supply of food and provisions on hand, a friend flew his plane over to be sure they were all right. They tromped out the message "OK" in the snow. The pilot dropped a pack of magazines from his plane first, for the purpose of finding the right drop zone. The next pass he dropped the mail right next to the house. The air mail delivery brought news from friends and their kids from all over and lifted their spirits. It was cold all across the United States and *Life* magazine ran a picture on the front page of a steer frozen standing up against a fence.

In the spring of 1949 Evelyn took her students to Greystone where Esther Campbell gave them their tests to see if they met the requirements to be promoted. Esther had a teaching certificate so was qualified to give these tests. She gave Lonnie his eighth grade tests and he graduated to high school.

The three younger kids did most of the riding and cattle work that summer. Pat would occasionally take time off his job at the K-Ranch and ride over to help catch up on the ranching work. They always traded branding work with Haslems, so it became more fun than work. Queeda was needed at the home place to help her mother most of the time and really relished the few times she got to be a cowboy.

Lonnie vividly recalled that summer.

I inherited Pat's saddle when he went to work for Pierre at the K-Ranch and bought his own. Tim had an old hand-me-down saddle he rode.

When Pat and Potch left to work outside the ranch Tim and I subsequently inherited the dwindling ranch work. Dwindling because the government cut the operation down and more and more fences made the riding less important.

We were about ten and thirteen or eleven and fourteen one summer day when we ran in the range horses. Stud, mares, colts and unbroke geldings. Being the head cowboys we decided we just as well break some of these wild eyed geldings. We cut them away from the mares and had about ten or twelve big five to eight-year-old geldings that weren't even halter broke. We would have to halter break these big buggers and then go to riding them. They snorted and broke by us and burned our hands on our ropes in the round corral several times before we had a conference and decided maybe we didn't have time to break them and agreed maybe we shouldn't mention the notion we had had to anyone.

About a year later Dad sold that bunch of horses to Alex Blair for bucking horse prospects. Alex put them in the draw at the Baggs rodeo in early September of 1948. The draw was for saddle broncs and every bronc rider drew a Mantle horse. That year every bronc rider was paid ground money (all got bucked off, but the judging

Tim, age ten and Lonnie, age thirteen. They broke horses as they did the ranch work.

was on who made the best ride for the longest time they stayed in the saddle) including Pat. Tim, and I made a good decision when we opened the gate and let them out the summer before. That winter they all died because of the hard winter and no knowledge of the new country they were wintering in.

The cattle ranching was a cow/calf operation that steadily increased in number from the Bar Diamond cows Dad bought in the late 30's. The number of cows increased yearly till the winter of '48 and '49 took about half the herd. The last of the big steers or steers over three years old were sold about 1945. A few two year olds were shipped till 1950, when the feed lots started operating and grass fat steers were replaced by grain fed beef on America's tables.

After 1950 only yearlings were sold. When the National Park Service took over grazing in 1960 any animal over 6 months of age became adult cattle and was counted as such on our grazing permit. During the 50's we held the yearling heifers off the mountain away from the bulls and bred them as two year olds to calve as threes with a much better calving percent and much less calving loss. The NPS six-months law put this whole yearling operation in a new light and basically reduced the actual breeding cow numbers by nearly one third. Steers had to be shipped to summer pasture in the Steamboat area to get them off the ranch.

Cows were bred to calve in April so they would have grass for milk when the calves were born. The shove up (to pasture on Blue Mountain) usually started about the 20th of June. The cattle on Red Rock were usually moved off about mid March and the drift fence gate shut to keep the cattle east of Hells Canyon. Pat had built a drift fence on the west rim of Hells Canyon which encouraged the cattle to move out east to graze rather than hang around the water and over-graze the Red Rock area.

About the 20th of June we would take our horses and camp outfit to Johnson and camp. For two or three days we would ride the east end of the allotment and shove the cattle west and lock them with closed gates west of Johnson.

A rain shower was always welcome because we needed the rain to blot out old tracks and thus be able to track out and gather the stragglers who were usually the wild ones. They were Cedar runners and would not leave the cedars easily. We would always leave the gates open in the Johnson drift fence when we left in the morning. We would hit the fresh tracks and follow the tracks sometimes all day through cedars and brush till they finally surfaced in open country. We would then drive them to Johnson after calming them down. Sometimes, we would trail the wild cows for two days before they finally quit the cedars and headed for Blue Mountain. Invariably these wild cows ran in families and were recognizable because of their family look. Once they were shoved west of Johnson they would be the lead cattle on the next move which went around Martha's peak and onto Blue Mountain.

The Fourth of July celebrations usually started on the second and we always wanted to make some of those rodeos. We always tried to time our shove-up so that we were finished in time to make those rodeos. If you crowded the wild cows too hard a calf would quit its mother, necessitating twenty-four hours for them to get back together and a subsequent day or two to calm them and work them out onto Blue Mountain. We learned that you handle those old wild cows with care. At the same time the river usually went down far enough to get the bulls out of Hardings hole pasture and put them with the cows about July 1.

After the fourth of July we would ride and gather our cattle off of Wolf Creek and throw all our cows over into Martha's Hole and onto Turner Creek where we could gather them and start branding calves. At the same time we would distribute the bulls to get as many cows bred to calve at the same time as possible. We traded branding help with Haslems. Haslems were always happy to see two or three of us young strong boys to flank down and tie the calves. We would alternately rodeo week ends and gather and brand straggler calves for the rest of the summer.

Potch was in southern Utah and Arizona. He had made quite a name for himself in rodeo. Evelyn was proud of his achievements, but worried that he would get crippled up before he ever got his fill of it.

Eva sent an almanac in the Christmas box. It was very useful for all kinds of information, and Evelyn even referred to it from time to time for school projects. Charley had the most interest in it, though. A spark of desire was growing within him to see some of the world before he died. The almanac told him how to get a passport, and he made up his mind to do that as soon as possible. His attitude was grim and surly most of the time now, anyway. His world was falling apart on him, and he just couldn't seem to make any progress. The Department of Interior threatened his grazing permits and livestock water with asinine government regulations. The Bureau of Reclamation was going to flood him out. Every move he made was monitored by some bureaucrat. The paper work alone was more than a man could handle. He had a dream of finding a place in some other country where his boys could work and build a life without getting it taken away from them.

36

Joe Dies, 1949-50

ANCY SENT WORD THAT THEIR BROTHER JOE WAS NEAR DEATH in Nevada, with pneumonia. The nurses had called the Stockton, California police to find Nancy. Tab, Nancy's son, was on the police force there, and soon figured out that the message was for his mother. When Nancy got to Nevada Joe was in an oxygen tent and very bad, but eventually recovered enough to travel to Stockton. Nancy's doctor did all he could for Joe, but he had silicosis from years of working in the hard-rock mines, and each breath was a struggle. His kidneys were not functioning properly, either and liquid was backing up into his thighs and legs. The doctor advised that he be moved to a dryer climate where breathing would be easier.

Joe asked Nancy if she could possibly get him to Charley's ranch in Colorado. The happiest times of his life had been spent there and that's where he wished to end his days. They finally got him to the ranch. He stood the trip just fine and for the first week he actually seemed to improve, but then his condition gradually began to deteriorate. His care became a terrible ordeal; he was unable to even swallow a drink of water and had to get moisture by sucking it through a piece of wet cloth. Everything choked him and his breathing was so labored it could be heard all over the house. It was a hard battle and it was inevitable that they would lose him. Charley, who had last seen Joe in 1921, visited his brother only once; he wanted no part of his care and stayed on the mountain. Joe was only four when their parents died and he had been put with one family after another until he was old enough to be on his own. When his death was very near Queeda got the help of a young archaeologist named Bud Best that was working on the site. They drove out in the Jeep to tell Charley, who managed to at least be with his brother the last few minutes of his life. Joe died the last of August, at the young age of forty-eight. He had been badly crippled up in a mine accident and was badly bent over. He still had rock splinters embedded in his head and nose.

Charley had arranged with Pat and Earl Gadd to send them a smoke signal that could be seen from the top of the mountain upon Joe's death. Pat and Earl, along with the proper officials came for a home burial. They made a wooden casket for Joe, lined it with a new sheet and nailed it shut. They hauled him to one of his favorite spots, the highest cliff overlooking the old homestead, and buried him there.

On September third, Evelyn took Queeda and Lonnie to school at Wasatch in the old Jeep. All of them were worn out and not really ready, but fortunately all the clothes Evelyn had ordered for Navvy from Montgomery Ward fit perfectly. Navvy had to become Lonnie and the new identity was hard for him to get used to. However, he was tough and resilient and not wanting to be a homesick sissy in front of his sister he bravely moved into the off-campus boarding house provided and fit in right away with all the students.

The boys' dorm mother loved to play checkers. There was nobody that could beat her. Many had tried. She was the undisputed checker champion and very proud and jealous of her fame. Lonnie set his jaw in the way he did when he was screwing up his courage for combat and knocked on her door. She answered the door and in her sweetest voice said, "Oh hello, you are the new boy, Lonnie Mantle. What do you need?" He said, "I can beat you at checkers." She chuckled and invited him to play her a game that evening in the lounge. A small crowd gathered and couldn't believe it when he beat her. She was humiliated beyond words and invited him back for a rematch the next evening. This time an even larger crowd gathered to watch. He won three more rematches and finally she grudgingly admitted he was better than she at checkers. From then on, he was the reigning checker champion all through high school.

Lonnie wrote of his Wasatch years:

I went to school at Wasatch in 1949 in September. My first year
I lived off campus at a rooming house. I can't remember the name.
I do remember we had assigned jobs at the school and my first one was
janitor at the gym. I had a little trouble adjusting to the pecking order
at school and had black eyes most of my first year there. I gradually
learned what was causing them and they diminished as each year took
me closer to graduation. I took a paying job as breakfast cook my last
two years in school, which helped pay my tuition. I had to get up at
four a.m. each day and lived with a saxophone player, a drummer, and
the school sound effects man. I got so I could do my homework and go
sound asleep by 9 p.m. each night.

When Evelyn got back to summer camp on September seventh, she found Charley and eleven-year-old Tim ready to start the beef drive. They didn't have enough hands to do it. She got recruited to follow behind the cattle drive with the Jeep and the camp equipment. Shorty Chambers showed up to help, which then made it possible to get the herd to market. Evelyn had fun doing it even though it was a tough drive. Two nights in a row the herd stampeded and they lost two days gathering them back up. That made the following days very long to make up for lost time, as they had a deadline to meet.

Sleeping out on the ground and being busy cured Evelyn of the sleepless nights and jumpy nerves she had been experiencing. They got the steers to

Craig in time to load them on the train for Denver. Charley pleaded with her to come along to Denver with him to sell the beef. Aunt Nancy and Uncle Bill were taking care of things at the Ranch, so she felt that she could be away a little longer and jumped at the chance to go. It turned out to be a dream trip. They bought tickets on the same train the steers were on. It was the first time Evelyn had been through the famous Moffat Tunnel, and she was thrilled. When they broke out onto the east side of the mountain the great flat plains stretched out to the skyline below them.

Juanita Hammond, Walt's wife, met them at the train station. They had not had much chance to see her after Walt's funeral, because she had sold the house and moved to Denver after his suicide. They put the steers in pens, choosing pens that cattle buyers would pass by first as they came to look over cattle to buy. They watered and fed them and calmed them the best they could, then locked the gates. Juanita took them to City Park on Sunday, and they had dinner and visited into the night.

On Monday Charlene Scoggin and her four year old son, Charles (nickname Chill) came up from Boulder. Little blond Chill reminded them so much of their precious friend Scoggin, his father, that they could not take their eyes off him. Earl Gadd's beef had come in on the train, too. Monday buyers would be stopping by the pens, so Charley and Earl would have to stick around to sell their steers. Charlene and Chill, Juanita, Earl, Charley and Evelyn spent the day at the stock yards visiting and selling steers. In the evening they all were invited to Joe Doak's in Denver for dinner. He was also a friend they had entertained at the ranch and become fond of.

Monday evening Charley and Evelyn went to Boulder with Charlene. They were grateful for the comfortable beds and scented baths that Charlene prepared for them. Tuesday morning Charlene's mother, Louise, fixed them a huge breakfast of bacon, sausage, eggs, and hot biscuits. Charlene assured them she was their guide for the day. She took them to the University campus and showed them every part of it, expressing hope that Queeda would come here to college. They visited the University of Colorado Museum where the Mantle cave artifacts were on display. Their old friend Hugo Rodeck was the director of the museum and proudly showed them what he had done with all the treasures that had been excavated from the cave, as well as the many items Evelyn had loaned him from her personal collection.

Charlene took them on to visit their friends, the Earl Morrises, Bob Burgh, Helen Rodeck, and Dick Jones. All these people had fallen in love with the Mantle Ranch, having worked there as archaeologists, eaten many meals at the Mantle's table, and enjoyed their hospitality. It was a grand day of visiting with good friends.

Charlene tore them away just in time to make it to a western store before closing time. There they bought Charley a western suit. Charlene patted and hugged him and praised his good looks while several choices were tried on and considered. Finally Charlene told him he must buy one suit that she and Evelyn particularly liked because he looked just like a movie star in it. Giggling like happy kids, they returned to Charlene's home called Sunset Ranch. Along the way Charley told Charlene, "You are just too good lookin' a woman to stay single. What's the matter with these Boulder men?"

Charlene's parents, Louise and Henry Knutson were wealthy, gracious farmers who had moved to Boulder to take care of Charlene and Chill after Scoggin was killed in the war. Outspoken, salty, brutally frank, and a true comic, Louise and Charley took to each other right off. They told funny stories and laughed uproariously with each other from the beginning. Henry was a quiet, gentle man who thoroughly enjoyed all their antics. They accepted Evelyn as their best friend and confidant at first sight and she felt the same about them. They knew the hard life she had lived. They also knew she came from a genteel life in New York and enjoyed seafood and frog legs. Most of all, they knew of the ache in her heart for her only daughter who would be going away to college next year.

Louise and Henry took them out to a dinner of fried oysters that night. Then they took them on a drive up Flagstaff Mountain for a view of the lights of Boulder and expressed their hope that Queeda would come here to college. But the magical day was not over yet. That evening they went to a movie and stayed the night with Charlene and her family. At 6:30 the next morning, Adair Feldman, another friend they had met at the ranch and for whom they cared deeply, came to see them and visited while they ate the wonderful breakfast Louise prepared. Adair relived the days he had spent with them as a young archaeologist. He had played with the Mantle kids so much he felt like they were his own. Adair had given Tim a Remington bb gun. Charley told him of all the hours of fun and sacks of bb's Tim had had with the gun. Tim used to tell tall tales about how far he could shoot with it accurately, after pumping the weapon an incredible number of times.

They fell in love with Boulder and the University. They felt that with all these good people looking after her this would be the best college for Queeda to attend. Both the Rodecks and Charlene insisted that Queeda live with them when she came to the university the next year. How sweet it was to have such good friends!

Charlene drove them back to Denver, via Golden. They hoped that Lonnie would go to the School of Mines there when he finished high school. They made a quick tour of the campus, as their time was running out. They had tickets on the Trailways bus that was leaving for Craig at 8:45 and caught it with two minutes to spare. They were totally exhausted and anxious to get home.

The bus broke down out of Denver and a replacement finally came out of Denver to pick them up for the rest of the trip. Originally they were supposed to get in to Craig about midnight. They arrived at 4:30 a.m. Maude Toole had been waiting all that time at the station for them. She took them right to her home and put them to bed, but they were up early with only a few hours of sleep. Maude cooked breakfast for them and they made plans for the day. They were very worried about Tim and things at home.

Maude and Dick drove them to summer camp. Tim and Shorty had come home in the Jeep from Craig and were waiting for them on the mountain at summer camp. They all enjoyed a fine dinner Tim fixed of fried meat, taters, and big fluffy sour dough biscuits. Maude and Dick went on home, promising to come fishing in the spring just as soon as the river fell.

The next day Evelyn drove home, and was joyfully received by Nancy and Charley's Uncle Bill who had been holding down the home base. They didn't know all the things Evelyn had done in the meantime, but both were ready to get out of there, so she took them out that very day. Nancy was still a nervous wreck from the ordeal with Joe. She had insisted that she wanted to be alone, but Evelyn could see it hadn't helped any. She had been with Joe for two months and it had taken a terrible toll.

Evelyn dived into the mountain of work at home. She had to wash all the bedding and clothes, clean the dirty house and try to get bad memories of Joe's death behind her. She was angry and baffled at Charley's treatment of his brother. She was all alone and loneliness began to creep up on her. Somehow they just had to find a way to not stay here through the long lonely winters.

An old school chum of Evelyn's from high school came to visit. They had played basketball together and been best friends at Hayden High. What a wonderful visit they had. Evelyn felt refreshed after Alley's visit. Alley had also seen Evelyn's parents in Oak Creek and Evelyn was relieved to get any news at all of them.

Supplies had to be gotten in and Tim had to start school. Pat had come over from his job at K-Ranch to help with the cattle. He and Charley were shoving cattle off the mountain. They heard that Calder was trying to sell his two ranches, so Pat would likely not have that job at K-Ranch again this winter. The "Dam" people, as the Mantles referred to the people pushing for the Echo Park Dam project were meeting again and no telling what was in store for the ranch there, but surely nothing good.

A whole box of *Popular Mechanics* Magazines arrived from Eva. Tim and Evelyn could hardly wait to get their hands on them. They would just have to wait, though, until they could get secured for the winter and school in session.

Just before Thanksgiving Charley bought a new blue Ford Pickup. Charley's driving skills had not improved. Everybody in the country was fearful he was going to tear up the brand new engine before it got broken-in. He stomped on the gas and released the clutch at the same time, causing great grasshopper leaps every time he started up. When he stopped he just let the truck die in whatever gear it was in while he held his foot on the brake. He didn't have a driver's license and couldn't drive on public roads, so Evelyn drove. Thanksgiving found Charley, Evelyn, and Tim in the new pickup, headed to Wasatch to visit Lonnie and Queeda for the long weekend. Wherever they went they camped. Charley had bought a brand new tarp and he would string it up to some trees near fresh water, and they would set up camp for the night under the tarp. They had brought along a leg of fresh meat, and that fresh meat with dutchoven biscuits and campfire coffee sure tasted good to the school kids, who had been eating cafeteria food for a couple of months. They drove from Wasatch to St. George, Utah, through Zion National Park. In Zion they were amazed at the tunnel a mile long, with apertures ever so often where one could look into the canyon below. From St. George they went up to Nephi, then across the mountains to Maroni and Mt. Pleasant. They had a wonderful, refreshing time. They were all proud of the new pickup, and the kids all thought it was great to get to ride in the back and wave at everybody they saw. After dropping off the kids at school they returned via Price, and across to Myton. Charley had spent time in this country as a young man, but it was Evelyn's first chance to see it.

Potch had a job working for Rial Chew for the winter. They expected Pat would be home after Christmas. The K Ranch was for sale again. Pierre very much wanted it back, but Calder quoted him a price of $75,000. The price was for the bare ground, without livestock, machinery, and the house was in terrible condition. They wanted it very badly, but that was a lot of money, and they were going to think it over until January. Pat was alone at the run down ranch, hired as cowboy/caretaker. His good friends the Earl Gadds, moved from Pops Place to Blue Mountain, and that was just too far for him to neighbor much with them any more. He was lonesome and discouraged.

There were so many Uintah Basin students at Wasatch Academy that year that the bus company put on a charter bus to bring them home for Christmas vacation. The bus brought Lonnie and Queeda as far as Vernal. Charley and Evelyn drove out the east way to get them because hunters had rutted up the west road so badly it was almost impassable. It started to snow on them on the return trip, and they barely made it home before the road became impassable.

Tim and Nav were so glad to see each other that they clung together like Siamese Twins. They played checkers until finally one of them won the sudden death game. Then, since Nav had become a pretty good ping pong player, they got out the old set and played until they wore out the ball. Pat was home, and everybody had a wonderful, renewing Christmas. They skated, sledded, hunted arrowheads, and played cards and board games way into the nights. Somebody would always go to the apple cellar for a big bowl of apples of various kinds. Somebody else would pop a dishpan full of popcorn and pour rich melted butter over it. Charley, Pat, Queeda, and Lonnie rode out over Moose Head to the K Ranch on New Years' day to put the kids on the bus back to school.

Evelyn and Tim had to get back to the business of his school. With one teacher and one student, they could really progress fast. He was an excellent student, and enjoyed learning. He loved to read, and everyone knew it, so everybody that came by all summer had given him books. In his aloneness, Tim became a scholar. He delved deeply into subjects and stored up a great deal of knowledge.

Queeda had not told them when her Easter vacation would be. She had a plane drop their mail and a message to them when she got to Vernal. Heartbroken, Charley and Evelyn tried to get out in the Jeep to get her. In their haste to leave they forgot the axe and found two big cedar trees fallen over the road in Sand Canyon. They managed to push and pull and shove them until they could squeeze by. Next was a nightmare of mud on Iron Springs Bench. They shovelled rocks under the wheels and pulled and piled brush under the wheels until they finally made it out on top of Blue Mountain. They were met by drifts literally hanging over the edge of the mountain in the road. Thinking it was just wind drifts and it would be better past that point they toiled on. It wasn't better, and by this time they were too exhausted to fight the running-board high snow any more. They turned around and arrived home at 9:30 completely worn out.

The next day Pat managed to ride over the mountain from the K Ranch bringing word that the next day there was going to be an important range meeting with the sheep man over the summer range dispute the next day and Charley had better be there or else forfeit his position. Charley saddled up and made the twenty-mile trip to find he was the only one that came.

Evelyn was at the sewing machine almost constantly, along with her other work. She made shirts for her boys for the rodeos that all their friends envied. She made Queeda a beautiful white dress for graduation. She made herself a pretty dress to wear at the graduation. She sewed for Hilda and Maude Tool, and for Mrs. Gadd. These ladies were the ones the Mantle family stayed with when they came out for supplies. It was Evelyn's way of repaying them for their hospitality. As well as all her other work Evelyn decided she wanted to learn to type. She taught herself touch typing from a teacher's handbook.

Graduation at Wasatch Academy was over Memorial Day weekend, May 26-29. Charley, Evelyn and Tim arrived in the pickup. The lady that Queeda had roomed with her freshman year invited them to stay at her house, which they did. It was convenient and right across the street from campus, so they could attend all the many activities and award ceremonies of commencement week. Lonnie and Tim were so glad to be together again that they could hardly contain themselves. Lonnie showed his family all around campus and introduced them to his many friends and teachers. The extraordinary faculty and staff of Wasatch Academy made every student feel special and every parent feel like royalty. It was a wonderful time of feeling good about their accomplishments for the whole Mantle family. At the Awards Ceremony Queeda proudly read her essay "Adventure" which had won first place in the F.C. Jensen Literary Contest. It was a sad day for her when she left Wasatch. It had been a refuge from the real world with all its sadness and difficulties.

37

Last School, 1950-51

I T WAS A TOUGH SUMMER FOR EVERYONE. No sooner had they returned from Mt. Pleasant than the well below the house quit producing water. The shallow, hand-dug well watered the big garden Evelyn had prepared and planted below the house. The garden was essential to the survival of this family.

So Lonnie went to Rangely and bought enough two-inch steel pipe from an oil well salvage to reach from the river to the house. The pipe was plugged with oil, however, which would not allow the passage of water. He dragged a lot of wood and laid lengths of pipe on top of it and set it on fire. It took several days of stoking the fire under the tilted pipes, but finally all the oil was burned out and the pipe now carried water. He screwed the pipe joints together from the river to the house, with a diversion gate at the garden so the flow could be controlled. A five-horse Briggs and Stratton pump located in the river finished the job and the garden was saved just in time, as were the lawn and trees at the house.

Queeda had been accepted at the University of Colorado. She thought about not going, however, because her mother had gotten some bad news. Evelyn had been feeling droopy and short of breath and finally went to see Doctor Monahan in Craig, who told her that she had a heart condition. He said she absolutely must slow down and not work so hard. She was forty-three and her body was protesting at the gruelling, grinding work she had been doing for twenty-five years. A letter from Julia, Evelyn's mother, via Eva told her that her mother was now bedridden and had to have someone else write for her. Evan was drinking uncontrollably. They still lived in Oak Creek and barely made it through each day. Evelyn had still not told her children after all these years that their grandparents were alive and lived in Oak Creek. Charley had insisted on her complete separation of them from his family; nobody but he and Evelyn would ever know why.

Life was filled with sadness and tension. Evelyn continued to irrigate and weed, to can and wash clothes, and to make clothes. She tried to slow down, but there was just so much to do. The Korean War and the fear for her boys was always with her! Queeda was frantic trying to help and not feeling that she really was. Her mother had lapsed into a deep sadness and hardly ever talked. They were both lonely and distant from each other.

Charley had recently suffered another serious back injury. He was riding along checking for cattle in Schoonover, fifteen miles away from home when his horse, Star, suddenly tore into a fierce bucking frenzy. Taken by surprise and off balance, Charley hung on for a while, then was slammed to the ground on his back in a pile of rocks. He thought his back was broken, but finally enough feeling returned for him to crawl on his hands and knees. Thinking to catch his horse, he crawled toward him, but the wily horse stayed just out of reach as he started down the trail toward home. Charley managed to make it out of Schoonover and dragged himself to the road. Still Star stayed near but out of reach. He waited there all day for someone to come looking for him. He had always chastised Evelyn for worrying and made fun of her for checking on anyone who was missing longer than she felt they should have been. She waited and worried until almost dark and still he wasn't home, so risking his wrath she took the Jeep and went searching for him. He was never so glad to see anybody in his life, but nonetheless chastised her bitterly for not coming looking for him sooner. Charley's back was very painful and he spent days lying on the cot in the living room reading and dreaming over moving to a better ranching country. He read about Argentina and Australia and imagined his boys would have a better future there. The Echo Park Dam was almost certainly going to be built, and the ranch covered by 200 feet of water. He had had enough experience with condemnation of property to know that he would be forced to sell out, and be paid almost nothing for his ranch.

Finally the pain let up enough that Charley felt he could get away from the ranch for a while and he needed to do that. In June, he and Evelyn took a week long trip to see the Ekker family on their ranch in Green River, Utah. Queeda stayed home to work on her college wardrobe and to watch things at the ranch. No sooner had they had left than Pete Peruzic showed up. Pete was an old bachelor in his sixties, almost a hermit, who lived on Douglas Mountain. He knew the Mantles had a daughter of marrying age and he had come over to look over the situation. Queeda had no choice but to let him stay, since he had walked all the way over. She was scared to death of him, she slept with a gun and had booby traps set up to wake her if he got to prowling around at night. He stayed until Charley and Evelyn returned and Charley sent him home. Pete wrote a letter of proposal to Evelyn addressed to Queeda after he got home. "Dear Queeda, I didn't want to ask you to share my home until you had a chance to look it over." The invitation and the proposal were declined.

Evelyn dreaded Queeda leaving for college. All kinds of evils lurked out there for young girls and she worried about every one of them. Yet, she was determined that her daughter was going to get an education that would give her a chance in life that she had never had. She was going to be well dressed enough to not be embarrassed, too. She got two sewing machines running, and she and Queeda sewed non-stop on Queeda's college wardrobe. Eva had searched until she found a buttonhole attachment for her that would work on

L to R: Aunt Nancy Ayres, Queeda, and Doris Karren, on the back porch.

both machines. In the past Evelyn had made all the buttonholes by hand. This wonderful attachment even made keyhole buttonholes! She made beautiful dresses and coordinated several outfits until she felt she had done the best she could.

They made several new western shirts for Lonnie. He liked wild, bright colors, so they were fun to make. Evelyn ordered underwear and shoes and pants for him from the catalog. She felt that he was pretty well outfitted for school. She didn't see much of him that summer, because with their Dad laid up with a bad back Lonnie and Tim did all the cowboy work.

Old friend, Earl Gadd, insisted on entering Queeda in the Rodeo Queen contest in Craig. Earl had a beautiful dark chestnut sorrel horse named Sox. He had a huge white blaze and four white socks to his knees and hocks. He was well trained, and so beautiful he could probably have won the contest all by himself. Earl would fix her up with all the equipment, too. He wanted to do it so bad that he couldn't be refused. So, for the first time in her life Queeda got to go up on the mountain to summer camp and be a cowboy. That was so Charley could teach her the proper way to get on and off a horse with a saddle, and generally make herself and the horse look good. She had ridden bareback since she was three and used a saddle on a couple of long trips, so she just needed some polish. Charley ordered her a pair of hand-made boots and somebody gave her a hat. She felt very guilty about leaving her mother alone at home with all that work. She had a great time, though.

Doris Karren and Queeda spent a great deal of time together that summer. They would ride back and forth to each other's summer camps and spend a few nights together. They swam in dirty reservoirs, talked about each other's brothers they were in love with and nearly rode their horses to death. One day

Stella, Doris' mother, drove Doris to the Mantle cabin with the intention of dropping her off to stay for a few days. Out by the hitch rack sitting on the ground was Queeda, hard at work skinning a prairie dog she had shot and hung up by its hind legs on the hitching rack. Her intention was to test a theory she had heard that the fat from prairie dogs was the best preserver and softener you could get for leather and she was going to oil her saddle. Stella's horrified eyes were glued on the sight of the skinned prairie dog hanging on the hitching rack when Charley's sharp eyes took in the situation. Never one to miss a chance to bugger somebody, he said, "Come on in. You're just in time for supper." Stella floor boarded the gas pedal, backed the car in a tight turn and left in a streak of dust.

Doris returned later and told the story between fits of laughter from herself and her audience of trying to convince her mother that we were not really going to eat that prairie dog. Finally Stella was fairly well convinced and let her come back.

Some old friends of Charley's made Queeda braided reins, head stalls, quirts, and tapaderos. They gave her a pretty bit and spurs, and looked forward to the contest with great anticipation. The worst thing they could imagine was that Charley Mantle's daughter wouldn't win in a riding contest. They had Queeda in a state of jitters when the time finally arrived. There were sixteen candidates. Queeda won the contest. She rode in the parade and grand entries in a state of shy numbness. There has probably never been before or since a rodeo queen who couldn't dance a step. Everyone was gracious and excited for her, and gave her every honor imaginable. It was a very exciting time for her.

Before Lonnie went to school he and Tim gathered the beef and put them at Martha's Hole. They had to do a whole lot of work on the spring there because the water supply was diminishing. Tim would keep an eye on it and keep the steers there to eat the abundant grass and get good and fat. At shipping time, Pat would come and help. Lonnie went off to school feeling like he had dumped too much on Tim.

Charley and Evelyn loaded up the pickup and set out for Boulder to put Queeda in school. They set up a bank account with enough money to pay her first expenses. Queeda had never written a check before, so it was a frightening experience to pay her bills. She felt extravagant and selfish, but she got enrolled in school and ready for classes. Evelyn and Charley bade their daughter a tearful goodbye then left so they could get Lonnie to school at Wasatch.

Tim and Evelyn started up the canyon school again in the living room. Evelyn had already decided that this would be her last year of teaching. She didn't feel it was fair to Tim to be all alone. He could attend the eighth grade in Wasatch and she thought he would get a better education there than she could give him, but the sacrifice made her cry just to think of it. Her baby would be leaving, and she would be all alone for the rest of her life in this lonely canyon. On top of that her health remained poor and her one goal in life had been to get her children educated. If she were to have a heart attack and die, all the kids would be set to finish their education. Charley wasn't get-

Queeda, rodeo queen in Craig.

ting any better from his back injury either. Evelyn wished with all her heart and soul that they could find some way to take care of the cattle so they could get out of Hells Hole for the winters.

Charley, Evelyn and Tim drove to Wasatch. They had Thanksgiving dinner at Wasatch with Lonnie and Queeda and her Wasatch friends from college, then all drove on to Green River and had Thanksgiving dinner again with the Ekker family the next day. It was a grand trip.

When she got home Evelyn was thrilled to find that her order of eight wool blankets from Baron Woollen Mills had arrived. She had bought wool from Rial and sent it in to them. The blankets were pure wool, generous, and luxurious. She felt so lucky to get them, because nearly all private industry was manufacturing supplies for the Korean War now, and she felt sure these would be the last wool blankets available for a while.

Pat had received his draft notice from the Army, with a notice to report in March. It seemed possible, though, that he would have to go earlier. Through the grapevine they heard that Potch had joined the Navy. They also heard that he won day money (an amount earned by each winning contestant each day) at Madison Square Garden during the National Rodeo earlier in the summer. Nearly every young man they knew had either been called up, or had his date set definitely. Utah seemed to have an unusually high number of boys being called up.

An upriver view of the Mantle home about 1945.

For Christmas Charley gave Evelyn yards and yards of beautiful wine col-ored velvet to make herself a dress. He stressed, however, that it was for herself, not Queeda. Evelyn snickered to herself as she thought of wearing velvet con-sidering the life she led. Inside the huge box of Christmas presents Eva sent for the family were books, useful items, and clothes. Eva sent Evelyn soup spoons to fill out her set of Oneida silver plate that Eva had sent her last year. It was all lovingly polished and the table set with it and the good china for Christmas dinner. The big Oak table was waxed 'till it glowed, and pulled out to full length in the dining room.

On February 18, Evelyn's forty-third birthday, she was excited by the beau-tiful day with such promise of spring. However, the radio battery was low that there was no reception during the day and they could only get the news in the evening. Evelyn was frantic for news from all the children. It had been seven weeks since they got any mail.

Charley planned to ride out with the mail on horseback. The battery in the Jeep was dead, so he couldn't drive it out. At the last minute Rial came over and invited Charley to ride out with him, as he was driving out in his Jeep the next day. Charley gladly accepted, as his back still hurt terribly, and it would be a long horseback ride out and back.

Evelyn had gotten out her carpenter tools again to pass the time. She built a floor to ceiling sewing cupboard in the master bedroom. She made eight drawers, some divided for tapes, another for patterns. Three shelves were for cloth and things to alter. The back side of the door was a spool rack with two trays for pins, etc. It turned out to be beautiful and very usable. She was very proud of her work. Also, she took on the job of making a sewing machine cabinet for her friend, Hazel Ekker. She made the entire cabinet, complete with drawers and fold down sewing machine storage and finished it off with an extra long working surface. She sanded and filled and put layer after layer of finish on both pieces until they were perfect.

Evelyn also took up knitting. She attempted knitting Barbara's baby a sacque, but it turned out big enough for Barbara. She had only a number five needle and asked Eva which was the larger, a number one or a number five. After this shaky beginning she knitted many beautiful things. While the fall and winter catalog was still in effect she decided to order Tim's school needs for next year. The price "nearly knocked my hat off and I've only just begun," she declared.

Tim passed his exams easily and was promoted to eighth grade. This would be his last year of school at home. He was excited about the prospect of going to Wasatch Academy.

It was August 22, 1951. Evelyn and Queeda had altered, cleaned and pressed eighteen pairs of pants, getting the boys ready for school. Tim got Nav's outgrown pants. Nav got Pat's. Evelyn guessed that she and Queeda must be next in line for Tim's outgrown pants. Queeda stayed home to finish up some sewing for herself and to clean up the house. Evelyn still had to make three white shirts for Nav, but she had two important jobs to do before she could get to it. In their haste to get everything packed for the boys they had let everything slide and the house was a mess.

Evelyn's rode out to summer camp with Charley. They went out the east way with a pickup load of cedar posts. They fought mud the entire thirty-five miles. Evelyn had accompanied Charley to see that he didn't allow his temper to get the best of him; that was her number one job on this trip. The range war with the sheep man over the grazing land had reached the boiling point, and she feared that violence was going to erupt.

Pat, Nav and Tim had gathered horses on Blue Mountain. They sorted out the big, tough, mean horses that just wouldn't be handled. There was a mean strain there somewhere and it would be a big relief to Evelyn when that bunch got sold. Seeing that they got sold was her number two objective. Her boys were always "messing" with those vicious horses and she feared they would get hurt or killed. This bunch of horses had honed the Mantle boys into the toughest competitors in the rodeos all around the area. The horses were in the corral and they were waiting for Deputy Sheriff Earl Gadd to do a brand inspection. The rodeo stock contractor was expected any minute to pick them up in his truck. They just hoped he wouldn't change his mind and not come because of all the mud. Everybody heaved a sigh of relief and regret as the load of horses pulled out.

38

Mexico, 1951-52

I T SEEMED LIKE THERE WAS JUST TOO MUCH GOING ON. Evelyn had three kids to outfit for school away from home, the festivities of the rodeo in Craig, and too much work to do on the ranch. Charley could barely get around because he had such excruciating pain in his back, let alone be able to do any heavy work. He was grumpy and sad all the time, too.

The range controversy between the Mantles and a neighboring sheep rancher added stress to their lives. Grazing officials, lawyers, and law enforcement officers were already involved. If not resolved very soon it could lead to big trouble. The violent sheep and cattle wars that took place in Browns Park hovered in Evelyn's memory. She would do all she could to keep her boys and Charley from getting involved in such a thing.

Evelyn's mother had surgery for a strangulated hernia. It was not until ten days after the surgery that Evelyn finally learned what had happened and she had heard nothing since. The mines at Oak Creek where her father had worked for so long shut down on the first of May. She worried about how her parents were making a living, but was unable to help them.

Charley finally made an appointment with a doctor in Ogden, Utah to look at his back. The doctor did some manipulating and helped it a great deal. He told him to rest his back and not to do any hard work. Pat had gotten a six-month deferment until November when he was to appear for induction into the Army. In November they were able to get him another six months until the following May. Pat insisted that Charley take the trip of his dreams to Mexico this winter and he would take care of the ranch. Charley was elated at the thought and planned on doing it right after Christmas.

Charley and Evelyn got Tim and Lonnie settled in at Wasatch and felt pretty good about Tim's first year there because Lonnie was around to help him get settled. Besides, Tim was a people person and made friends easily. Evelyn knew he had good study habits, but time would tell if he could resist playing at the expense of his school work.

They shipped the beef to market in Denver on September 15, and delivered Queeda to college in Boulder at the same time. She rented a room very near campus and got a job at the rooming house, which consisted of closing up each night, shooing dates out, and doing room check. For this she got free breakfast. She also waited table for two hours during the noon rush at Joe's Highland Inn, a small cafe nearby in the college commercial area. She got a small salary and twenty percent off her meals, all of which helped pay expenses.

Lonnie loved sports. He was one of the champions in an early tennis tourney. He was working out for football at the same time and easily made the team. By the end of the season the team won the league football championship. Lonnie was one of the captains and was very proud to get his name engraved on the championship cup which would be forever on display in the main hall at Wasatch.

That year Lonnie landed the job of "breakfast boy" at the school cafeteria. He got up at five and cooked breakfast for the school. Another boy from Hawaii worked with him. Lonnie baked bread, cooked bacon and eggs, and the other boy poured juices, dished up jams or whatever preparations needed to be made. The cook, from the night before, laid out their menus for the next morning. This was not one of the regular jobs students were assigned to. He got paid for this job and besides that he could have anything he wanted for breakfast regardless of what the others were served and it was usually ham and eggs and hot cakes. The school set up a special schedule for him so that he slept during sixth and seventh periods. He was growing fast and Evelyn was relieved to know that he was getting his full quota of rest.

Tim had an accident. He fell and rammed his arm through a window and cut his wrist rather badly. He had to go to the infirmary to get stitches, which was just one more new experience to him. He was exuberant and happy at school and seemed to be doing well in his classes. Evelyn was grateful to Wasatch for its requirement that each student write his or her parents every Sunday afternoon. Both boys were good about writing. They worried about their parents being lonely and wrote lively, interesting letters that they knew Charley and Evelyn would take great joy and comfort from.

Some good news: Dinosaur Monument hired two county road graders to come in on the east road. Charley and Evelyn picked out loose rocks that had gotten left on the road after the graders finished and now they could drive the forty miles to Elk Springs in two and a half hours, whereas before it had taken at least twice as long. Also, the graders scraped off an airplane landing strip for them just off the road on the west side of Hells Canyon. The Park Service was also going to let them use one of their two way radio transmitters this winter, so they wouldn't feel so completely and hopelessly isolated from their children.

Charley continued to read books on Mexico and study the Spanish dictionary, learning new words. Pat was there to wean the calves and distribute the cattle around. However, early in the winter heavy snows began to fall, with all the signs of a hard winter coming. Pat kept assuring his dad that he could handle it and not to worry, just go on with his plans to go to Mexico. He wanted him to get his back rested up, as well as have a well earned vacation. Pat and Evelyn played Canasta in the evenings. It became a very lively contest. Charley had never liked playing cards or board games and didn't join them. His pet project was babying the chickens with hot food and warm water. He got their production up to eight to ten eggs a day, which is really good for winter. He felt a little silly about it, but he really did enjoy the excited welcome the hens gave him each time he showed up. Even the rooster crowed like a champion at the sight of him.

When it came time to go out and pick up the kids for Christmas vacation. Charley, Evelyn, and Pat left one morning and soon found that conditions were the worst they had ever tackled in a vehicle. They fought drifts and worked out of ruts they slid into, and wore out three sets of chains. They worked the Jeep so hard that they emptied the gas tank, plus they used the five gallons of emergency gas they always carried. They were completely out of gas and Pat had to walk six miles through the drifted, blowing snow for more. The rancher he got the gas from brought him back and filled the gas tank for them. Pat 's feet were badly frost bitten. They finally got to Gadd's house in Blue Mountain at 2:30 a.m. Once more they had narrowly escaped death in the continuing struggle to educate their children.

Nav, Tim, and Queeda arrived at Gadds on December 21st. They would all head for the ranch the next morning. Shorty was riding in with them for Christmas. They had the Jeep and pickup both, so hoped it would be easier than the trip out. It was not. In fact the whole family nearly perished on the trip to the ranch. They spent twenty two hours shoveling every step of the way over the mountain. The winds had made the road so drifted it was impassable. They could barely find the road most of the time. Everybody shoveled until they were exhausted. The sweat from the exertion froze on their bodies so they would have to get back in a vehicle to warm up before going to work again. They had been without food since early morning. Charley and Pat exerted themselves far beyond the endurance of any man and finally as they were about resigned to their fate they reached the crest of Blue Mountain and it was down hill and less snow from then on and they were able to make it the rest of the way home.

One by one everybody came down sick. The freezing air that had seared their lungs and the total exhaustion of their bodies took them down one by one. Pat kept the wood box full and milked the cow. Evelyn was able to keep hot food prepared and snow melted for water, but it soon became evident that Charley was developing pneumonia. Eva had sent a bottle of Penicillin pills in her Christmas package. They were likely the only thing that saved Charley's life, along with the mustard plasters that Evelyn kept on his chest and the steaming kettle she kept on the stove to moisturize the air for him. She never went to bed.

Queeda stayed a week over her vacation time so they could get on their feet a little for the rough ride out. Pat took on the job of getting Lonnie, Tim and Queeda out on horseback over the west end of the mountain. They left at 8:30 in the morning and fought snow drifts all day, reaching Jensen at 6:30 that night. It was twenty degrees below zero, and Nav froze his feet bad. Pat made the ride back quickly before his trail could drift shut again. He had four horses to take turns breaking trail and made it although there had been considerable drifting since the first trip. He was desperate to get back as soon as he could because it was obvious his mother was going to be needing all the help she could get to save Charley's life.

As Queeda went through Craig she called Henry Mobley and asked him to send in a snow plow for Charley. He called Dick Toole and they were on their way to the rescue within the hour. It took Dick and five crew members plus an old friend, Roy Templeton sixteen hours from Elk Springs to the head of Hells Canyon with two cats and dozers and two pickups. They managed to get into the canyon with one cat and dozed the road down the canyon and right up to the house. It turned out they had to leave that one cat there until the road dried because it was liable to slip sideways into the bottom of the canyon if they tried to drive it out the steep slick dougway (or dugway, a steep incline). Evelyn marveled at how big those machines were. Dick told her confidentially and with a big smile that when they came in to get it next spring they would probably have to improve the road considerably to get it out.

Dick walked into Charley's bedroom at 1:30 a.m. and woke them. Everybody rested, ate, and got ready for the trip out. The penicillin and Evelyn's nursing had Charley better as far as pneumonia was concerned, but swollen sinuses had caused one eye to nearly pop out of his head and caused severe headaches. Dick drove the cat, pulling quite an assortment of vehicles behind him. First was the Mantle's pickup, then Dick's pickup, and finally, Roy's pickup. Dick cleared the road and at the same time pulled the three pickups which were left in neutral. Charley got awfully tired, but took a box of aspirin and a pint of whiskey one of the crew had and made it. They got into Craig at 2:30 a.m. Tuesday morning, January 14, 1952.

The doctor soon had Charley feeling better. Maude and Dick put him and Evelyn both to bed at their house and saw to it they rested. Evelyn had coughed so much with her cold that she developed a pain in her lower left rib area. The pain was so intense that she was not able to drive until it finally got better. A bottle of twenty four Areomycin capsules at $13.00 a bottle plus penicillin shots brought howling protests from Charley about the cost, but by February fourth he was eating and sleeping well and feeling fairly strong. Since he could see that he was in no shape to be any help to Pat anyway, he prepared to go to Mexico. Pat was insistent that they go. He and Rial both assured them that they would be working together a lot and would look after each other. There were thirteen inches of snow on the ground at the ranch, with deeper, drifted snow on the mountain. Around Artesia and Blue Mountain they had twenty six inches of snow. The Gadds were having misery gathering their cattle. They had to get a plane to spot them first, then go after them horseback.

Pat suffered all winter from his frost bitten feet, but never let up on the enormous task he had taken on of trying to get the livestock through the winter. Lonnie, too, suffered pain in his feet for the rest of his life as a result of having them frozen that winter. When Queeda finally got to school she was sick in bed for another week.

Charley supervised Dick and Evelyn in making a chuck box to fit in the back of the pickup. He planned to have everything they needed in that box for camping out in Mexico. Pierre and Hilda came by on their way back from the School of Mines where Tommy was enrolled. They decided to go along with Charley and Evelyn to Mexico. On February 18, Evelyn's birthday, they took off with their two pickups and all their camping supplies to see Mexico. At the last minute, word from Lonnie came that his frozen feet were going to be all right, meaning he wouldn't lose any toes. It was most welcome news. Somehow, all managed to survive that terrible ordeal. Everyone knew that Pat was the one who would ultimately suffer the most trying to keep the livestock alive.

They left Craig on February 18, with a chuck box full of food, a barrel of water and a barrel of gas. They had a great time and of course no road was too much of a challenge if they could get to see some new country. Charley wanted to see it all, because this just might be the place he dreamed of where he could buy a ranch for his boys where they could find a better life.

A letter from Charley and Evelyn postmarked from Alamos, Sonora, Mexico dated February 24, 1952 told of driving the back roads, of poor cows, poorer horses, of burros that survive anything, and endless sights that thrilled them. In Alamos they camped inside the walls of a hacienda. It was owned by a friend of a friend who was a reporter for the *Los Angeles Times* and had been to the ranch and written about the Mantle family.

They crossed the border on Easter Sunday and left Mexico. They drove up through Utah and stopped off to see the boys at school on Wednesday afternoon. The boys had good grades and were happy, so Evelyn and Charley felt really pleased as they drove on to Vernal. However, as they drove through the countryside they came to the full realization of the severity of the winter they had missed. Snow was just melting and the mountains were still so deep and white that the rivers would be in flood all summer. At every stop they heard grim stories of starving livestock.

Snows had been much deeper and it was generally a worse winter than that of 1949. They learned that a March blizzard had been really devastating. Everyone was on the ragged edge of losing all their livestock. They couldn't learn much of Pat other than that he had "Hell and then some." Irma Chew had sent a plane in for Rial around April first and it had landed on two feet of snow in the field by their house. Pat and Rial had been sort of looking out for each other, but both were up against it. Hardly anybody they talked to believed that either of them could have saved any livestock at all.

They called the Moffat County road man who had gotten them out last January. He said it had been too bad for them to go in for the other cat yet, but would make a try the first of the week. Charley's back was weak again, but they figured that probably not riding in the pickup for awhile plus a good rest would help him more than anything.

39

Tourists, 1952-53

HARLEY AND EVELYN FINALLY GOT HOME, following a snow plow. Pat was haggard and thin and had the look of one who has seen too much death. Rial's cheeks were sunken and his whiskers and hair were nearly snow white. His eyes had a frantic look in them. The huge snow pack was melting fast, and when it was time for the kids to come home from school in June there was a real danger from floods. Bridges and highways were being flooded out. Towns all along the rivers were barricading their banks hoping to keep from being flooded. At home the upper park across the river from the house was under water, and the river was a foot from running over its banks at the orchard.

They scoured the canyons and benches for living cattle and horses. Pat found thirty cattle dead in one bunch. Many more were missing or found dead. All but three brood mares had perished. The chestnut stallion they depended on so much had died. So many of the saddle horses had died that it would be hard to get together enough horses to do the ranch work the following summer. The team had lived because they had been near enough for Pat to reach and feed them hay. The snow had come so fast and been so deep that Pat simply had not been able to reach the livestock. It was totally heartbreaking for him.

The floods were terrible in the river and in Hells Canyon. It took all the ingenuity they could muster to save the orchard from flooding away. Great patches of willows along the river banks were all that saved the fields. The growth along the river was mostly wiped out and would not be there another year to save the banks. The dam had to be rebuilt and the ditches repaired to get irrigation water on the fields and the orchard.

Hells Canyon was left a wide, deeply trenched boulder field from the upper end to the Vee at the east end of Castle Rock. You could hardly get a horse out of it, let alone a wheeled vehicle. The kids all had to come home horseback because Evelyn couldn't drive the truck out to get them.

Dinosaur Monument and Moffat County were working closely together on road repairs and maintenance. One or both of them authorized a major repair of the road in Hells Canyon. They rerouted the creek onto the west side of the canyon, and made a good, high, secure bank for it. Then they graded a

Boaters on the Yampa River.

nice road down on the east side of the canyon. They even hauled in dirt and covered the rocks with a nice smooth surface, put in culverts, and repaired the rest of the Bench road where it had great slashes through it.

When it came time to turn out the bulls the river was still flooding and Charley and the boys couldn't get into the parks below Hardings Hole to get them out. The river was crawling with boaters. Some stopped by and visited. One such group told Charley that on a certain date a National Geographic photographer was coming down the river to take pictures for a story he was doing on Dinosaur. Not wanting to miss his chance, Charley and his sons were sitting on the banks of the Yampa River when the group arrived in Hardings Hole. The boaters were glad to help out and the photographers were ecstatic over getting to photograph it as the cowboys boarded the boats and the horses swam behind from crossing to crossing until they reached the bulls. Then the cowboys mounted their horses and jumped the bulls into the deep river and they swam out crossing by crossing while the cowboys rode in the boats and their horses swam behind. It was a fine day's work and the boat party went on their way with still plenty of daylight to make it to the Mantle Ranch and make camp that night. The boat crew cooked up a big supper and invited all the Mantles. The story of all the adventures of the day got better and better as everybody added a little bit. Charley, of course, was the star of the day and also the best story teller.

The severe winter and near death of the Mantle family was written up in the local newspapers. Friends offered to help in any way they could. A man from Vernal decided to try out the new airstrip west of Hells Canyon near the Bench Road. He wanted them to have a way of escape and to get help in the future. One clear day in early December he buzzed the ranch house to alert them he was going to land at the airstrip. They jumped in the Jeep and drove out to meet him. He had landed all right, but found the airstrip to be too close to the mountain and not long enough. He invited them to help him find the perfect spot for the airstrip. They drove west on the Bench Road examining every prospective place. Finally, just east of Red Rock on a long smooth bench the pilot announced that this was a perfect spot. To reach it from the ranch house they could drive the road if it was passable, or they could ride horseback up Red Rock Canyon.

They took the pilot back to his plane. He barely made it off the ground from the short strip, then tipped his wings as he circled around and flew off to the west. He had promised to come back and try out the new strip soon. Pat, Charley and Evelyn cleared and smoothed the strip in two days with the horse drawn grader. Sure enough, the pilot returned. He landed smoothly with plenty of room to spare and pronounced the landing strip perfect. He offered to give private lessons on their own field below the house if any of them would like to learn to fly. Evelyn's heart raced at the possibility, and she asked him to let her think about it.

Their walkie-talkie was not working right. They could pick up Rocky Mountain National Park in Estes Park pretty clear, but only faintly got Dinosaur Monument headquarters in Jensen. Dinosaur had promised them a working radio and once again they were very disappointed to find themselves with no way of communicating with the outside world.

Plans were made to go out and get the three kids coming in from school for Christmas vacation. Pat was looking forward to staying out for a few days to spend some time with his young friends. However, he got a swelling in his neck and had a sore throat, which worsened the next day. The swelling was so huge it deformed his face and he felt terrible. Evelyn looked up his symptoms in her "doctor" book and pronounced it mumps. He had to stay home, which made him feel even worse.

While they were out they learned that the Chews were selling out. Rial was trying to sell to the National Park Service. County Assessor, Hank Mobley, was at the Mantle Ranch making an appraisal right now. They picked up the kids and hurried home so they could see Hank. He spent the night with them and they got a good visit and got caught up on Craig news. They knew that Rial's health was not good and that Irma enjoyed living in Vernal, but they could hardly stand the thought of losing their good old neighbor and friend.

The winter had been too long and lonely and all their life's work seemed so fruitless. By March, Evelyn was deeply depressed. Rial had been in serious danger with a hernia. He finally had an operation when the pain got too much to bear and he feared it would rupture. While Rial was recovering, Pat, now over the mumps, moved over to the Chew ranch to take care of the livestock; Evelyn missed his loving presence. There was also much more than this to add to her melancholy.

Evelyn next to Lonnie at his graduation from Wasatch in 1953.

Pat had returned from the Denver Western Stock Show on the sixth of February, bringing Evelyn a telegram from her father, that had been lying in their mail box. The telegram informed Evelyn that her mother had died and she had not even been able to attend the funeral. Worse yet, Charley had been out to check the mail and knew about the telegram, but had purposely avoided telling her. She felt betrayed, angry, and guilty.

She had just spent two days washing, and now had a week's ironing to do with the old flatirons. The Jeep was falling apart. It needed new tires. The last one she mended was patches on patches. It was not running well and Charley wouldn't get it repaired. It really needed replacing, since it was seven years old and it had done constant hard, grinding work; five kids and Charley had all learned to drive on it. She figured that when it broke down someplace with Charley in it and he had to walk home, he'd fix it.

She felt all alone and weak. For the first time in her life, Evelyn had to search for a purpose to her life. She told Eva her only goal was to see her kids through. She said perhaps being forty-six had something to do with her sad state.

It was a beautiful spring. Evelyn wished desperately for some farm equipment so she would be able to tend the fields and nurse the ranch to greater production. The hens were laying everywhere, the wild geese had just returned and the blue birds had been around for quite a while. All were cheery heralds of spring. Charley had sprayed the horses and the milk cows for ticks and lice. Charley's arthritis had his whole left arm practically paralyzed. Hopefully the storms would pass soon and he would feel better.

All the heavy work was up to Evelyn, Nav and Tim, as Pat would surely have to go into the Army this spring. He refused to ask for any more deferments. He thought it was wrong, and Evelyn said if she were in his place she would think it wrong, too. Eisenhower was president now, and Mantles felt that at least if Pat did have to go he would have a commander-in-chief who knew what he was doing. Pat would be twenty-three years old in August and had already lived through as many crises as most men do in an entire lifetime.

It was the last of May 1953 and Lonnie was graduating from Wasatch Academy. The commencement week was a grand celebration, a time to honor the graduates and Evelyn wanted to enjoy it. She was excited and proud to watch her son graduate. Always the lady, Evelyn looked well dressed, calm and lovely. Never would anyone guess the life she lived. Lonnie liked graduating all right, but mostly he couldn't wait to get back to the hills. He and Tim had many plans for the summer, like rodeoing and cowboying, and dancing with girls. After all they would be the head honchos of the ranch now with Pat in the Army.

On June 25, Evelyn wrote:

> Two hundred seventy five people have been here since June began.
> Three groups of Sierra Club were one hundred seventy. Boaters—sev-
> enty-two camped last night, sixty-eight last week,
> and about the same the next. All have to give us the once over. We
> also had two overnight guests from Vernal. We can't even get the
> kids trunks unpacked or washing done. We have to think of some-
> thing to make this pay, for it takes all our time. Charley and the
> boys are haying today.
> Queeda goes to Echo Park tonight to pick up our (inflatable)
> boat. Some writers couldn't get into the Sierra Club group because
> they were too full, so they rented our boat. We just got our boat,
> paid thirty-five dollars, and they rented it for twenty dollars for two
> days.

The grasshoppers were very bad that summer, but Evelyn still had fruit. She canned and entertained tourists and entertained some more. They were very nosy, curious people, and she was a curiosity to them. She was exhausted by the time the river finally got too low for the boaters to float it any more.

Lonnie enrolled in college at Colorado A&M in Fort Collins that fall. Jack Haslem was already there and got Lonnie a job at the stable cleaning stalls. They lived at a motel about three blocks away from campus, and Lonnie walked to school each day and worked morning and evening at the stable. Soon he had saved enough money to buy a car. A 1947 DeSoto. Wheels! He had dreamed of this day.

Pat was home on furlough the first ten days of November. He was being transferred from Fort Sill, Oklahoma back to Camp Chaffee, Arkansas. He was overwhelmed by the constant crisis conditions for his parents and his inability to help them.

Road workers had been boarding with the Mantles for the last ten days. They had mended the east road so it was usable again. Trying to help them,

Charley pulled a ligament in his shoulder, which gave him lots of night pain. He tossed and turned and walked the nights away. At age sixty, Charley was no longer able to work as hard as he once did.

On December 15, Charley and Evelyn went out to get Lonnie for Christmas vacation. When time came to go, however, they found that the batteries were dead in both the Jeep and the pickup. Evelyn had to catch a horse and ride the ten miles to Rial's to get him to come over and give them a pull to get started. They took out both the Jeep and the pickup; hooked up with Lonnie in Artesia, and stayed overnight at Eddie Ledford's house.

Eddie and Irma Ledford had recently moved to Artesia and opened a liquor store. Eddie was the brother of Walt Hammond's wife, so they had known him for a long time. He had been blinded while working on construction of the Moffat Tunnel. Irma was a very attractive, quiet lady who could move mountains. The Ledfords and Mantles had become fast friends. Evelyn and Irma were especially fond of each other. The Ledford children, Barry and Cynthia, were also dearly loved by all of the Mantles and became an important part of their life. Barry became a cowboy and proudly rode herd on the cattle of the Mantle Ranch during his growing up years. Cynthia became like a second daughter to Evelyn and Charley. Although blind, Eddie was always cheerful, a great prankster and ran a successful business. The Mantles left the Jeep at Ledfords that day and took the pickup home. Queeda and Tim would be in a few days later and they could drive the Jeep home.

While the boys were home they cut up enough wood to last the winter. They weaned the calves and got the livestock placed around for the winter. Evelyn glowed with pride that Lonnie's grades were very good his first quarter in college. Even better, he didn't look thin and tired from his heavy schedule of school and work.

When Lonnie and Tim got home from school that spring they went right to work. Lonnie had a young little black horse he was breaking. He called him Buggs and he was a cracker jack of a prospect for a saddle horse. He was sure-footed, wiry and tough as nails. He quickly learned everything Lonnie taught him. Most horses could only endure a morning's hard work and a fresh horse would have to be saddled for the afternoon work. Lonnie never needed to change horses at noon when the riding was hard because Buggs was able to go hard all day.

Lonnie had ridden Buggs for about thirty or forty days and the little horse was perfect in every respect. He was the best cow pony Lonnie had ever had. Not to be satisfied, Lonnie decided he would see if Buggs could buck. A bronc rider needs practice to stay good so Lonnie was pleased to find that if he spurred Buggs in the shoulders he gave him a pretty good buck. The next time he decided on a little buckin' horse practice out of Buggs Lonnie was just barely able to stay aboard. He thought maybe he better not press the issue so just went back to riding him. Well Buggs had evidently been thinking, too, because about half way through the next day's ride he fired off without any persuasion and bucked Lonnie off soundly. Lonnie lost ground from then on and the only way he could ride Buggs was to cheat. He found that Buggs didn't like to buck in the rough terrain, so he would ride through a rock pile rather than through some flat ground any time he could.

Lonnie was riding the bottom of the canyon, where Turner Creek turns into Hells Canyon on Blue Mountain. This was a place known as "Bob Cat," under the east face of Round Top. He had ridden Buggs off in there from North Fork Draw to cut sign for some cattle the neighbors had reported seeing there. This was tough country so he felt real secure riding Buggs in there. Buggs got real fidgety as they rode under a big old cedar tree down in the bottom, but it was out of character for him to start anything in such rough country. Lonnie looked up and there were three or four baby bob cats in that tree. He got off and knocked one out cold with a rock. Quickly pulling his saddle off Buggs, he rolled that little cat up in the saddle blanket and tied it on the back of the saddle. After a losing battle Lonnie finally had to blindfold Buggs to get that saddle and the screeching cat back on him. Lonnie was tired by then so he sat down under the cat tree and studied Buggs' reaction to the live cat behind the saddle. He thoughtfully considered where he was, the distance back to camp, and the mile and a half of real flat ground he had to cover to reach camp after he got out of the canyon. He solemnly considered that he couldn't ride that damn horse even without a cat behind the saddle, so he pulled the saddle off, turned the cat loose and got home without a wreck. Buggs had won. Lonnie later sold Buggs to Edgar Wilson to use in his string of bucking horses. Edgar later said the rodeo riders rode Buggs just once, in four years, and that was in the mud.

40

Change, 1954-55

INETEEN FIFTY-FOUR DAWNED DRY AND WARM. This would prove to be the year of the greatest changes in the lives of Charley and Evelyn. The ice went out in the river on February 6. There was no snow, just endless dust. By June, the weather experts were saying that this drought had already surpassed the 1934 record. The Mantles, however, were having plenty of trouble with mud where it wasn't needed. On February 18, Eddyjo Ekker, a good friend and pilot, decided to deliver mail to the Mantles. He landed in Artesia, picked up their mail, then landed on the airstrip. He had buzzed the house to signal that he would be landing at the air strip, so they drove out to meet him. He hadn't planned on staying, but the landing strip was so muddy he couldn't take off and had to stay the night and take off on the frozen crust early the next morning.

A letter from Pat in Fort Hood said he had put in for his release from the Army on the grounds of hardships at home, but hadn't gotten a reply yet. Charley had sent a formal letter to the Department of Defense stating that Pat was desperately needed at home. Charley's inability to work would have meant the end of the ranch if a bad winter had come.

On January 21, at one-twenty p.m. Evelyn was standing in the middle of the living room floor when all at once the windows rattled and the chairs and curtains danced furiously on the floor. A strange noise came from the chimney. She felt like she needed sea legs to stand up. Frightened, knowing it was an earthquake, she waited for the house to collapse and the cliffs to fall. It was over quickly, with no visible damage. She called Dinosaur headquarters and they said there had been tremors in Wyoming, too.

The Mantle's old friends, Dick and Maude Toole, paid a surprise visit a few days later. It was unusual for them to visit in January, but boy were they a welcome sight. It was so lonely and quiet with just Charley and Evelyn there. Dick had a very bad back and bad knees and Maude couldn't get around very well either, so when they left in their pickup to go home Evelyn was very worried about them driving around this isolated country by themselves. This time of the year there was no traffic on the road so they would be in big trouble if they broke down. She offered to drive out with them, but Dick refused because that would have left Evelyn to return home alone.

Evelyn's worst fears were realized. The starter stuck on the Toole's pickup at the foot of the switch-backs. It was too far and too cold to try walking out to Elk Springs, so they decided on the twenty-mile walk back to the Mantle Ranch. They made it to Johnson's Draw by dark and were nearly spent, but on they trudged through the inky darkness. Dick's knee went out and he was in agony. He tried to get Maude to go on without him, but she refused and they limped on together. It took them sixteen hours, but somehow they made it, though just barely. Charley and Evelyn clasped them and sobbed at the thought of what might have been.

The next morning Evelyn called out on the two-way radio and had a mechanic from Craig come and fix their pickup. Then she drove them to their pickup and traveled behind them until they were almost to Elk Springs. When Dick got home he immediately bought a little house trailer and pulled it down to Dry Woman and set it up. He stocked it with food, warm bedding, and an extra propane bottle. He said that never again along that lonely road would anyone be in danger of losing their life as he and Maude almost did. Now there would be shelter. The trailer was a welcome addition and replaced the winter camp in the cave at Schoonover. It was a great relief to Evelyn because now she wouldn't have the constant worry about the men when they were working cattle up there during the winter months.

When spring arrived, Charley was feeling pretty good as long as he didn't do anything that involved bending or lifting. Cynthia Ledford spent a lot of the summer helping Evelyn at the ranch. Evelyn was doing a lot of sewing for her. Cynthia was a sweet girl and having her to do sewing for helped Evelyn through her terrible loneliness for Queeda. Just she and Charley were at home now. Could five children have grown up and gone so quickly?

On April 14, the first boat party arrived. It was the Superintendent of Dinosaur, along with some of his staff and boating guide outfitters, looking over potential campsites for the coming summer. The building of the Echo Park Dam was such an imminent danger that the Mantles were willing to cooperate in any way they could to keep up the river travel and recreational uses in the area. Representative Saylor of Pennsylvania had come through and visited and promised he would lead the fight against the dam. He was doing a magnificent job of defeating plans to rush the project through. He was also gaining increasing support from powerful environmental groups. He was truly a man of his word. The Echo Park dam was never built.

The worst floods in years came roaring down Hells Canyon and took out so much of the the road that even the Jeep couldn't make it out. On a trip out before the floods the pickup had come up with a broken rear axle at the head of Hells Canyon and they had to abandon it. The flooding was so bad they couldn't even get to it to get it repaired.

There was no clear water to be had. It had been too cold to use the pump in the well, as it would have frozen. The river was muddy and full of trash, and the creek was a churning mess of mud as well. Charley and Evelyn had been trying to repair the crib by the dam, but the floods came too early. A beaver had undermined the crib protecting the bank the summer before, and when the floods came the whirling water took out the rest of the crib, leaving no bank. The flood waters filled the ditches so full the fields were soon covered, and the little lake below the house got so full it was about to run into the river. Evelyn couldn't wash clothes and any water for use at the house had to be carried from a small well she dug by the river bank where the muddy water filtered through sand, clearing it up before it got to the well. Even with the filtering Evelyn still boiled their drinking water.

Lonnie and Tim came to Artesia for their spring break. The roads were so muddy and torn up that Charley and Evelyn stayed with the boys rather than battling the mud three more trips. They had a good time visiting friends, driving here and there, and just getting to be with each other. Lonnie had been trampled by a horse and had thirteen stitches in one of his fingers and was glad for the inactivity. Just before he left for vacation his counselor told him that he was in the top one-third of his class, and thus eligible for a scholarship and helped Lonnie fill out the application forms. If he got the scholarship it would be around $500, which could be applied toward his schooling in any way he wished. He was thrilled for the help since he paid nearly all his own expenses for college.

The ranch was swarming with strangers that spring of 1954. Boaters on the river and tourists on the road streamed in daily. They tromped the hay fields, picked the fruit from the orchard, let the kids chase the chickens and the cows, and left gates open. Charley felt he just couldn't go to Queeda's college graduation and leave the ranch alone, so he stayed home. Irma Ledford and Barry were driving to Denver so Evelyn and Tim rode out with her then caught the bus to Boulder. Lonnie came down from Fort Collins to join them and they all went to the graduation ceremony together.

Pat got his discharge from the army and came right home and started work. First he gathered the steers to take to pasture above Steamboat. There was a terrible drought on, and they were getting as many cattle off the range as possible. The steers should grow a lot this summer on the lush pasture of the high country. They planned to keep the cows on Blue Mountain for only thirty days, just for the breeding season. By that time all the feed would be gone. Pat was also digging out sluggish springs and putting in troughs to utilize every drop of water. Lonnie and Tim were wild to get home and help him.

Queeda decided not to come home after graduation. She made the agonizing decision to get a job and put her university education to work. With a degree in business, she accepted a position as secretary to the chairman of the history department at the University of Colorado. She feared that if she just came home she would never leave, and would miss this opportunity. Evelyn was comforted to know she would be where their friends could check on her.

It sure looked like all their combined efforts had failed; that the Echo Park Dam was going to be approved after all, and their ranch would be drowned out. All were disheartened, but the fight would not be over until the water

Queeda's graduation from the University of Colorado, June 1954. Looking on with pride are Pat, Tim, and Lonnie.

started backing up over their property. Meanwhile, Evelyn was keeping up the home place, while Charley just sat and suffered, in pain most of the time. He studied Spanish and poured over world maps. He wanted so much to get away from this place. It was a constant and losing fight to continue the ranching operation under the heavy hand of the National Park Service and now the Department of Interior was going to build a dam and drown him out like a rat. He thought surely there was some other country where he could find ranches with a future for his boys. There surely was no chance for them here any more. The Paradise they had worked so hard and sacrificed so much for was going to be lost.

That summer of 1954 Lonnie was offered a job on the 101 Dude Ranch up the White River from Meeker. He helped Tim finish up the branding on Blue Mountain then headed for his new job breaking horses at the 101. Lonnie got paid $150 a month and about that much in tips from tourists he guided. If you added winning a little each weekend at a rodeo or two he had a pretty good stake to start school with. Lonnie figured out he could generate more money by rodeoing hard all summer between school sessions than he could with a regular job.

It was so hot it really took courage to have fire enough in the stove to cook meals. Eddy and Irma gave Evelyn a gasoline camp stove she used most of the time except when baking. One day she fired up the wood cook stove, baked some apple pies, a devils food cake and a sour cream cake to take to the boys at summer camp. Barry Ledford had come up to cowboy with them for a while and was enrolled at Wasatch with Tim for that fall. Evelyn had made five shirts

Charley, Pat, Tim, Lonnie, the men of the Mantle ranch in 1954.

for Barry and wanted to get them delivered so his mother could pack them. Her spirits lifted as she drove up Hells Canyon.

October 24 found Charley, Evelyn and Pat at Summer Camp. It was hunting season, and the opening weekend was good. They took hunters all over the area, up oak brush draws, into craggy canyons, through sagebrush flats, and to the tops of high ridges. They packed deer out of difficult to impossible places all weekend. Their paying hunters had all filled up and left, and they had locked the gate behind them so no straying hunters could come in. The following Saturday at daylight they were worn out and were not happy when they looked out the cabin window and saw a shiny red convertible car and Jeep parked down by the locked gate. Four occupied sleeping bags lay around the car when Pat went down to check on it. He let out a Pat Mantle yell which jerked everybody awake thinking death was upon them. The first head to pop up was his sister's. Professor Bob Lacher, his wife Dickie, together with Queeda and a young man had all driven over from Boulder last night.

They drove up to the cabin, and the Mantles met Rex Walker, Queeda's future husband, for the first time. Before the day was out Lonnie and two buddies from college, plus Tim and the Ledford family showed up. Irma had gone to Wasatch and picked up Tim and Barry. Four hunters were camped in a trailer house and five more in a tent, so the place was humming. Everybody got their deer.

There was no end to cooking for all those people, but Evelyn wanted to go hunting with everybody else, so when they got in late in the afternoon everybody pitched in and cooked. Pat made his famous wonderful sour dough biscuits, Charley and Lonnie cooked huge stacks of venison steaks, and Tim fried potatoes. After the steaks were done Evelyn made milk gravy in the drippings. The feast was on! Everybody was starved after tromping the hills all day. They filled their plates and found a place to squat and eat. Those who didn't cook cleaned up after supper.

Charley looked Rex Walker over real well then said, "Throw your bed roll down out there in the brush." A Texan in a fancy car just wasn't high on his list for a son-in-law. Rex had never seen such good hunting. He thought he had died and gone to heaven and was willing to sleep anywhere Charley put him just to get in on the hunting.

On Tuesday Charley and Evelyn went home to check on a milk cow they were expecting to calve. These milk cows gave much more milk than the calves were able to consume, so it was essential that they milk her right away after the calf was born. Otherwise her udder would become engorged and feverish and diseased, ruining her as a milk cow forever. After searching for her, Charley finally waded across the river and found her there. Her calf was about fifteen minutes old, so their timing was good.

Next day Charley and Evelyn both waded across the river to bring Mustard and her baby home. The wobbly baby calf couldn't wade across the river. Charley tied its feet together, then slipped a pole between its legs and they carried him swinging upside down from the pole they carried on their shoulders. Mustard was so distressed that she kept her snorting nose and bellering mouth right in Evelyn's hip pocket. Evelyn had the back end of the pole and did a high stepping dance all the way across the river to keep Mustard from tripping her, making her stumble and dunk the calf.

Charley was not doing well. He was having black-outs. He would stand up, stagger a little, and fall over. His face would flush and from this Evelyn guessed he had high blood pressure. Evelyn didn't dare leave him alone at all. By the end of December he was a little better, but refused to see a doctor. He was getting fat around his stomach. He quit eating butter and other fat, hoping that would help. He lost weight and did feel somewhat better.

In Lonnie's own words:

One time during the slow cattle prices in the 50's Tim and I decided to go into the deer hunting and guiding business on the old ranch on top of Blue Mountain. It was the time when there was a great overpopulation of deer in the country. We set up a tent, locked off all the access to the Martha's Hole and Hamblin properties and started advertising for hunters.

We met some Portuguese hunters in a bar in Artesia and tried to get them to go hunting. Well, they agreed to go look. They wanted big bucks and if we could show them some they would sign up. We made a run through the back country in an old Jeep and saw so many bucks they couldn't wait to sign up.

We put them in the tent for the night with an old wood stove to take the chill off. We kept the stove behind the cow camp when it wasn't in use. We had lots of wood cut and stoked up the stove for them and everybody went to bed. Just got to sleep and "boom!" Sounded like a bomb hit us. Tim and I ran outside and the tent was leaking Portuguese out the front, under , and out the back. Smoke and sparks were coming out of that tent everywhere along with five or six Portuguese who had forgotten how to speak English. Well Tim and I lit a lantern and after the smoke had cleared a little we went in the tent. The stove had the front door and the oven door blown off and coals were all over everything. About then I remembered that summer I had been dynamiting several springs in the back country. I hid the dynamite caps in the back of that old stove so the kids that were there wouldn't play with them.

The Portuguese finally decided to stay but wouldn't sleep in the tent. We hunted with them for about three days and it was a three deer per person area. We got them fifteen bucks and nothing smaller than three points. In spite of the terrific hunting they never came back another year.

41

Alone, 1955-56

AT, LONNIE, TIM, AND LONNIE'S GOOD FRIEND JIM CARMEN were all home for Christmas in 1954. Queeda had a new job with Shell Oil Company and could only get three days off, so she spent Christmas in Goodland Kansas at the home a friend. The four boys were rowdy and boisterous, bringing joy and life back into the ranch house. They ate huge beef steaks chopped off the frozen quarters with an axe, popped popcorn and ate apples from the cellar. They played cards and told stories late into the nights.

The boys caught up on all the work around the place. They weaned the calves, built corrals, cut wood and butchered a beef. Charley just wasn't up to doing all that work himself and was greatly relieved to have it done. Both Charley and Evelyn felt renewed and able to face the winter alone that lay ahead by the time Lonnie and Tim left for school.

This was Tim's last year at Wasatch. Charley and Evelyn reminisced about how hard it had been to scrape together the $700 per year, per child to attend school there. Although expensive, Wasatch had educated their children well and they had been safe and happy there. They felt like they were leaving a dependable old friend behind.

In January, just as cabin fever and loneliness were setting in, Dick and Maude surprised them with a two-week visit. They fed cotton seed cake to the weaners and did some other work that required riding a horse. Dick lamented that his pimples and sore spots had finally made calluses and now he had to go home and wouldn't ride a horse again for another year. When it came time for them to leave Evelyn alerted Dinosaur headquarters by radio that Tooles were headed out, so if they didn't make it when they were supposed to, someone would come after them, but they made it without any trouble.

The winter wore on with little mail from the kids. Unable to stand it any longer, Evelyn went to Boulder in April and spent a week with Queeda, who had just returned from spending spring vacation with Rex in Texas. Evelyn was surprised and distressed to find that they were planning a June wedding in Boulder. Evelyn's heart ached as she thought of her daughter getting married to a stranger from a completely different life style, and whom she had known for such a short time. Worse yet, Rex would be graduating from the university in June with a degree in geology, and had accepted a job in Caracas, Venezuela,

Jean Rodeck, Cynthia Ledford , Cynthia's cousin, Cheryl (left), at the ranch.

working for Socony Vacuum Oil Company. Thus the big rush, because his job started in July. He had signed a contract for a two year hitch in Venezuela. Evelyn thought her heart would break.

Tim graduated from Wasatch at the end of May. He was only sixteen and had been accepted at Colorado A&M for the fall semester.

On Friday, June 10, 1955, Rex graduated from the University of Colorado. He and Queeda were married in Boulder the next day. Evelyn wrote to Eva about the beautiful wedding and the fabulous gifts, especially a grand reception given by Charlene, Henry, and Louise Knudsen at their home. Pat and Charley looked grand in their tuxedoes. Evelyn wrote: "Rex has a job as Jr. Geologist with Socony Vacuum Company and they leave for Caracas, Venezuela, July fifteenth to be stationed there for two years. His salary is fabulous. I only hope they both have sense enough to know they aren't worth it. They will fly down and the company will ship their belongings for them. Both are really excited over the venture."

During that summer Hugo Rodeck's daughter, Jean, visited at the ranch several times. Her parents had been so very good to Queeda while she was at college. Jean and Queeda had become fast friends. Charley and Evelyn felt like she was one of the family. One time she got word to them that she wanted a ride in on a certain day. Charley showed up to get her in the old yellow Jeep and they set out for the ranch. It was soon obvious to Jean that Charley wasn't the best driver in the world. He roared the motor with the clutch in, then took his foot off the clutch and they literally jumped through every gate she opened, then jumped again when they started back up. In between stops they speeded along until the whole jeep shook and the front end lunged around furiously all over the road. Jean finally realized that they weren't going so fast, but something was amiss under the hood, causing the Jeep to shake all over the road, making a terrible racket. On one steep slope in Sand Canyon the Jeep somehow left the road and lunged to a stop clinging to the hillside at a spectacular angle. Jean was on the upper side and Charley said, "Get out, I don't think we're gonnna mak'er." Jean said, "If I get out you'll tip over." He jammed the Jeep in gear, popped the clutch, rocketed back onto the road, and never stopped until he had to let Jean out to open the gate in Sand Canyon.

Tim started college in September. He and Lonnie batched together. They bought one hundred pounds of pintos beans and put three deer in the locker. They figured that would take care of their food needs for the semester. Evelyn and Charley were pleased that the boys were so happy. Charley's habit was to write out a check in the fall to each boy to cover tuition and housing and that was it until next year. Lonnie always said it was a good thing they were cattlemen, because they were used to getting a check once a year and it had to last until the next year or you starved.

Pat was still running the ranch, waiting for Lonnie to graduate, when it would be his turn to manage the ranch and Pat would be free to do something else. He was in love with a girl named Sue Wooley in Meeker and had to make up his mind what to do about her. He didn't want any woman to have to live like his mother had on the ranch, but he had nothing else to offer her. He struggled with the problem of how to get on with his life, yet care for his family like he always had.

The boys were all home for Christmas. Lonnie had just finished a forging and welding class at college, so did a lot of work around the ranch. The weather had been so nice that beavers were building dams everywhere. They even tried to dam off the spring and the ditches. The boys caught one that was the main offender, but another moved into his territory the minute he was gone. Evelyn had plans to put him out of business just as soon as everyone left.

Lonnie and Tim both made the college rodeo team that fall at C.S.U. They were both such good saddle-bronc riders that it seemed they took turns winning first place in that event at the college competitions. Both of them held down jobs as well as maintaining a good enough grade point average to qualify for the rodeo team. Evelyn worried that they might be overdoing it and harming their health. Charley, however, was happy with the deal because he was pretty sure they got better grades because they *got to* rodeo, not *in spite of* rodeoing.

Evelyn had begun suffering with the problems that came with menopause that winter. She had high blood pressure and problems keeping her emotions in control. She wrote to Eva, who was having the same problem, "When "it" is passed we will feel wonderful again providing we live through it, (and those around us)."

Lonely and restless, Evelyn got out her carpenter tools again. Last winter she built a counter in the kitchen with drawers underneath and had carved out the sink hole in the counter top. This winter she set in the sink and got the counter top covered with linoleum. Then she built a two-section dish cupboard above it, with a medicine cabinet between and a dish cupboard on each side. She measured and planed, then sanded and sawed, finishing off every shelf perfectly. Finally she painted it and hung a mirror on the front of the medicine cabinet. Ever a perfectionist, her kitchen was finished perfectly—except that there was no water.

One day Evelyn asked Charley to help her with some difficult boards she couldn't hold and pound all at the same time. He didn't often help with the carpentry work but agreed to on this occasion. She held the boards in place and he pounded. He accidentally hit her finger a terrible blow with the hammer. Evelyn yelped and jigged and the boards toppled down with a great clatter. Charley, red in the face, didn't know whether to swear or laugh, so just got red in the face, and said, "You always will think that was an accident."

Pat told his mother that he had found her a refrigerator that operated on kerosene. She joyfully prepared a place in anticipation of its arrival just as soon as the roads permitted.

Winter was over, and spring arrived with a huge quick meltdown on Blue Mountain. Big floods washed out the dam and the road in Hells Canyon. Afterward, the road was still passable, but so rough that they broke a spring on the pickup. Unfortunately, the $16,000-road Dinosaur had just built into Echo Park all flooded out and had to be replaced, so there would be no money in the budget to fix Mantle's end of the road. Charley was now sixty-three and Evelyn forty-nine. They were weary of fighting the floods in Hells Canyon and this time they dreaded repairing the damaged road and irrigation system for their crops more than they ever had before.

42

We Did It, 1957-60

OFFAT COUNTY DILIGENTLY KEPT THE ROAD to the Mantle Ranch graded and passable during the summer months. On April 16, 1957, Rex and Queeda drove in to the ranch in their car. They had just returned from Venezuela. On the way through Craig, Queeda had visited the doctor and found that they were going to have a baby in December. Pat, meanwhile, had gotten married and was already a father. Queeda and Rex came by way of Meeker to pick up Sue and meet little Stephen Rex, Pat and Sue's baby. Sue rode into the ranch with them, but they left Steve with his grandparents in Meeker since they didn't know how the roads would be. Rex only stayed long enough for a short visit, then left for Texas to see his family and tend to some business. The roads were dry so they knew he would be able to get out with no trouble.

Pat and Sue went out the following week and brought Steve back. What a reception he got. He got passed around and carried and pampered, grinning and smiling through it all. He got bundled up to go feed and rode a horse with his father every day. They stayed for a month. When they left Charley and Evelyn missed them terribly. Evelyn had become very fond of Sue, too, and missed her companionship. They had done a lot of sewing and cooking and Evelyn had delighted in the interest Sue took in all the photographs she had taken over the years.

Rex got back from Texas just in time for Lonnie's graduation from college. Evelyn, Cynthia Ledford, Sue and Queeda rode the bus to Denver, where Lonnie, Tim and Rex met them. The graduation ceremony was marvelous and Evelyn was so proud of her son. It seemed that everyone at C.S.U. knew Lonnie. When he went up on the platform to accept his diploma a great shout went up. After the graduation ceremony Rex got reservations in Denver for everyone for the new movie, *Around the World in 80 days*. It was a wild ride but they made it from Fort Collins to Denver and were only fifteen minutes late.

Lonnie went out to Denver for his pre-induction physical and passed. He was talking of enlisting rather than waiting to be drafted. There was so much cutting of the armed forces going on, however, that Evelyn and Charley hoped he wouldn't have to go at all.

Irma Ledford got a great offer on the liquor store and sold it. She made a profit and was glad to be rid of the burden. She still kept her business of selling tires, however. She and Evelyn were each other's crutch. Each had such a heavy burden to bear that they felt they couldn't have borne it one without the other. Evelyn had feared they might leave Artesia, and was greatly relieved when they didn't.

Rex and Queeda drove to Colorado again for hunting season the last of October. Evelyn rode back to Texas with them to stay until the baby came. It was the first time she had been away from the ranch for any length of time since she was married in 1926.

Charley was sinking farther and farther into a dark, brooding existence. He seldom shaved, talked to himself constantly, and dreamed of "leaving this god-damned ranch and finding a country where a man can still make a living." When she went to Texas it was the first time Evelyn had ever left him alone. He dreaded her going, but could not be coaxed into going along. Evelyn only knew she must be with her daughter for the birth of her first baby.

The time dragged for Evelyn in Tyler. She felt like she was in a foreign land, although everyone was wonderful to her. She and Freda, Rex's mother, became fast friends. At last, on December 12, 1957, Cindy Evelyn Walker was born. She was a big baby and there were complications. Queeda was weak and needy on through Christmas, so Evelyn had plenty to do. Christmas was especially hard for her, being away from Charley, the boys, and her beloved home.

A bombshell that shook both families came from Rex. He felt he needed advanced training in geology to ever be successful in the oil business. He wanted to take his training at his old school, the University of Colorado. He knew that Queeda wanted desperately to get back to Colorado, too. Rex found that he could enroll in graduate school and start on his masters degree immediately if he could make it to Boulder by January fifth.

Evelyn, always ready to launch herself full tilt at any problem, over-worked herself tending the baby, keeping Queeda from over exerting and packing them up for the move. Freda took over all the meals for everyone. Rex's Uncle Ham and Aunt June took them through the trade center in Fort Worth where they picked out all the household things they were going to need to set up housekeeping.

Ham struck out for Colorado with his pickup overloaded with all their belongings. Right behind him came the red Oldsmobile with Evelyn, Rex, Queeda, two week old Cindy, and Bugger, the German Shepherd dog. Evelyn was the only one who realized the insanity of what they were doing. A fragile two-week-old baby had no business being driven up Highway 287 through the bleak, dangerous plains of Texas and Oklahoma, then half way through Colorado on New Years Day. They didn't even have a home awaiting their arrival.

It was a two day trip, and luckily all went well. Ham and Evelyn got them moved into a rental house out east of Boulder on a small farm, after which both of them had to go home to tend to their long neglected homes and busi-

Cynthia Ledford, Irma Ledford, and Evelyn.

nesses. Evelyn took the bus to Irma's house and from there Lonnie took her home. She wanted to kiss the ground she was so happy to be home. However, when the aftershock of all she had been through settled in on her, she was tired to the bone. She couldn't seem to get enough rest.

Lonnie was drafted into the army in February 1958 and was sent to Fort Hood, Texas for basic training. Charley had been stationed there and knew how much Lonnie was going to hate it. Evelyn felt the loneliness settle in over her like a shroud. She rested in bed as much as she could, but felt terrible. By March she was feeling a little stronger, but remained listless and weak. Charley had the two Shefstead boys, Guy and Holmes, down visiting him on the ranch, so she was kept busy cooking for them. Holmes and Charley talked non-stop about South America and getting away to go see that part of the world.

Evelyn was just beginning to feel better when one day she was struck down. She fell in a dead faint on the floor. Charley put her into bed and frantically tended to her, but she didn't respond well. She had all the symptoms of a heart attack. Charley couldn't leave her to go for help, and they figured there wasn't anything anyone could do anyway, so Evelyn was just "resting it out." Charley finally got a chance to send out word to Irma that he considered Evelyn's condition critical.

Irma called and wrote to all the children. Pat, Tim, and Lonnie came immediately. Charley was near exhaustion from overwork and anxiety. Tim had to get back to school, but Pat and Lonnie got the outside work caught up, then Pat had to get back to his job. Lonnie was on emergency leave and was able to stay for only a week, but he kept in contact with Irma on the two-way radio about Evelyn's condition. Queeda and baby Cindy came and stayed for three weeks. Just the presence of the baby was like a strong tonic to both Charley and Evelyn. Charley happily entertained the baby so Queeda could clean up the house, cook, and get the laundry caught up.

Evelyn improved, but very slowly. She could get out of bed for only a short time each day. Finally, by the middle of May she felt she could travel. Irma came and put Evelyn in her Suburban. She arranged a bed for Evelyn in the back so that when she felt tired she could lie down. It was a very hard trip on Evelyn and when she got to Irma's house she was in bed for another week.

Pat was worried about his mother travelling to Craig to see the doctor, so he got Dr. Monahan to come to Artesia to see her. He had treated many heart patients in his practice and had been Charley's doctor when he had pneumonia, so he understood how and where Evelyn lived. He felt that there was no permanent damage to her heart and that in time she would be well again. He sent back some iron pills which began making her feel stronger right away. He also gave her some medicine for the spells she had when her throat felt very constricted. His main prescription was that she should rest in bed, then reduce her work load drastically for the rest of her life. He strongly recommended that she move to town where living was easier.

Lonnie was shipped out to Butzbaach, Germany in June. On the ship ride over he was seasick from beginning to end. In spite of being sick, though, he was very excited about having an opportunity to go overseas.

June 14, 1958, found Evelyn still at Irma's. She was better but still very weak. Pat and Tim had been over to gather the steers, which were really scattered. Charley was home alone, and Evelyn felt guilty being so content with Irma and the kids. She had been there for four weeks. She was improving, but still had to stay in bed much of the time. She went to Craig to see the doctor once more before going home. He said that she had made amazing improvement. There was no enlargement of her heart, her blood pressure was down, and her blood count up, so he felt she could safely begin living a more active life again. However, he cautioned her about ever again doing any hard labor.

Queeda and baby Cindy came to stay at the ranch and help with the work and keep Charley and Evelyn company. They were there for only a week when Cindy got sick with allergies and a cough. Evelyn was so worried about the baby that Queeda felt she had to leave as she was doing Evelyn more harm than good by staying.

On July 14 Evelyn had a setback. She had picked up a virus and had a very hard time. Once again, Irma drove in to the ranch and got her. She stayed at

Irma's for a week until she could get around again. Irma had a supply of anti-
biotics that seemed to help.

Charley, Pat, and Tim had all been on the mountain for most of the summer. Cattle were besieged with pink eye, especially the yearlings. It was a constant chore to keep them treated. They were so wild that they started running
the minute they saw a horse and rider and had to be chased down, roped, and
doctored on the range.

The men had a huge project they were working on in addition to doctoring the pink eye. They were laying a mile of plastic pipe from Quaker Spring
to Serviceberry Gap. There was a new plastic pipe available that only weighed
twenty-three pounds for each two hundred foot roll. Quaker Spring is very
high on the north slope of Blue Mountain. It is so rough and rocky that the
cattle can't climb to it for water, making the abundant water of little use at its
natural location. The grazing area around Serviceberry Gap, on the other
hand, is good, but unusable because there is no water. So they were piping the
water from Quaker Spring around the side of the mountain for a full mile to
Serviceberry Gap. There they set up a six hundred-gallon tank for storage.
When the storage tank filled up it then drained on demand into a trough
equipped with a float. This water system would open up a lot of new pasture
area.

Meantime, the men were trying to keep the garden and yard watered at home.
They were getting pretty run down themselves. The river was very low, as was the
water level in the well and depleted quickly when pumped. The garden was now
located below the house and depended on the well for water. By August 26 Evelyn
was home again. She was still very weak, but getting around and determined to keep
up the work around home. No amount of persuasion could get her to let it be and
rest, whether it be at home, with Irma, or with Queeda.

Charley was still camping at Serviceberry Gap and holding the cattle on
the new pasture. He had to maintain a constant vigil to keep them from coming down into the winter country too early. That feed just had to be saved for
winter. He came home about every second night, but went right back up early
the next morning. The cows and calves were looking much better, so the close
herding was paying off. Pat and Tim, meanwhile, were gathering dry cows and
trucking them to sales in Vernal.

Lonnie was faithful about writing from Germany. He was having a very
good time and taking full advantage of his experience. His job with the Army
had him working in an office. In his spare time he started cutting hair and
built up a nice clientel. Unfortunately, he wasn't popular with the black sol-
diers because of a serious mistake he made early on in his barbering career. A
black soldier came to him for a hair cut, saying it was too long. Lonnie got out
his shears, set the height gauge, and flipped them on. The shears stalled out
in the kinky hair, so Lonnie applied a little forward pressure, but they wouldn't
move. Then he tried to pull them out of the hair. No luck. He finally had to
cut the shears loose with the scissors. There was a lot of yelling and cussing and
thrashing around by the victim during the whole procedure and even more

Tim's graduation from C.S.U., June 1960

when he saw the jagged hole in his hair. Lonnie tried to give him his money back, but he said he just wanted to get away from him.

A soldier was transferred and had to sell his car in a hurry, so Lonnie bought it. He was anxiously awaiting his buddy who was getting transferred to Frankfort from Fort Hood. They had big plans to do some traveling.

Evelyn had a hard winter, with little strength and the usual chores to do, but was finally feeling better. She had bought a new Necchi sewing machine while in Boulder. They had converted it from electric to treadle operation. It did zigzag, plus an endless number of fancy stitches. She cut squares of soft white cloth and machine embroidered and appliquéd children's motifs on them and made a magnificent little quilt for baby Cindy. Charley got interested in the project, too, and it passed many peaceful hours for them.

In April Lonnie and his buddy finally got a leave and the opportunity for which they had planned so long. They took off in Lonnie's car for a tour of northern Germany and Denmark. Lonnie bought a fine German camera and took pictures everywhere they went. He sent his pictures home with great stories of all they had seen and done.

In June, 1959, Pat and Rex started a business venture together. They bought five horses and an old truck and rented the horses to a kids camp for the summer. They were pretty excited about it and were open to a deal offered by a guy to invest in a riding stable in Estes Park. Trouble is they had to build it first. The location was terrific. They put up a small barn. They bought a few horses, some saddles and bridles and on July 3, 1959, rented out their first horse. They could hardly believe their good luck to get a dollar-fifty an hour rent for a horse. Not only that, but business was brisk and they were going to need more horses.

Pat Mantle and Rex Walker became partners in the horse business, building the 7-11 Rodeo Company and Sombrero Ranches.

In 1960 Dinosaur National Monument was expanded. It had now swallowed up the Red Rock Ranch into the boundaries of the Monument and all of the Mantle grazing permit was within the boundaries of the Monument. Immediate restrictions were put into effect on grazing and ranching activities on the Mantle Ranch. It was like a last blow to Charley. The heart was out of him.

In February, 1960, Lonnie was discharged from the army. He came right home to take over the duties of running the ranch and release Pat from that burden. Pat was very busy with his new business, which he and Rex named Sombrero Ranches. Pat also had put together a rodeo string, which he named The Seven Eleven Rodeo Company.

At last the day for which Evelyn and Charley had struggled and sacrificed for thirty-six years arrived. In June, 1960, Tim graduated from Colorado State University. Everything seemed worth it to Evelyn as she tearfully watched her youngest child, draped in his graduation robe and mortar board step up on the podium to receive his college degree. Tim was inducted into the Army almost immediately after graduation. Lonnie ran the ranch for the next two years while Tim served his hitch in the Army.

Charley Mantle, 1960

Charley couldn't stand it any longer. He just had to get away and do some investigating of the world. It seemed to him that the ranch had gone to hell in spite of all his lifelong efforts. He left home and flew into the remote Amazon country of Brazil during the winter of 1960–1961. He had his camp outfit with him, so all he needed to do was buy a riding horse and a pack horse. That done, he set off through the jungles to find a better country. But that is another story. Evelyn was crushed that he would go off like that and she felt that he would surely die down there. Evelyn spent the winter in Boulder with Rex and Queeda, but that, too, is the beginning of another story.

Evelyn Mantle, 1960

This unlikely marriage between a cowboy from the wildest west and a much younger city girl from New York had yielded many trials and many victories. They had accomplished their fondest dream. That dream was to get their children educated. All five of their children had gone as far in their education as they would. Three of them had graduated from college. Charley and Evelyn were very proud of their accomplishments. Their children were very proud of their parents.

CPSIA information can be obtained
at www.ICGtesting.com
Printed in the USA
FSOW03n2123150218
44670FS